4/23/2003

To Andrew —

With best wishes

David Cave

Judy Barrett Litoff

Fighting Fascism in Europe

WORLD WAR II: THE GLOBAL, HUMAN,
AND ETHICAL DIMENSION

Series Editor: G. Kurt Piehler
University of Tennessee
Knoxville

Lawrence Cane, circa 1935.

Fighting Fascism in Europe

*The World War II Letters
of an American Veteran
of the Spanish Civil War*

LAWRENCE CANE

Edited by
DAVID E. CANE,
JUDY BARRETT LITOFF,
and DAVID C. SMITH

FORDHAM UNIVERSITY PRESS
New York
2003

World War II: The Global, Human, and Ethical Dimension No. 1
G. Kurt Piehler, series editor
ISSN 1541–0293

Library of Congress Cataloging-in-Publication Data

Cane, Lawrence, 1912–1976.
  Fighting fascism in Europe : the World War II letters of an
American veteran of the Spanish Civil War / Lawrence Cane ; edited
by David E. Cane, Judy Barrett Litoff, and David C. Smith—1st ed.
    p.   cm.—(World War II—the global, human, and ethical
dimension ; 1)
  Includes bibliographical references and index.
  ISBN 0-8232-2251-9 (hardcover : alk. paper)—
  ISBN 0-8232-2252-7 (pbk. : alk. paper)
    1. Cane, Lawrence, 1912–1976—Correspondence.   2. World
War, 1939–1945—Personal narratives, American.   3. Spain—
History—Civil War, 1936–1939—Veterans—United States—
Correspondence.   4. United States. Army—Officers—
Correspondence.   5. World War, 1939–1945—Campaigns—
Western Front.   I. Cane, David E., 1944–   II. Litoff, Judy
Barrett.   III. Smith, David C. (David Clayton), 1929–
IV. Title.   V. Series.
D811.C257 A3   2003
940.54′21′092—dc21
[B]   2002040894

Printed in the United States of America
03   04   05   06   07   5   4   3   2   1
First Edition

For Grace Singer Cane Mason

CONTENTS

Appendixes

ACKNOWLEDGMENTS

G. KURT PIEHLER, professor of history at the University of Tennessee and general editor of Fordham University Press's World War II Series, has provided us with invaluable guidance. His prodding questions and careful attention to detail have added immensely to the quality of this work. We deeply appreciate his enthusiastic support and encouragement. We would also like to thank Frank Mathias, professor emeritus of history at the University of Dayton and a World War II veteran, for his careful reading and thoughtful comments on the original manuscript. Melvin Small, professor of history at Wayne State University and Marcus G. Singer, professor of philosophy at the University of Wisconsin, each read the original transcripts of Lawrence Cane's letters and provided critical guidance and advice. Professor Singer, Grace Singer Cane's brother, was also a source of important first-hand information about the lives of Lawrence and Grace Cane. Dr. Vartan Gregorian, then president of Brown University, read the transcripts in 1995 and was the first to suggest that the letters be published. Lt. Col. (ret.) John B. Wong shared valuable information about Lawrence Cane's entry into the 238th Engineer Combat Battalion and his actions during and after Operation Cobra. Robert W. Kenny, military researcher at the John Hay Library at Brown University, was generous with his time and expertise. The research staff of the Hodgson Memorial Library at Bryant College, in particular Colleen Anderson and Paul Roske, creatively fulfilled our numerous research requests. Linda Asselin, a faculty coordinator at Bryant, patiently corrected errors, formatted chapters, and took care of numerous and tedious details that made our work far easier and allowed us to complete this book in a timely fashion. Bryant student Mark Danisewicz helped our Macs and P.C.s to talk to one another. David Lux, chair of Bryant's history department, deserves particular thanks for his abiding support. Documentary film maker and journalist David J. Boardman broadened our understanding of the Spanish Civil War by introducing us to Ken Loach's provocative film, "Land and Freedom."

David Cane's children, Rachel and Eli Cane, helped to transcribe the original letters, and in so doing they got to know the grandfather that they never met. David's wife, Suzanne Cane, transcribed many of the letters and much of the supplemental material. She has been a constant source of insight, advice, encouragement, and love. Nadja Pisula-Litoff and Alyssa Barrett Litoff have been a part of their mother's quest for the human stories of World War II all of their lives. Their continued encouragement, scholarly advice, and love are greatly appreciated. David Smith's immediate family—Sylvia, Clayton, Kit, Jamie, and Joshua—have been equally supportive of this effort to bring to life the stories of the World War II generation. To our families, we offer our heartfelt thanks and love.

D.E.C.
J.B.L.
D.C.S.

INTRODUCTION: LAWRENCE CANE'S FIGHT AGAINST FASCISM

Judy Barrett Litoff and David C. Smith

As most Americans grappled with the challenges of the Great Depression of the 1930s, the political left looked beyond the economic problems of the nation and recognized that a greater threat, the rise of fascist and totalitarian governments, loomed on the horizon. Americans who embraced the ideals of the left expressed grave alarm at the ease with which fascism and totalitarianism had gained popularity and power in Europe and in Asia. In July 1936, with the outbreak of the Spanish Civil War, many on the left feared that all of Europe would soon fall to fascism. Right-wing General Francisco Franco, with the support of Adolph Hitler and Benito Mussolini, quickly defeated many of the Republican forces in Spain. As the situation deteriorated, antifascists from around the world, spurred on by the Third Communist International (Comintern) in Moscow, rushed to help the Spanish Republicans. Eventually, 35,000 antifascists from fifty-two countries joined with their Spanish comrades to oppose Franco. Three thousand of this group came from the United States where they fought for the mostly English-speaking Fifteenth International Brigade. One of these Americans was Lawrence Cane.[1]

Lawrence Cane was born on August 8, 1912 in New York

---

[1] The literature on the Spanish Civil War is voluminous. The starting point for researchers is Hugh Thomas, *The Spanish Civil War* (New York: Harper and Row, 1977). Three important works on the American experience are Peter N. Carroll, *The Odyssey of the Abraham Lincoln Brigade: Americans in the Spanish Civil War* (Stanford: Stanford University Press, 1994); Cary Nelson and Jefferson Hendricks, eds., *Madrid 1937: Letters of the Abraham Lincoln Brigade from the Spanish Civil War* (London: Routledge, 1996); Robert A. Rosenstone, *Crusade of the Left: The Lincoln Battalion in the Spanish Civil War* (Lanham, Md.: University Press of America, 1980).

City, the eldest son of working-class, Russian-Jewish immigrants, Abraham and Faye Cohen.[2] He grew up in East Harlem where he was deeply influenced by the radicalism of the eastern European, mostly Jewish, immigrants who lived in his neighborhood. After graduating from DeWitt Clinton High School in 1930, he enrolled at City College at the 23rd St. Campus School of Commerce, a progressive institution that attracted many left-wing Jewish students. While at City College, he participated actively in several sports, including boxing and wrestling, was elected an officer of the student council, and served as editor of the college newspaper, *The Ticker,* where he wrote anti-Nazi editorials. As a supporter of the student antifascist movement, he helped organize protests against the German-American Bund and other Nazi activities in the United States.

Larry Cane was an inquisitive person who liked to see things for himself. While a student at City College, he once crossed the United States hobo-style, "riding the blinds." This trip gave him a new and vibrant look at the people of the United States, as it did other sojourners, such as Justice William O. Douglas and journalist Eric Severeid.[3]

Following his graduation from City College in 1935 Cane worked at a variety of jobs until shortly after the outbreak of the Spanish Civil War in July 1936. Motivated by his antifascist beliefs, he went to Spain as a volunteer for the International Brigades in the summer of 1937. In a February 12, 1972 radio interview in New York City, Cane talked about why he chose to go to Spain. He noted that mainstream Americans of the 1930s simply did not recognize the powerful threat that fascism posed to the world. By contrast, those who volunteered for Spain understood "that the fascist powers, led by Hitler and Mussolini, were bound on world conquest." By joining in this effort, Cane became part of the initial military endeavor to bring an end to fascism.[4]

---

[2] Lawrence Cohen changed his name to Cane in early 1939 following his return to the United States after the Spanish Civil War.

[3] William O. Douglas, *Go East, Young Man: The Early Years, An Autobiography* (New York, Random House, 1974) and Eric Severeid, *Not So Wild A Dream* (Columbia: University of Missouri Press, 1995), originally published in 1946.

[4] WBAI-New York radio interview, February 12, 1972. See Appendix H.

By the time Cane volunteered for the International Brigades, the U.S. State Department had banned travel to Spain, and during the war American passports were stamped, "Not Valid for Travel in Spain." Consequently, getting to Spain involved an arduous and illegal journey. Cane, in fact, did not tell his parents about his decision to go to Spain until after he arrived in Europe, when he then wrote them a letter and informed them of his plans. In a contemplative letter to his wife, written on V-E Day, May 8, 1945, he reminisced about his journey to Spain aboard the *Acquitania* and the "romantic and exciting secret moves via the [French] underground railroad. The hike over the Pyrenees and finally the thrill of being stopped by Spanish sentries."

Upon arrival in Spain, he enlisted at Albacete, where international volunteers underwent basic training. Cane was assigned to the mostly Canadian Mackenzie-Papineau Battalion, where he trained for about six weeks. The Mac-Paps, as the battalion was called, was named after William Lyon Mackenzie (1795–1861) and Louis-Joseph Papineau (1786–1871), two leaders in the 1837 independence movement in Canada. In fact, most of the international battalions chose names that honored leftist heroes in their nations' past. For example, the most famous United States battalion was the Abraham Lincoln Battalion, usually referred to as the Abraham Lincoln Brigade or simply the Lincolns.

From the late summer of 1937 until the autumn of 1938 Cane, who attained the rank of lieutenant, endured heavy combat. Throughout this period, the Mac-Paps and the Lincolns often fought side-by-side, and Cane established many strong and lasting friendships with men in both battalions. During the Aragon offensive of August–October 1937, he experienced difficult street fighting in Quinto and Belchite and acted as a sniper at the Battle of Fuentes del Ebro where he was wounded. Later hospitalized for typhus, he left his sick bed to join in the punishing warfare at the Battle of Teruel (December 1937–February 1938).

Throughout the dreadful retreat from Aragon in the spring of 1938 the Mac-Paps experienced heavy casualties. Upon reaching the banks of the Ebro River, they swam to the other shore, towing their weapons and one non-swimmer with them. After a month in bivouac, the Mac-Paps returned across the Ebro and began to assemble for a new attack against the fascist forces. On

July 26, 1938, near the town of Corbera, Cane and several other Mac-Paps stole some horses and went on a wild cavalry ride, driving out the fascist forces while securing a large supply depot. The next day, the Fifteenth Brigade, with the Major Atlee (British battalion) on the left, the Mac-Paps in the center, and the Lincolns on the right, undertook a full-scale charge on enemy positions. This was the last full-scale charge of any International Brigade. Casualties were extremely heavy over the next two months. Finally, on September 24, the bedraggled last remnants of the Fifteenth International Brigade, including Larry Cane, slowly crossed the plank bridge over the Ebro and eventually headed home.[5]

As the Fifteenth International Brigade retreated for the last time, the news of the appeasement of Hitler at Munich reached the weary soldiers, further adding to their gloom. These soldiers would carry their memories of Spain and their fight against fascism with them for the rest of their lives. Of the 3,000 American volunteers who had gone to Spain, more than 800 died. This staggering death toll equaled more than one-quarter of those who fought. Larry Cane was one of the survivors.

Only one fragment of a letter written by Cane from the Spanish front is known to exist. But that letter, written on November 20, 1937, describing the events at the Battle of Fuentes del Ebro, reverberates with the horrors of combat. Cane wrote: ". . . you've read about the horrors of war. So have I. But, it takes just about thirty seconds of charging in the face of machine-gun fire to understand what it really means. . . . Men fell all around. . . . Somehow or other, I can't figure why or how, the bullets missed me this time. . . . It was impossible to reach the fascist trenches—the fire was too heavy. So, we halted, utilizing the cover of slight rise in the ground."[6]

Cane returned to the United States in January 1939. For the

---

[5] For specific information on the Mac-Paps, see Victor Howard and Mac Reynolds, *The Mackenzie-Papineau Battalion: The Canadian Contingent in the Spanish Civil War* (Ottawa: Carleton University Press, 1986) and William C. Beeching, *Canadian Volunteers: Spain, 1936–1939* (Saskatchewan: Canadian Plains Research Centre, University of Regina, 1989).

[6] Lawrence Cane to "Jean-Jean," a friend in New York, November 20, 1937. Letter in the possession of David Cane.

next few years, he worked as a lathe operator at Liquidometer Corporation in Long Island City where he was a member of the United Electrical, Radio, and Machine Workers Union. During this time, he met and fell in love with Grace Singer. On June 16, 1940 Larry and Grace were married.

Following the Japanese attack on Pearl Harbor in December 1941 Cane tried repeatedly to enlist, but because of poor vision, he was rejected by the military. Finally, advised to enlist through his local draft board, he entered the U.S. Army in August 1942 at the age of 30. After processing at Fort Dix, New Jersey, he was sent to Geiger Field in Spokane, Washington for basic training as an aviation engineer attached to the Army Air Corps. Larry and Grace would spend much of the next three years apart. Yet their marriage and love continued to grow as they wrote hundreds of detailed letters to each other. Grace's letters did not survive the war years. Fortunately, the letters of Larry Cane did survive, and a selection of his letters form the core of this book.[7]

After the United States entered World War II, veterans of the Spanish Civil War quickly responded to the nation's call to arms. Of the 2,200 who had survived that conflict, at least 425 served in the armed forces and another 100 sailed in the merchant marine. Of course, many veterans returned with injuries that prevented them from serving in World War II, and others were simply too old for combat.

For the veterans of the Spanish Civil War, fighting for the United States against fascism and totalitarianism was the logical extension of their struggle for the Republican cause. Whether fighting along the Ebro River, going ashore on D-Day in Normandy, or battling the Japanese in the South Pacific, their objective was the same: the complete defeat of fascism.

What these veterans who served in World War II did not realize is that they would be routinely discriminated against by the military for being "premature anti-fascists." Spanish Civil War veterans were often assigned to noncombatant duties, denied commissions and other promotions, and prevented from going overseas. Historian Peter N. Carroll has argued that "recent his-

---

[7] The complete set of World War II letters of Lawrence Cane are in the possession of his oldest son, David Cane, who lives in Providence, Rhode Island.

torical scholarship, facilitated by the Freedom of Information Act, reveals that the systematic discrimination against Lincoln [and other] veterans in the armed services reflected a deliberate military policy formulated in the War Department against 'potentially subversive personnel.'"[8] Even in the face of this discrimination, however, veterans volunteered for dangerous duty, earned many decorations for valor, received battlefield promotions, and one veteran, Herman Bottcher, was awarded two Distinguished Service Crosses.[9]

It is uncertain to what extent Larry Cane experienced the type of discrimination so often endured by Spanish Civil War veterans. He rapidly advanced when he first entered the service, was commissioned as a 2nd lieutenant, volunteered for hazardous duty, took part in the assault wave with the combat engineers at Utah Beach on D-Day, and was awarded the Silver Star for gallantry in action against the enemy. During his interview for officer candidate school, the only questions about Spain the review board asked him dealt with technical military matters. No political questions were asked.

In fact, Cane's extensive combat experience in Spain prompted his commanding officers to turn to him regularly for advice and counsel. During basic training, he was almost immediately made an acting staff sergeant and sent to Non-Commissioned Officer School. In addition, he was frequently asked to lecture on his combat experiences. Although he enjoyed giving these lectures, his left-wing beliefs and his political acumen caused him to note in a September 12, 1942 letter to his wife that "of course, any political questions will have to be handled with tact. No one has told me that, but I'm sure that would be correct in such a situation." On September 23, 1942 he reported to Grace: "I've mentioned it before, but it's become part of the routine in my company. Any time there's a lecture by the company commander or any of the lieutenants, I'm called on to add to the discussions and illustrate from experience." Cane's extensive first-hand knowledge of combat also led to his being nominated for Officer

---

[8] Carroll, *The Odyssey of the Abraham Lincoln Brigade,* p. 262.

[9] For the remarkable story of Herman Bottcher, see Michael D. Haydock, "Born and raised in Germany, Herman J.F. Bottcher gave his life for his adopted country," *World War II* (March 1998): 8, 12, 14.

Candidate School (OCS) at the end of September. On the other hand, Cane encountered significant difficulties in getting assigned to a combat unit, but whether this was due to deliberate opposition or simply Army bureaucracy is unclear.

Cane was proud to be part of the fight against fascism. In his first full-length letter to his wife, written from Fort Dix, New Jersey on August 28, 1942, he complimented the Army for the "enormous job" that it was doing in processing "thousands of men" each day. However, he cautioned that there were two things about Army life that he didn't like. The first was the "segregation of Negro troops. It hits you in the puss the minute you step off the train."[10] The second was "something that doesn't happen. . . . Nobody has told us what this war is about and why we have to win it." He wrote that the welcoming speeches had included "not a word about fascism, about Hitler, about Japanese militarism." In his early letters to Grace, he continued to reiterate that "what this Army really needs is an educational system which would indoctrinate the men—officers as well—with a true spirit of fighting democracy."[11] For Larry Cane, the annihilation of fascism was the essence of the battle now being waged, and he wanted every American to understand this.

The mammoth two-volume study by Samuel Stouffer and his associates demonstrates that most servicemen of World War II made little attempt "to give the war meaning in terms of principles and causes involved, and [had] little apparent desire for such formulations."[12] In Larry Cane's case, however, quite the contrary was true: ideology remained the central motivating factor in his intense desire to serve his country in an effective way during the Second World War.

---

[10] Throughout World War II, the armed forces, like most of American society remained segregated. Not until June 26, 1948, when President Harry S. Truman issued Executive Order 9981, did desegregation of the military begin to occur.

[11] Lawrence Cane to Grace Cane, 6 September 1942.

[12] Samuel A. Stouffer, et al., *The American Soldier: Adjustment During Army Life.* Vol. I (Princeton: Princeton University Press, 1949), p. 433. Others who have emphasized this include Stephen E. Ambrose, *Citizen Soldiers* (New York: Simon & Schuster, 1997); Lee Kennett, *G.I.: The American Soldier in World War II* (New York: Charles Scribner's Sons, 1987); and William L. O'Neill, *A Democracy at War: America's Fight at Home and Abroad in World War II* (New York: Free Press, 1993).

Two months after arriving in Geiger Field, he made perceptive comments about his fellow G.I.s that are remarkably similar to what Stephen Ambrose would later call the "citizen soldiers" of World War II.[13] In an October 24, 1942 letter to Grace, he remarked: "Maybe they haven't got much book-larnin', maybe their table manners aren't so good, maybe some of them are slow to catch on. But they're honest and generous and wise-cracking guys. They're America and they're ready to go. The People Yes."

In early November Cane was transferred from Geiger Field to duty at Fort Belvoir, Virginia, Army Engineers Officer Candidate School where he was commissioned as a second lieutenant on March 3, 1943. He was sent for further training to the Military Intelligence School at Camp Ritchie, Maryland where he was stationed from March 10 until late June 1943. He was then briefly reassigned to Fort Belvoir. During this period, he made frequent weekend trips home to see Grace in New York City, but he also continued to write regularly to her. In a March 21, 1943 letter, he expressed special pride upon learning that Grace had begun work as a lathe operator. Acknowledging the important role to be played by women workers on the home front, he observed: "Well, 'Keep 'Em Rolling' has a new meaning for me now. It'll be my wife breaking her back over a whirring chuck—my wife and the millions of other working stiffs back home."

Throughout his letters, Cane expressed enthusiastic support for the Russian war effort. On January 20, 1943 he wrote, "Darling, aren't those Russians the stuff? They take so much and then they strike back and crush Nazis. What people!" Indeed, prior to the D-Day assault of June 6, 1944, Russians on the Eastern Front took the brunt of casualties in Europe. This was the period of the horrific fighting at the Battle of Stalingrad (winter of 1942–1943), the siege of Leningrad (September 1941–January 1944), Kursk (July–August 1943), and Kharkov (1941–1943).

Cane continued his January 20 letter by emphasizing, "Just think, the thing that makes them [Russians] that way is the same belief that you and I have. The belief in a better world, a finer and cleaner world, a place where people like you and me can make a wonderful life together without worrying about insecurity

---

[13] Ambrose, *Citizen Soldiers*.

and war." This theme is one that Cane would reiterate throughout his letters. As a member of the political left, Cane had strong
empathy for the Russian people and their struggle against fascism,
and he sincerely believed that the American wartime alliance with
the Soviet Union would lead to the creation of a better world
for all.

By the spring of 1943 Cane had become increasingly frustrated
over the fact that he had not been assigned to a combat unit. In a
May 18, 1943 letter to Grace, after learning that he had been
asked to stay on at Camp Ritchie as an instructor, he groused:
"My place isn't here—buried in the Blue Ridge Mountains giving boring lectures on some damn fool subject like staff duties.
My job's at the front, where men will be shaping the world's
destiny with guns." On July 4, 1943, when he learned of his
new assignment at Camp Claiborne, Louisiana, where he was to
command a unit of black troops in the 582nd Engineer Dump
Truck Company, he grumbled: "I'm really disgusted for fair this
time. ME, in an Engineer DUMP TRUCK Co! Probably spend
the rest of the war hauling manure across the swamps of Louisiana. I don't know the first goddam thing about a truck, never
drove one, can just about tell the hood from the ass end, and they
give me such an assignment. Well, if that's how they treat men
who know something about combat, and who are anxious to
fight the hell with them."

In an effort to attain a transfer to a combat unit, Cane wrote
and spoke to several officers whom he knew, and he implored
them to intervene on his behalf. Although the officers expressed
concern that this combat veteran was not being properly utilized,
they were unable to help him. Cane also wrote a letter to the
Chief of Engineers, U.S. Army, requesting reassignment to a
combat outfit, but that effort failed as well.[14]

Once it became clear that Larry would not be transferred to a
combat unit, he and Grace decided that she should become a
"camp follower" and join him at his new assignment in Camp
Claiborne, Louisiana. In making this decision, they did not differ
from other young couples of their generation. Millions of people

---

[14] Lawrence Cane to Chief of Engineers, U.S. Army, 17 July 1943. Letter in
the possession of David Cane.

were on the move in the United States as one of the major demo-
graphic shifts of the twentieth century took place. The Census
Bureau estimated that 15,300,000 civilians moved during the war,
over half of them across state lines. People hurried to new jobs
opening up in shipyards and war plants. Families sought out the
precious times they could steal together "for the duration" or as
long as would be granted them at the military bases where their
husbands and fathers were in training.[15]

On July 27, 1943, shortly before leaving for Camp Claiborne,
Larry commented on the segregated conditions they would experience while in Louisiana, informing Grace that "Claiborne is
going to be made an all-Negro Camp by the end of the summer.
. . . It's a helluva thing to have to say, but we're going to be living
in a part of the country where white chauvinism will blow in our
faces like a bad breath continuously." Cane, being the progressive
individual that he was, certainly did not oppose serving with black
troops. In Spain, for example, the troops of the International Brigades were integrated. What bothered him about the Louisiana
assignment was that it took him one step further away from
combat.

Larry and Grace were together during his six-month assignment at Camp Claiborne, and there are no letters from Cane
during this time period other than an August 1943 letter he wrote
to the Chief of Engineers, U.S. Army, in which he reiterated
his desire for "reassignment to any combat or airborne engineer
battalion." Cane emphasized that his prior combat experience in
the Spanish Civil War and his "practical and theoretical experience together with his enthusiasm for combat work qualif[ied]
him to contribute much more to the Service in a Combat or
Airborne battalion." He went on to state that "since a man's performance as a leader of soldiers depends chiefly on his enthusiasm
for his work and 'knowing his stuff,' the [said] officer, despite a
conscientious attitude, feels that he is handicapped. He will be
able to function only at a fraction of his capacity in his present
assignment."[16] This request was also rejected, and for the next

---

[15] For example, see Barbara Klaw, *Camp Follower: The Story of A Soldier's Wife*
(New York: Random House, 1943; reprint, 1944) and Agnes Meyer, *Journey
Through Chaos* (New York: Harcourt, Brace and Company, 1944).

[16] Lawrence Cane to Chief of Engineers, U.S. Army, August 1943. See Appendix B. Letter in the possession of David Cane.

six months, Cane remained at Camp Claiborne with the 582nd Engineer Dump Truck Company.

A letter that Grace wrote from Camp Claiborne to her younger brother, Mark, who had recently enlisted in the Army Air Forces, suggests that Larry's assignment to the 582nd may have been a deliberate effort by the Army to keep him out of combat. She reported to her brother that "Larry's now Mess and Supply Officer of his company—they've been giving him the old one-two and he's pretty disgusted. They don't seem to like men from Spain. We feel they intend to bury him in Louisiana for the duration. For a while they took him away from the troops and gave him a run of crappy assignments—but now he's back with his company. But he'd prefer to be in the fight over there. Oh well, maybe he'll get the breaks soon! Who knows."[17]

In January 1944 the 582nd received orders to go to England. Cane was now one step closer to actual combat. By that time, Grace was in the early stages of pregnancy. She returned alone by train to New York City so that she could be near family and friends as she awaited the birth of their first child. Cane traveled north with his company, leaving Louisiana on January 31, 1944 where he served as quartermaster of the troop train on the way to their departure point at Camp Shanks, New York.

Writing from the troop train, Cane underscored his progressive principles when he sarcastically reported on the segregation policy of the Army. "We're traveling with a white outfit on the same train—they in one section, we in another. In good old Army fashion we have separate messes and separate cars." Cane, however, seized the situation on the train as an opportunity to advance social justice. In this same letter, he told Grace how he was able to get the black and white mess sergeants together to plan menus and exchange ideas, commenting that "each thinks the other is a pretty good guy. (Not very much, but it's something.)"

Cane and the 582nd Dump Truck Company arrived in England on February 21, 1944 as part of the massive build-up of American troops and supplies prior to the anticipated cross-chan-

---

[17] Grace Cane to Mark Singer, November 11, 1943. This is one of five letters that Grace wrote to her brother during World War II that survived the war years. Letters in the possession of David Cane.

nel attack into Nazi-occupied France. By the time of the June 6, 1944 D-Day invasion of Normandy, more than 1.5 million American troops were in England. Over the next several months, Cane and the 582nd moved supplies for the impending attack.

On the day of his arrival in England, Larry wrote to Grace and proudly reported that "the first thing we got when we got off the boat was a speech of welcome which told us briefly and unequivocally why we were here. There was no monkey business about it. Everything right on the line. We're here to invade the continent." He then continued, "To me, the most thrilling remarks and those which practically floored the gentlemen from the South, were deliberate and blunt orders that in this theater there will be no racial discrimination whatsoever." His letters from England contained vivid accounts of the English people and their willingness "to fight to the death," the destruction caused by the Blitz, and the immense history that surrounded him.

Even with all the training and preparations required for the D-Day invasion, there was still time for relaxation and entertainment. On February 27, 1944 Larry wrote Grace about an integrated dance at the local post of the British Legion. He told how the men of the 582nd were, at first, reluctant to ask British women to dance even though "we had told them that the English did not have the same attitude toward mixed association." After "the first pioneer hesitatingly asked a girl to dance," others joined in and "the evening was, for them, a memorable occasion." The evening also provided an opportunity for Larry Cane to draw some prescient conclusions for a fellow officer who was "shocked" by the night's events. He told the officer that he "better get used to it. And so had a lot of others. Because tens of thousands of Negroes will come home with a lot of new ideas when this is over."

On March 20, Larry reported to Grace that he was attending a school located in a large English manor house. Because of censorship regulations, he could not provide additional information except to say that "it's one of those places Jerry [the Germans] is probably very much interested in. No, it's not Cp. Ritchie stuff." In fact, Cane attended a school at Overcourt Manor in Bristol on bomb reconnaissance where he was taught how to defuse the enemy's ordnance. Sometime in April he volunteered to take part in the D-Day landings when the 582nd Dump Truck Company was assigned as the trucking outfit for the 1106th Engineer Combat Group which had been picked to carry out the assault engineer work in the landings on Utah Beach. In typical Cane fashion, he then used this new assignment as an opportunity to lobby, once again, for a permanent transfer to a combat unit.

In the final weeks leading up to D-Day, Cane's work increased dramatically, and he did not have time to write as often as he would have liked. In a May 3 letter to Grace, he wrote, "I hope you haven't been worried by the sudden gap in my letters. We've been terrifically busy recently. What we've been doing and where we've been is, of course, impossible for me to describe—you'll understand."

As the invasion date drew near, the sending and receiving of letters became increasingly important to Americans stationed in England and loved ones on the home front. On May 26, Cane lamented "that the mailman didn't bring me one of those blue envelopes from you that always makes my heart skip a beat." Grace received even fewer letters in the weeks preceding D-Day as mail from England was held back because of the fear that someone might give away important information about the forthcoming events.

Throughout the wartime years, mail was universally recognized to be the number one morale builder in a service person's life. Ernie Pyle, whose wartime dispatches most accurately captured what life was like for the ordinary frontline soldier, placed "good mail service" at the head of his list of soldiers' needs. Larry Cane certainly agreed with this observation. Grace's letters would sustain him in the coming months of hard combat, and his letters would be equally important to her.[18]

On the early morning of June 6 Cane landed on Utah Beach with eight of his men from the 582nd Dump Truck Company along with the first assault waves of the 238th Engineer Combat Battalion. He participated in the demolition of beach obstacles and the storming of beach defenses, and he helped secure the

---

[18] Judy Barrett Litoff and David C. Smith, " 'Will He Get My Letter?' Popular Portrayals of Mail and Morale During World War II," *Journal of Popular Culture*: 23 (Spring 1990): 21–44.

beach for the invasion forces that were to follow. Cane was the only Spanish Civil War veteran from the United States to participate in the assault wave on D-Day.

By mid-morning of June 6 American troops had penetrated well inland of Utah Beach. The job of Cane and the other combat engineers who had removed the mines and other obstacles from the beach to clear a way for the initial landings was essentially over. Cane dug in along the line of dunes at the edge of the beach, enjoying a cigarette, and watching the rest of the invasion stream ashore. Looking down the beach he recognized a colonel whom he had met several weeks before. This same colonel had interviewed him when he had volunteered to take part in the landings. Following the interview, Cane had told him about his repeated attempts to be assigned to a combat unit and had solicited the colonel's help. The colonel responded that if he got off the invasion beach alive, he would be able to "write [his] own ticket." Now the colonel was hunkering down in the sand, trying to make himself as small as possible while the beach was taking enemy shell fire and occasionally being strafed by the odd German plane. Crawling over to the colonel, Cane shouted to him, "Hey colonel, remember me? Lieutenant Cane. How about that transfer?" To which the colonel replied, "Jesus Christ, Cane! Can't you at least wait until the paper and pencils come ashore?"[19]

In total, some 175,000 men and their equipment crossed the English Channel on June 6, supported by 5,333 ships and some 11,000 airplanes, as part of the greatest amphibious invasion in the history of warfare, landing on the Normandy coast and smashing through the formidable German coastal defense.[20] During the first three days immediately following the invasion, the 238th opened and maintained the roads on the entire Utah Beach area.[21]

On D-Day plus four, Cane dashed off a brief V-Mail to Grace

---

[19] Lawrence Cane as told to David Cane. Interview with David Cane, February 10, 2001.

[20] Stephen E. Ambrose, *D-Day, June 6, 1944: The Climactic Battle of World War II* (New York: Simon & Schuster, 1994), pp. 24–25.

[21] After/After Action Reports, Headquarters, 238th Engineer Combat Battalion, June 1–30, 1944, National Archives at College Park, Maryland, World War II Operations Reports, Record Group 407, Box 18763.

to let her know that he had survived the invasion.[22] The next day he wrote a much longer letter in which he fleshed out the details of the events of June 6. While describing these events, he reminded Grace of his anxiety about "getting into some real action—about being up front where people like us should always be. Well, darling, I should never have worried about it. Somehow, I always get to where the fighting is hottest."

The capture of Carentan by the 101st Airborne on June 11 made it possible for the 238th to construct a Treadway Bridge over the Douve River. The bridge, which played a vital part in the linkup between the American beachheads at Utah and Omaha Beaches, was the first military bridge constructed in France during the invasion.[23] Writing to Grace from a foxhole on June 13, Larry talked about the capture of Carentan and arriving at the bridge site on the outskirts of town where he was greeted by an elderly woman who "crept out of a pile of rubble that had formerly been her home" and "carried something close to her breast and painfully struggled up the debris until she stood at the highest part of the mound. Then gently and proudly she shook what she had in her hands, and out fluttered the tri-color of France." Cane's next few letters described "pushing ahead, foot by foot. Painful + slow, but sure" as they drove the Nazis out of France.[24]

During the hard, slogging fighting of the summer of 1944 Cane's revulsion for the Nazis only intensified. In a June 24 letter he angrily remarked: "One word is engraved in my heart when we go after those bastards, 'REVENGE.' For Spain and my maimed and dead comrades, for my people, the Jews, for the destruction, the devastation, the suffering of all the peoples of the

---

[22] In order to save space in scarce wartime transport, the government introduced V-Mail, a process that involved photographing letters that were written on specially designed $8^1/2 \times 11$ inch stationery available at post offices. When the V-Mail film was developed, the letter was delivered to the recipient in the form of a $4 \times 5^1/2$ inch photograph. Letters with a bulk weight of 2,575 pounds could be reduced to a mere 445 pounds when processed in this manner. More than one billion V-Mail letters were dispatched during the war years.

[23] After/After Action Reports, Headquarters, 238th Engineer Combat Battalion, June 1–30, 1944, National Archives at College Park, Maryland, World War II Operations Reports, Record Group 407, Box 18763.

[24] Lawrence Cane to Grace Cane, June 15, 1944.

world. It's a terrible thing to say, perhaps, but I am full of hate and my soul cries with the Russians, 'DEATH TO THE GERMANS. DEATH TO THE NAZI DESPOILERS.'"

By the middle of June Cane was back with the 582nd. He wrote to Grace on June 18 that "they've got me trucking again. If that's the way they want it, so be it. I got in some damn good licks, anyway." In a June 19 letter Larry told of the news that broke his heart when he had to burn all of Grace's letters. "You know," he wrote to his wife, "up to now, I saved every letter I ever received from you. C'est la guerre." During this period, his letters also contained many references to Grace's health and how the course of her pregnancy was progressing.

On July 4 Cane excitedly announced that he was about to get what he had "hoped and dreamed for so long": transfer to "the best battalion in the outfit." On July 5 he reported that he had been permanently transferred to the 238th Engineer Combat Battalion. However, he also mentioned that he had ambivalent feelings about leaving the 582nd, and he wrote to Grace that "much as I wanted to leave my old outfit, when the time came to say goodbye, I felt kinda funny. I had been with them so long, I'd become attached to them more than I had realized. The new battalion that I'm in, is, of course, not a Negro outfit. So, I guess I'll have to learn all over again how to get along with white soldiers."

Cane was assigned to the 1st Platoon of Company C of the 238th Engineer Combat Battalion, commanded by Lt. John B. Wong. Upon their first meeting Wong asked him, "Cane, can you shoot?" to which he replied, "Hell yes." Lt. Wong then told him that he wanted him to qualify every man in the platoon in firing the .30 caliber and .50 caliber machine guns. "That is my specialty," replied Cane. "I can do that with my eyes closed." Over the next three weeks, while the 238th cleared mines and booby traps, improved and maintained roads, and continued to build bridges, the 1st Platoon of Company C also practiced in the use of automatic weapons and prepared for the coming offensive.[25]

---

[25] David Cane interview with John B. Wong, Oakland, California, June 8, 2002.

From July 27 to 30, 1944 the 238th Engineer Combat Battalion took part in Operation Cobra, a coordinated attack preceded by an air and artillery bombardment of unprecedented magnitude designed to obliterate a segment of the German front along a passage through which the American Army was to pass. This battle resulted in the massive American breakout at St. Lo from the Normandy bocage country and into the open plain, beginning the rout of the German Army in France and opening the way to the Seine and beyond.

The 1st Platoon of Company C was assigned to the point of Combat Command B, 2nd Battalion of the 67th Armored Regiment (see Map 2, Operation Cobra, p. 106). For much of the time during the three days and nights of Cobra, the point was 10–20 miles in front of the main body of Combat Command B. On July 28 Lt. Wong assigned Lt. Cane to a reconnaissance mission, northwest towards the village of Roncey, from which direction the retreating armor and infantry of the German Seventh Army were moving as they attempted to avoid encirclement and destruction. For more than four hours Lt. Cane and his squad tracked the leading elements of this force from their jeep without revealing their own positions, relaying information about the enemy movements to the point of Combat Command B whose armor, infantry, and artillery waited in ambush. The ensuing attack destroyed the advance elements of the German armored column, resulting in an enormous two- to three-mile backup of the enemy column along the narrow Normandy roads and leading to the annihilation of the entire column by massive American artillery and air attacks. On the night of July 29–30, as part of the running battles with German armor in the vicinity of the villages of Grismesnil and Lengronne, the point of Combat Command B found itself in danger of encirclement by German forces attempting to break out of the trap. At great personal risk and under direct enemy fire, Larry Cane successfully reconnoitered a safe route of withdrawal for the American Armored unit. For his actions during Operation Cobra, Cane was awarded the Silver Star, the third-highest combat decoration for gallantry in action. The 1st Platoon of Company C received a Distinguished Unit Citation, and each man in the platoon was awarded the French Croix de Guerre with Palm for their leading role in the American breakout.[26]

In the following weeks, Cane served at the front in the dramatic race across France. From August 25 to 27, his company ferried infantry across the Seine River at Evry Pont Bourg near Corbeil, 30 kilometers south southeast of Paris and constructed a Class 40 steel Treadway Bridge. Several more bridges were constructed across the Marne River near Meaux, 44 kilometers east of Paris, from August 28 to 31. Over the next few days, the battalion advanced north through Soissons (Aisne River) and Chavignon (Ailett River), bridging the Oise River with a 110-foot, Class 40 Bailey Bridge at Etréaupont near the Belgian frontier. After crossing into Belgium, the battalion reached Namur on September 6 and moved rapidly through Liège and Herve to enter Nazi Germany in front of Aachen on September 15, 1944.[27]

During this difficult fighting, Larry wrote to Grace at every chance that he could get. On August 12 he told her about the "job" that got him the recommendation for the Silver Star. He matter-of-factly reported that "there were a lot of tanks + equipment that were in danger of falling into enemy hands. So, I volunteered to get them out. With some luck, I managed to take about a hundred armored vehicles, including thirty medium tanks through enemy held territory." But Cane saved most of his praise for the men of his battalion, writing on August 20 that "they're 100% G.I. Joes and they're wonderful. . . . Like most of the American Army, they're not much on spit and polish—and they never will be, no matter how much the West Pointers tear their hair. But they're tough, and they stay with it no matter how hard the going."

As the 238th moved rapidly across France toward the German

---

[26] For an account of the 2nd Armored Division during Operation Cobra as well as the role played by the 238th Engineer Combat Battalion, including Lts. John Wong and Larry Cane, see Mark Bando, *Breakout at Normandy: The 2nd Armored Division in the Land of the Dead* (Osceola, Wisc.: MBI Publishing Co., 1999). A copy of Cane's Silver Star citation is included in Appendix D.

[27] After/After Action Reports, Headquarters, 238th Engineer Combat Battalion, August 1–31, 1944, September 1–30, 1944, National Archives at College Park, Maryland, World War II Operations Reports, Record Group 407, Box 18763.

border, Cane wrote of the enthusiastic greetings the troops received from thankful French peasants who welcomed their liberators with wine, food, flowers, songs, and kisses. He reported with special pride about the French Forces of the Interior and the heroic work of the French underground.

Yet even in the midst of these historic days of World War II what most concerned Larry Cane was his "darling" Grace and his unabated love for her and their unborn child. Despite the suffering and misery of war, he often reminded Grace that "for me the worst thing is terrible loneliness and longing—the heartrending yearning that I have for you." As the September 20 due date of the birth drew near, he expressed special concern for Grace's health and well-being, telling her that "no matter what I'm doing or where I am, I'll be pacing that hospital floor."[28] On September 11 he wrote, "I keep thinking about the 20th of this month. I know, of course, that babies don't run on train schedules—but the 20th is a good reference date. Very possibly you may get this letter after the event. You may even be lying in a hospital bed reading this right now."

Larry's first letter to Grace after stepping on German soil, written on September 15, began with an anxious statement about the impending birth and his abiding love for his wife: "I've said it many times before, but it still goes, I wish I could be with you darling. I'm so lonesome and homesick for you. Each letter I receive from you is like being home for a few minutes." In this same letter, he also returned to the political theme of antifascism and its growing importance to America's fighting forces, noting that as "we progressed through France and Belgium, the men saw what Nazism actually meant to the people. Most of them, in my outfit anyway, are conscious anti-fascists now."

Shortly after crossing into Germany on September 15 the 238th Engineer Combat Battalion was temporarily placed in the line as infantry, 2 kilometers southwest of Aachen, on the border between Germany and Belgium. Bitter fighting continued along the Siegfried Line, Germany's western fortified frontier, until noon on October 21 when the German garrison at Aachen finally surrendered.

---

[28] Lawrence Cane to Grace Cane, 13, 18 August 1944.

For the next three to four weeks the battalion was engaged in clearing mines and repairing streets in Aachen, as well as undergoing additional training. The 238th entered the fighting in the Hurtgen Forest around November 26, bivouacking in the town of Eschweiler on the Inde River east of Aachen, where it constructed more bridges. On November 28, Cane was transferred to the battalion staff and named assistant S-2 (intelligence officer). Several weeks later, he was appointed acting S-2.[29]

On September 19 Cane jubilantly headlined his letter to Grace, "Somewhere in GERMANY!!" He told her that "this Siegfried Line is no joke, but we're busting our way through. . . . The people here are no longer friendly. This is Naziland and they hate us. We are no longer 'Liberateurs,' we are now 'Invaders.'" But what he seemed most concerned about was the impending birth of their child. In this same letter he wrote, "Today is the day before the deadline [due date], and darling so help me, I'm a lot less worried about Jerry's artillery than I am about you."

Not until October 4 did Cane learn that his son, David Earl, had been born on September 22, 1944. Grace's sister, Marjorie, had sent Larry a telegram with the news of the birth, but it was delayed. The telegram, along with a letter from Grace, arrived at about the same time. Even the news of the birth of his son could not assuage Larry's apprehension, however, and he wrote to Grace on October 7, "Same old story, I'm consumed with anxiety."

Over the next few weeks, Larry wrote of sharing the good news of the birth of David with his fellow officers, and how he proudly circulated the photographs that Grace sent him to his friends. In his November 11 letter, in which he described the ceremony when he received the Silver Star, he lamented, "I wish you could have seen the ceremony. You would have been so proud. All through the proceedings I kept thinking, If only my Gracie could be here, holding David in her arms, and drinking it all in."

In November, as Larry and the men of the 238th cleared the

---

[29] After/After Action Reports, Headquarters, 238th Engineer Combat Battalion, October 1–31, 1944, November 1–30, 1944, National Archives at College Park, Maryland, World War II Operations Reports, Record Group 407, Box 18763.

mines and repaired the streets of Aachen, he wrote a long letter to Grace in which he mused about the fate of postwar Germany. He expressed frustration with the mainstream analysis published in newspapers and journals such as *The Stars and Stripes, Life, Time,* and *Newsweek.* He urged Grace "to sit down and write me a long letter telling me about what we are going to do with Germany after the war." He continued by asking her "if anything is being said about it in Church these days, give me the dope—clippings, articles, etc." "Church" was their code name for the Communist Party, and Larry yearned for news from the left.[30]

On November 22, 1944, the day before Thanksgiving, Larry contemplated the meaning of giving thanks in the midst of war, writing that "there'll be rain tomorrow, just like today and the day after tomorrow, and there'll be mud and gunfire and bitter battle, and there'll be loneliness and longing." But after further thought, he added, "when our turkey's dished out (yes, we'll have turkey), I'm going to be thankful that I'm still alive, thankful for my wonderful wife and the baby I've never seen, thankful that I've been able to come from the maelstrom of the beach of Normandy on H-hour June 6th to the quagmire of the Siegfried Line, thankful that the world stands on the verge of victory over the horror that is fascism, thankful that I have been able to contribute my two bits to the struggle, thankful for the men around me and their courage and fortitude." The interlude of Thanksgiving was quite short, however, and within a few days Cane once again found himself in the thick of battle.

Beginning on December 16, 1944 American forces received the brunt of a massive German counterattack, popularly referred to as the Battle of the Bulge, along a 110-kilometer front that initially drove a deep salient into the Allied lines in the Ardennes Forest of Germany and Belgium. The 238th Engineer Combat Battalion took part in this fighting, initially moving from Eschweiler, Germany to Xhoris, Belgium to meet the German counterattack. Acting in conjunction with the 82nd Airborne Division, the battalion played a critical role in halting German advances near Manhay from December 23 to 25. The 238th continued to work for the next week in direct support of the 82nd

---

[30] Lawrence Cane to Grace Cane, 15 November 1944.

Airborne, preparing trees for abatis and bridges for demolition, putting in minefields, and constructing road blocks. Over the next month, the battalion constructed numerous bridges under enemy artillery fire in the Ardennes Forest of Belgium. As the enemy salient was reduced, the 238th constructed bridges, repaired and maintained the road in its sector, and removed numerous mines. All this occurred during one of the most severe winters of the century.[31]

Even as the Battle of the Bulge was raging, Cane realized that he was a participant in one of the great events of the twentieth century. In a letter to Grace on December 27, during the height of the battle, he wrote, "I'll bet you and everyone else back home has been hugging the radio and biting fingernails." He continued, "A great swirling battle is raging now—one which will go down in history as one of the great, decisive battles of all times. . . . Tell the folks back home, they can be proud of their boys. I've been in some shows the past few days that made me so proud I could have cried."

In a January 9, 1945 letter, he described his work as an intelligence officer where he gathered information needed for building bridges at the front. He told Grace that he felt like a "damn duck in a shooting gallery" during reconnaissance. As "some sonofabitch of a Krauthead" shot at him, he took out his "damn tape measure" and jotted down his findings. Cane then unpretentiously concluded, "That night a bridge goes in. The next morning tanks are rolling across."

By the middle of January, with the Germans finally pushed back, Cane could contemplate the day when American and Russian troops would be together in Berlin. He told Grace that "It'll be a great day when we can meet the 'Tovarische' in Berlin, and drink a couple of beers to the death of German Nazism."[32]

The fate of postwar Germany continued to trouble Cane, and on January 27, 1945 he wrote a long letter to Grace on this topic.

---

[31] After/After Action Reports, Headquarters, 238th Engineer Combat Battalion, December 1–31, 1944, January 1–31, 1945, National Archives at College Park, Maryland, World War II Operations Reports, Record Group 407, Box 18763.

[32] Lawrence Cane to Grace Cane, 16 January 1945.

But he concluded with the observation that he didn't "believe that the world will live happily ever after, merely as a result of the correct solution of the German problem. That's only part of the job. The living standard of the steel worker in Youngstown, Ohio, the well-being of a Chinese peasant standing barefoot in his flooded rice-paddies, the liberty enjoyed by the Untouchable Indian, the educational facilities at the disposal of a Negro share-cropper, are part and parcel of the problem of maintaining the Peace."

Interspersed with Cane's discerning political commentary were beautiful tributes to his darling "Gracie." On February 4, 1945 he plaintively wrote: "I miss you. Miss the smell of your hair, your head on my shoulder, the feel of your body at night. I miss the sound of your laugh, the perfume behind your ears, your warm lips under mine. I miss your biscuits, the way you walk into a room, the desk crammed full of your junk. I miss our constant exchange of thoughts and ideas, our growing up together, our dreaming of the future. And I wish I could see and hold our son—part of both of us."

Following the Battle of the Bulge the 238th supported the U.S. First and Ninth Armies as the Allies began a massive push through the Siegfried Line, first to the Roer River and then to the Rhine. The battalion continued to construct bridges, sometimes under heavy fire. On March 17, the 238th crossed the Rhine, the last major obstacle to the invasion of the German heartland. In the ensuing month, the battalion moved rapidly east as the German Army collapsed. During this period, the 238th constructed numerous bridges, cleared obstacles and mines, and carried out reconnaissance. One of Cane's duties as acting S-2 for the battalion was to screen the male population of German cities to identify those persons who had previously been part of the German military.

Shortly after the liberation of the Nordhausen concentration camp on April 12, fighting ceased on the battalion's front. By April 24 the 238th had taken over Military Government duties, with their headquarters at Helmsdorf. On April 30 the battalion was assigned responsibility for the city of Eisleben where it was located at the time of the final German surrender on May 8, 1945.[33]

During the spring of 1945, with the end of the war in Europe finally in sight, Cane wrote about the crumbling morale of retreating Nazi soldiers, the despicable behavior of the captured Nazi elite, the circumstances of fellow Spanish Civil War veterans, the integration of a few American infantry units, the death of Franklin D. Roosevelt, and his disappointment at being replaced as battalion S-2 by a West Pointer. On April 15, three days after the liberation of Nordhausen, he wrote about the "indescribable murder mills that have been running full blast since the Nazis came to power twelve years ago" and emphasized that "nothing in all the written history of man can equal, or even approach, the infamy and degradation, the sadistic depravity, the barbarism of Germany under Hitler."

He began his May Day letter of 1945 on a brighter note with "May Day greetings from the ruined citadel of Nazism!" In this same letter, he told of former Russian prisoners of war who were "celebrating May Day the old-fashioned way. They'd cut down some trees and constructed an archway over the entrance to their camp. The arch was painted red. On the top center was a huge red star. . . . Red flags were streaming in the brisk wind. An altogether stirring sight."

On V-E Day, May 8, he could finally write to Grace and say with relief, "We made it." He recalled the "long, hard, bitter road . . . the painful trek from Madrid to Berlin. So much suffering, so much heartbreaking loneliness and longing for you, so many comrades lost." He recited a litany of battles fought—his first days in Spain in the summer of 1937, the terrible retreat in Aragon, D-Day on Utah Beach, the Siegfried Line, the Battle of the Bulge, and the final linkup with the Russians. And he closed this letter with the plea, "If you've ever wished hard for anything, wish that I'm one of the lucky ones who comes home soon." Unfortunately, it would be almost six months before Larry, Grace, and David would be reunited.

---

[33] After/After Action Reports, Headquarters, 238th Engineer Combat Battalion, February 1–28, 1945, March 1–31, 1945, April 1–30, 1945, May 1–31, 1945, National Archives at College Park, Maryland, World War II Operations Reports, Record Group 407, Box 18763.

From May 9 until May 31 the 238th Engineer Combat Battalion carried out Military Government duties in Eisleben. Cane was placed on special assignment, opening a Counter Intelligence Corps (CIC) office in Eisleben staffed by four German-speaking enlisted men. In this capacity, he was responsible for the identification of Nazi officials, including members of the Gestapo and S.S. as well as German soldiers now trying to pass as civilians.[34]

On May 31 the CIC detachment was officially relieved. Three days later, on June 3, the Battalion moved by motor convoy to the Assembly Area Command in France, first at Camp Baltimore between Reims and Chalons sur Marne and then to Camp Oklahoma City in Sissonne on June 16. The 238th remained there for the next four months, initially preparing for transfer to the Pacific and then, following the Japanese surrender in August 1945, awaiting shipment back to the United States. Although given duties in camp construction and maintenance, the period between June and late October, when Cane began his journey home, was mostly spent marking time.

After V-E Day, Cane wrote about his first meeting with Russian soldiers where he exchanged a bottle of Scotch for a bottle of vodka. He provided a highly illuminating account of a conversation with two former functionaries of the Communist Party of Germany who had spent "twelve years in the infamous concentration camp for politicals at Buchenwald." Following his transfer to the Assembly Area Command in France in early June, about the only thing that kept him sane from all the boredom that he and the other men were experiencing was his reunion with Al Tanz, a fellow veteran from the Spanish Civil War. At their first meeting in early July, they "chewed the rag for a couple of hours, exchanging news." They talked about "church" and how it was hard "to arrive at an independent opinion over here." At another meeting, they had a "real old-fashioned bull session" where they "beat the Spanish War to death."[35]

When the atomic bombs were dropped on Hiroshima and Nagasaki in early August, Cane responded enthusiastically, knowing

---

[34] After/After Action Reports, Headquarters, 238th Engineer Combat Battalion, May 1–31, 1945, National Archives at College Park, Maryland, World War II Operations Reports, Record Group 407, Box 18763.

[35] Lawrence Cane to Grace Cane, 16 May, 3, 16 July 1945.

that the war would soon be over. He also recognized the great potential for the peaceful use of atomic power, telling Grace that "here is a source of power, which if harnessed, makes practically anything you can dream of possible—running through the air like Superman, taking a trip to the moon, anything." In response to the Russian entry into the Pacific War, Cane wrote that he looked forward to the "future friendship of the Russians and ourselves," and, in retrospect, he naively predicted that "we're going to be friends for a long time. Not that there won't be plenty of bastards who'll try their damnedest to split us." With the acceptance of unconditional surrender by the Japanese on August 14, Larry exclaimed in his next letter, "It's over! Really over! . . . Tell Davy his pop will be there to give him a piggy-back soon."[36]

The remainder of Cane's stay in Europe was a waiting game of "insufferable boredom and impatience." He frequently complained about the "confusion, inefficiency and stupidity" of the Assembly Area Command. He did experience a brief respite in mid-September when he went on a one-week Cook's tour of Switzerland in an effort to take "up the slack time." Even in Switzerland, he interjected politics into the tour when he visited "the biggest steel works in the country" and "had a fine time sticking my nose everywhere and talking production with the plant managers, and wages, hours and unions with the workers." Upon returning to Camp Oklahoma City, he sarcastically remarked to Grace, "Well, back to Alcatraz. . . ."[37]

Finally, on October 10, 1945, Cane could exclaim: "Stop the mails! Poppa's coming home!" He sailed from Le Havre in late October, returning to the United States in November 1945 where he rejoined his wife, Grace, and their 14 month-old son, David Earl, whom he had never seen. He was discharged from the Army in February 1946 with the rank of captain. In addition to the Silver Star, his decorations included the Good Conduct Medal, the World War II Victory Medal, the American Theater Ribbon, the European-African-Middle Eastern Theater Ribbon with five battle stars and bronze Arrowhead, and a Distinguished Unit Citation, as well as the Croix de Guerre with Palm from France.

---

[36] Lawrence Cane to Grace Cane, 12, 14 August 1945.

[37] Lawrence Cane to Grace Cane, 31 August, 15, 19, 26 September, 10 October 1945.

The published letters of Spanish Civil War veterans and the published letters of veterans of World War II have greatly expanded our understanding of the meaning of the experience of war in the twentieth century. But no book of wartime letters has so splendidly shown the ideological connection between fighting fascism in Spain and fighting fascism in the Second World War than this one. As much as we might lament that we have just a fragment of a letter from Larry Cane's Spanish Civil War correspondence, we can only marvel at the way that his World War II letters offer remarkable insights about why he fought for the Spanish Republic *and* for the United States during World War II.

Larry Cane's fight against fascism in Europe spanned eight years and two brutal wars. On many occasions, he risked his life for his ideals. As a civilian, Cane continued to take an active role in radical causes as he conscientiously worked for the creation of a better world. He responded bravely to the challenges of his time. *Fighting Fascism in Europe* is a testament to his enduring legacy.

REMEMBERING LAWRENCE CANE

David Cane

AS AN OFFICER IN THE American Army, my father, Lawrence Cane, participated in the liberation of the notorious Nordhausen concentration camp in the closing days of the Second World War. Some of the U.S. Army photographs that he brought home after the war documented scenes of starvation and death as well as attempts by the Nazis to cover up the evidence by burning some of the 3,000 dead that they left behind as they fled the victorious Allied armies. After the liberation of the camp, Germans from nearby Nordhausen had been forced by the American Army to come to the camp to witness what had happened in their midst and to bury the dead, and these scenes too were portrayed in the photos.

In the spring of 1995 I decided to donate these photographs to the Photo Archive of the United States Holocaust Memorial Museum, but first I wanted to learn more about the origins of the pictures. Unfortunately, I could no longer ask my father, since he had died in 1976 at the age of 64. Visiting my mother in Richmond, Virginia, I told her that I intended to donate the Nordhausen photos to the Holocaust Museum, and I asked her what she remembered about where the photographs came from. Her reply was completely unexpected. "Why don't you look at Daddy's letters?" she responded. "Perhaps you'll find the answer there." I had no idea what letters she was talking about. "I saved all the letters that he wrote to me while he was in the service," she explained. "I also kept a scrapbook at the time. They are all in a box in the attic."

In fact, there were just over 300 letters in all, written in the neat, clear handwriting that I knew so well. Most were one to three pages in length and together they covered the entire period of his Army service, beginning with his induction at Fort Dix, New Jersey at the end of August 1942, through his basic training at Geiger Field in Spokane, Washington, then the Engineer Officer's Candidate School (OCS) at Fort Belvoir, Virginia and Military Intelligence training at Camp Ritchie, Maryland, his training in England, and his entry into combat, starting with the D-Day landing on Utah Beach, the fighting in Normandy and the liberation of France and Belgium, the invasion of Germany, the Battle of the Bulge, the crossing of the Rhine and the collapse of the Reich, followed by military occupation service, and ending with the long wait pending demobilization and return to the States in November 1945. And indeed, among the letters was one that he wrote on April 15, 1945, three days after he had witnessed the nightmarish scenes at Nordhausen, mourning the death of President Roosevelt and describing his reaction to seeing the Camp:

> In my rather extensive career as a soldier I have seen much death and a great deal of suffering. But since this final push has been under way we have been overrunning some of the indescribable murder mills that have been running full blast since the Nazis came to power twelve years ago.
>
> Here were scenes so monstrous, so grisly that the imagination palls. Never, so long as I live, will I forget the horrible sights, the tales of the pitiful survivors whom we liberated.
>
> The worst one of all that I have seen was a concentration camp for politicals. Nothing in all the written history of man can equal, or even approach, the infamy and the degradation, the sadistic depravity, the barbarism of Germany under Hitler.

These letters opened up an entire world to me. Here was the man I had known through the eyes of a son, and yet here was much more. Here he was again as a young man—a veteran of the International Brigades and the Spanish Civil War for whom the fight against Franco and the war against Hitler and the Nazis were part of the same continuum, a struggle for freedom and basic human decency against tyranny and oppression and barbarism of a kind and extent unrivaled in all the sad, brutal history of the world. Here was his idealism, his intense interest in history and politics, his constant effort to see the larger picture. Here was his repeated frustration and despair over his many fruitless attempts to obtain a combat assignment, as well as his dedication and personal courage on the field of battle. Here, too, was his determination that when it came down to it, he would be where the action was and his vindication when his chance finally came and he was able to land in France on Utah Beach with the assault wave of the D-Day invasion, as well as his elation at finally obtaining a permanent transfer to the combat engineers. And running through all his letters, there was deep love for his young wife, Grace, his hopes and dreams for their future together, and his terrible longing for her even at the times of greatest triumph.

My mother, Grace Singer, was born in 1920 to David and Esther Singer, who lived near Central Park West and 92nd Street in New York City. Esther's parents had been born in Germany, David's in Hungary. David Singer, a successful lawyer, died in 1935 when Grace was only 15. By the age of 16, Grace had already become involved in the radical politics of the Depression. In December 1938, she was invited by a mutual friend to go down to the docks with Celia Cohen, whose brother, Larry, was coming home that day from Spain. When my father got off the boat, he greeted his sister and then turned to my mother and said "Hi, Gracie." Although he was eight years older than she was, he recalled having met her at a Communist Party gathering before he had left for Spain and immediately recognized her by her red hair. He soon began to court her and they fell deeply in love, marrying in June 1940.

When my father went into the Army in 1942 my mother had lived in Sunnyside, Long Island City, Queens and had worked as an organizer of volunteers for the Civilian Defense Volunteer Office of Greater New York. Once, Eleanor Roosevelt, who had become assistant director of the Office of Civil Defense (OCD), came to New York and gave a speech at the Macy's Auditorium to a group of OCD volunteers and leaders. My mother told me that, afterwards, Mrs. Roosevelt invited several of the women to accompany her back to her house at 29 Washington Square. They left the auditorium and walked all the way to Greenwich Village, trying to keep up with the first lady, who was marching ahead of everybody. Passersby stopped in their tracks as she suddenly strode by and called out, "It's Mrs. Roosevelt!" Arriving at 29 Washington Square, she gave my mother and the other OCD volunteers a tour of the house, including the President's Room, and then served them cookies and milk.

For several months in 1943 my mother joined my father in Louisiana where he was stationed at Camp Claiborne and where I was conceived. When he shipped out to England at the end of January 1944 she first lived in Great Neck, Long Island with her mother and sister, then moved to a small apartment on W. 77th St. in Manhattan. When I was born on September 22, 1944 the U.S. First Army had just invaded Germany and my father's Combat Engineer Battalion was about to go into the line as infantry in the fighting for Aachen. It was nearly two weeks before he received the telegram from my aunt announcing my birth. For the next year, he knew me only through photographs and from my mother's letters chronicling my growth. For my part, my mother had me say goodnight to his picture every night.

I first met my father in November 1945 when I was 14 months old. During the long months following the German surrender in May 1945, my parents waited impatiently to be reunited, uncertain when he would be allowed to return. At last, at the end of October 1945, his telegram arrived from Le Havre announcing his imminent departure from France. Finally came the long-awaited phone call in mid-November. He had landed in New York, had 24 hours' leave, and would be home as soon as possible. Early the next morning he was there. According to my mother, he kissed her so hard she couldn't hold her head straight for a week! But then, in mid-clench, he practically dropped her. With a tiny noise from my bed in the next room, I was announcing that I was there too. He walked into my room to meet his son. I looked at him, then handed him my toy telephone. So he said hello to me by phone. I was just learning to walk and could still hardly talk. With my Dad holding on to my upraised forefinger, I led him on a tour of the entire apartment, then consented to have him feed me my breakfast, after which I leaned forward in my high chair, planted a wet kiss on his cheek and said "Da-Da."

Following his discharge from the Army with the rank of captain and back in civilian life, my father did not return to his prewar job as a lathe operator at the Liquidometer Corporation, but began working as a salesman, first selling liquor, then housewares. As a manufacturer's representative, his work involved travel throughout much of southern New England. In August 1947 we moved to West Hartford, Connecticut, where he could be more centrally located for his work, and where he and my mother, who had both grown up in New York City, each had cousins.

We lived in a second floor, 3¹/₂-room apartment in a housing development of simple, two-story brick garden apartments built just after the war. Loomis Drive where we lived was a quiet street. Most of our neighbors were other families with young children, and we kids used the grounds of all the apartments as our playground, where we could join in games of hit-the-bat or pickup baseball, play cowboys and Indians, ride our bicycles, and sled in the winter. We could also explore the vacant field next to our building or the cemetery in back, as well as a nearby brook. In the summer, the daily arrival of the Good Humor ice cream truck was a major event.

I do not think most of my early childhood was much different from that of my friends. During that time my father worked and my mother stayed home to care for her children, first just me and then my sister, Lisa, after her birth in 1949. I went to a local nursery school and kindergarten, attended the Memorial Day parades that heralded the beginning of summer and that ended at the cemetery just behind our house with speeches and the firing of rifle salutes. I joined the Cub Scouts where my mother was a Den mother, attended day camp first at the local park and then at Camp Shalom, learned to swim, listened to the Lone Ranger and the Shadow on the radio, and went to the Saturday morning movies at the Central Theater (admission 10¢) to watch Roy Rogers, Gene Autry, and Commando Cody fight off bad guys. We had no TV at home until 1955.

There were some ways, however, in which my experiences as a young boy were clearly different, although in many cases I was only vaguely aware of these differences at the time. Like many veterans of the Spanish Civil War, my father kept his idealism, his passion for social justice, and his political activism all his life. He also brought back a lot of stirring songs. (Many years later the satirist Tom Lehrer would sing, "Though he [Franco] may have won all the battles, we had all the good songs."[1]) My first intro-

---

[1] Tom Lehrer, "The Folk Song Army," *That Was the Year That Was* (Warner, 1965).

duction to the Spanish Civil War was my father singing me to sleep in an alternately gentle and booming voice: "Viva la quince brigada, rumbala-rumbala-rumba-la." I can remember lying on his shoulder as he walked me around the room or rocked me in the chair in my parents room as he sang, "Die Heimat ist weit und wir sind bereit. Wir kämpfen und siegen für dich: FREIHEIT" (The homeland is far away and we are ready. We are struggling and will emerge victorious for you: FREE-DOM—a song learned from the German Internationals, the Thaelmanns, union men, socialists, intellectuals, and communists who were refugees from Nazi Germany and who had brought their struggle against fascism to Spain). He would sing "Si me quieres escribir, ya sabes mi paradero: en el frente de Gandesa, primera linea del fuego" (If you want to write to me, you'll know where to find me: on the Gandesa front, in the first line of fire). And that's where he had just come back from again—the front lines of some of the most cataclysmic battles in the history of the world as a soldier in the Allied armies that had smashed their way into occupied France and swept the Nazi oppressors back to their "Vaterland," finally crushing the once-proud and strutting mad-men who had brought unparalleled destruction and misery to tens of millions of people.

As a young boy, I of course knew my father had been a soldier and a war hero: that he had landed on Utah Beach on D-Day, June 6, 1944, and that he had been awarded the Silver Star for bravery in action. He rarely, if ever, talked with his family about actual battle, but we learned about the horrors of war—the cold-ness, the misery of living in constant rain, the deadly fatigue, the wanton destruction and waste. Growing up in a Jewish family, I learned very early about the Nazis and the Jews. I do not remember when I first saw the grisly pictures of the Nordhausen concentra-tion camp. There were also other mementos and souvenirs—some thrilling, others sinister: a pair of wooden shoes which he had purchased in the midst of the fighting for the port city of Cherbourg; an SS officer's dress sword; Wedgewood purchased while he was stationed in England; china taken from the ruined house of a high Nazi official; a large swatch of green camouflaged silk parachute that had been used by U.S. paratroops in the D-Day invasion; a German aviator's leather flight helmet; an American army bayonet; an SS helmet; a map from the D–Day landings; a huge obscene Swastika; and a handmade tricouleur, a French flag that had been sewn in secret by a young girl during the Nazi occupation and that she presented to my father when her village was liberated in August 1944.

Throughout my father's life, most of his closest friends were his fellow veterans of the Abraham Lincoln Brigade in Spain, men with whom he had a special bond based on an extraordinary shared experience and a life-long idealism and devotion to progressive causes. They would often get together and "refight the whole Spanish Civil War" as he would describe it, or argue about current political events, what was going on in Franco-dominated Spain, and what was happening at home in America. As far as I know, after World War II, he never kept contact with any of his fellow soldiers from the U.S. Army in Europe or classmates at OCS. Perhaps this was because he was considerably older than many of the troops and fellow officers with whom he had served. (He was already 30 years old when he enlisted in the U.S. Army in 1942. Many of his fellow soldiers were only 18 or 19.) Although he would occasionally put on his American uniform and medals (he had plenty—in addition to the Silver Star, five campaign ribbons, a Distinguished Unit Citation and the French Croix de Guerre) and walk in the Memorial Day parades when I was a boy, he was not interested in joining the VFW or the American Legion.

Even as a child I was aware that my parents' politics were different from those of my friends' parents. None of them had ever been on a picket line with their mother, or participated from a baby carriage at the age of 6 months in a rent strike. Both of my parents were active in the late 1940s and early 1950s in the Communist Party. Although they had read Marx and Lenin and had fervent, often heated, political discussions with other friends who I later would learn were also party members, the talk in our house was not about the Soviet Union or overthrowing the government. It was about union organizing, workers' rights—the right to strike, the right to health care, the right to a job—things which are so mainstream in America now it is almost inconceivable that they were once considered radical. We talked in my family about racism and segregation—I learned about the notorious Jim Crow laws, about lynchings and beatings of people whose only "offense" was the color of their skin, who had to have separate schools, separate toilets, separate water fountains. It never occurred to me at the time that it was unusual that my parents had black friends, not just at work, but friends who came to dinner or whose homes we visited and whose children were also my playmates. I was taught by my parents from the beginning that skin color was a result of the presence of a simple pigment and that prejudice—racial, religious, political—was evil. I was told, however, that politics was family business and that things that I overheard at home were not to be repeated to outsiders or discussed with my friends. At the age of five and six, I knew nothing about the FBI or informers, but I knew that my parents' political views were outside the mainstream.

Although I was a pretty happy child, I could also be very sensitive and it was easy for others to hurt my feelings. In fact, I could be a terrible crybaby. Another child had only to insult me or say something mean, and I would run home wailing. My father was a very tough guy and this drove him nuts. Young children can be bullies and unwittingly cruel, but to make matters worse, it turned out that one older man, who didn't like my parents because of their politics, took particular delight in hearing me cry. In fact, I soon learned that kids in the neighborhood could collect a nickel from him every time they sent me home crying. This went on for several weeks. Each time I came home in tears, my father would tell me and my mother that I had to fight my own battles. "But they're bigger than me," I would plead. "Don't be afraid of bullies," he would say. Finally I had had enough. One day another kid took a swing at me and instead of running home bawling, I punched him back in the nose, then jumped on top of him and gave him a pretty good, six-year-old beating until several adults pulled me off and scolded me for picking on him (he was about six inches taller and outweighed me by about fifteen to twenty pounds!). I told them what I thought of them too, then rang the old man's door and demanded *my* nickel. That was the end of the bullying and I learned a good lesson about standing up for myself.

In the fall of 1952 I was eight years old. Most of my friends were either supporting the Republican candidate, Dwight Eisenhower, or the Democrat, Adlai Stevenson, for U.S. president—as were of course their parents. My parents, by contrast, were supporting Vincent Hallinan, a renowned attorney who had defended labor leader Harry Bridges and was the candidate of the Progressive Party. (Vincent Hallinan's son is Terence Hallinan, the long-time populist district attorney in San Francisco.) In October 1952 we went to hear Vincent Hallinan speak. To a group of at most twenty-five to thirty people, he outlined his views. His running mate for vice-president, a black woman named Charlotta Bass who was a prominent journalist and well-respected civil rights leader, also spoke. Afterwards I met the candidate himself. (None of my more establishment friends got to meet Ike or Adlai when *they* came to Hartford.) I asked Mr. Hallinan if he was going to win and he laughed and said very kindly that he didn't think so. I wanted to know why then was he was running? To which he replied that it was the right thing to do. Needless to say, he didn't even come close. My mother was a poll watcher and on election night, I was with her at a polling station in Hartford where the results were being read out from each machine. A typical result was something like: Eisenhower 1,300, Stevenson 800, several candidates I had never heard of 20–100 votes each, and Hallinan 12. It was disappointing, but then at least the Dodgers had won the pennant that year—so 1952 wasn't a total loss.

Early in 1952, when I was seven years old, I had decided that I wanted to support a baseball team. Not wanting to root for the Yankees like many of my friends (even then I thought the Yankees were so corporate they were practically Republicans), I announced to my father that I was a Cardinals fan. "Really?" he asked, "why is that?" "Because I like the bird on their uniforms," I told him. "Oh," he said, "that's fine. But did you know that the Cardinals won't hire Negroes?" "All right," I said, "I'm not going to root for them. Who does hire Negroes?" He told me that although Jackie Robinson had broken the color line in 1947, there were still only four teams with Negro ballplayers—the Brooklyn Dodgers, the New York Giants, the Cleveland Indians, and the Chicago White Sox. "OK," I said, "then I am going to support them." Of course, I quickly learned that there was no way to be both a Dodger and a Giant. Within a few weeks, I had become a fanatical Dodgers fan, a passion that would stay with me for over twenty years.

In 1953 Julius and Ethel Rosenberg became the first and only U.S. civilians to be executed for wartime spying, having been convicted on charges of giving U.S. atomic secrets to the Soviet Union. My parents were actively involved throughout the year in activities aimed at winning them clemency from the president. The night the Rosenbergs went to the electric chair, my father was participating in an all-night vigil outside the White House.

It was about this time that I became aware of Senator Joseph McCarthy. The House Un-American Activities Committee and Richard Nixon were not highly thought of in my house, nor was J. Edgar Hoover a household icon, to say the least. My mother began to work at this time and I started to realize that from time to time my father would be out of a job. It was several years before I was told why. During the period of the Red Scare, members of the Communist Party, Veterans of the Lincoln Brigades, people with leftish ideas, liberals, intellectuais, people who had gone to world peace rallies even once in the 1930s, were the targets of a mass anti-Communist hysteria. Branded pinkos, com-symps, fellow travelers, or outright traitors, these people were hounded from their jobs, banned from their professions, ostracized by their communities. I learned later that some of our neighbors would report to the FBI the license numbers of cars of people visiting our apartment. Mail was intercepted and opened. Periodically the FBI would show up at my father's place of work and inform his boss that Larry Cane's loyalty was suspect. Never mind that he had served in the U.S. Army in World War II and been decorated for heroism. He had fought in Spain in the International Brigades, and was considered by the U.S. government to have been a "premature anti-fascist." The next day he would be out of work, often needing months to find a new job, continually going into debt trying to support a wife and two young children. My father told me years later that during his last few months in the Army he had been interviewed by Army Intelligence. They told him that with his American military record, combined with his service in Spain, they could arrange it so that he could go right to the top of the U.S. Communist Party! When he told them that he wasn't interested and that they could go to hell, they told him, "OK, you will regret it. We will get you." From that time on he knew that the party would be filled with informers. By the mid-1950s, it had become a standard joke that J. Edgar Hoover was one of the chief financial supporters of the CPUSA. From time to time, there would be arrests in Hartford for alleged violations of the Smith Act, followed by articles in the local paper filled with names of alleged Communists and sympathizers, with the informers turning out to be people who had been to our home and with whose kids I had played. After the unmasking of McCarthy by attorney Joseph Welch at the Army-McCarthy hearings and McCarthy's subsequent censure and humiliation by the Senate in 1954, the anti-Communist hysteria began to subside in the United States.

In the meantime, my parents, like many others, had become disillusioned with the party, finally leaving in disgust after Khrushchev's revelation of the atrocities that had been committed by Stalin and then the Soviet invasion of Hungary in 1956. By 1960, when a matching pair of FBI agents showed up for the last time at our house, making veiled threats to my mother that they might cause trouble for me at my high school and asking her to give them the names of the people who had recruited her to the party, my parents were supporting John F. Kennedy for president.

Sometime in the early 1950s the great black American actor and singer Paul Robeson came to Hartford to give a concert. Before turning to a successful career as a film and stage actor, concert performer, and recording artist, Robeson had been valedictorian of his Rutgers class where he had starred in four sports, including twice being named an All-American in football, and had also earned a law degree from Columbia University. He was outspoken on behalf of racial justice and world peace, African independence, and left-wing causes in general, earning him the enmity of conservative groups in the United States. By the time he came to perform in Hartford, the possibility of demonstrations and even violent disruptions was a serious concern. The sponsors of the concert therefore kept his movements secret and arranged for him to stay at an unannounced location in the North End of Hartford, at the home of Jim and Helen Tate, who were friends of my parents. It was also arranged that my father would be in charge of security for Paul Robeson's visit. We arrived at the Tates' apartment the afternoon of the concert. While Mr. Robeson was taking a nap, my friend, Buddy Tate, and I were sent outside to play, with strict instructions to *stay out of trouble*. Good intentions. As it turned out, a young black boy, who I suppose hadn't been filled in on what a cool white guy I was, picked a fight with me over something silly. Although our scuffle mostly consisted of circling each other warily, it began to attract a bit of a crowd. What I remember most was suddenly being lifted up by the scruff of my neck by Buddy's Mom, Helen, who, attracted by the noise in the street, had rushed outside when she saw the cause. I was hustled back upstairs and given a sound talking to. By this time, Mr. Robeson had awakened from his nap and I was introduced to this gentle giant of a man who shook my hand seriously, then laughed heartily when he learned what I had been fighting about. As it turned out, the concert that evening was a great success and went off without incident. Several of the concert-goers, however, seeing my father standing sternly in the back of the hall in his trenchcoat, giving everyone the once over, thought that *he* was the FBI!

In 1955 my parents bought their first house, in Windsor, Connecticut, financing the purchase under the G.I. Bill. My brother, Joshua, was born in 1956. My parents immersed themselves in fixing up their new home, and I learned alongside my father a great deal about how to paint a house, sweat solder a pipe, build a fence, and other skills of home maintenance. Both of these New York City natives enthusiastically took up gardening, with my mother focusing on her flower beds and my father tending the lawn and proudly caring for his vegetable garden. The bayonet he had brought back from the Army was put to use weeding dandelions and planting tomato sets—he liked to say he was beating his sword into a ploughshare.

In 1962, just after I graduated from high school and prepared to go off to college, my family moved back to the New York area. My father had become national sales manager for a company selling adhesive-backed wall coverings. Although his work required him to travel all around the country, the company itself was based in New York. He took advantage of his travels to maintain and re-establish contact with many of his buddies from the Abraham Lincoln Brigade, visiting with his old friends Butch Goldstein, Gabby Klein, and Sammy Nahman in Los Angeles, or

Saul Wellman in Detroit. He became increasingly active again in the Veterans of the Abraham Lincoln Brigade, supporting democracy in Spain before the death of Franco, speaking out against American support for Franco, and assisting Spanish refugees, many of them still in exile in France and other countries. He enthusiastically met with young scholars interested in the Spanish Civil War, was interviewed for several books on the period, and helped to organize outreach activities such as a speakers' service which sent vets to American schools and universities to promote education about the Spanish Civil War.[2]

During the Vietnam War, when many of my college friends had major conflicts with their parents due to fundamental differences in their attitudes toward the war, my parents strongly supported me in my own opposition to it. When my wife, Suzanne, and I traveled to Washington, D.C. in November 1969 for the March on Washington, my father joined us at this huge peace rally. He joked later, however, that many people there probably thought he was a veteran of the Spanish-American War, rather than the Spanish Civil War.

He always dreamed of going to back to a Franco-free Spain. By the early 1970s many of his friends had started to go back even though Franco was still alive, and in June 1972 I traveled with both my parents and my brother from Madrid to Barcelona. We visited many of the battlefields and other places where he had been during the Spanish Civil War. We saw the ruins of Belchite, the fields of Corbera, the Ebro River valley, the stark Sierra Pandols, and the cliffs outside Teruel where the brigade had fought a desperate holding battle during the terrible winter of 1938. We met with young Spanish leftists and intellectuals and my father was interviewed by a Spanish film crew making an underground film about Americans who had come to fight 35 years earlier for Spain's freedom.

Throughout his life he continued to read extensively. He had a voracious appetite for books on history, social movements, politics, and political thought. He loved the parry and thrust of discussion, delighted in ideas, had little patience with mushy

---

[2] See, for example, Arthur H. Landis, *The Abraham Lincoln Brigade* (New York: The Citadel Press, 1967).

thinking. Once when I had expounded some superficial theory of what was happening in the world, he quietly demurred. "You need to read a little more history, Son," he gently told me.

In the early 1970s, however, his health, which had been remarkably robust all his life, suddenly began to fail. He noticed increasing difficulty with his night vision and developed blind spots. He was diagnosed with retinitis pigmentosa, a congenital deterioration of the retinal pigment that eventually would have left him completely blind had he lived. He developed phlebitis in his legs from long periods sitting in airplanes, and excruciating pains in his feet that often made it difficult for him to walk, then suddenly went away. Finally, in late October 1976, he returned home from a business trip, exhausted and ill, and within a week he had died, apparently of a viral infection that was never identified. Suddenly this strong and indestructible man was gone.

A year after his death, his old friend and fellow Spanish Civil War vet, Sammy Nahman,[3] sent a letter to my mother which typified the way we all felt about my father:

October 8, 1977

Dear Grace:

To me Larry was always a personal hero from the time I first met him at 16 years old and he was 23 in 1936. My going to Spain was influenced in part by Larry's being there and I too went to the Mac-Paps when I went to Spain. While there I got wounded twice while he was going through the same battles and more, he never got wounded there and all the other battles in Spain[4] and he never forgave me for getting wounded and the perennial get-together with Larry, Butch Goldstein and myself almost every year brought out this thorn in his side.

---

[3] Sam Nahman, a Sephardic Jew, was born in East Harlem where Larry grew up. He went to Spain at 18 in 1938 and returned to a Spain that was free of General Francisco Franco (1892–1975) in September 1977 with seven other vets, all of whom were good friends of Larry's.

[4] In fact, my father was wounded in the battle of Fuentes del Ebro in October 1937. In a second action, he received a shrapnel wound in the head from a bullet that struck the front leg of a machine gun that he was firing.

"You little son of a bitch, Sammy," he would say. "You come 8 months to Spain, go through the biggest battles of the war, get wounded twice and then go home a hero." "While I don't even get a scratch and all I got to brag about is my yellow jaundice and that don't show."

"Some people are just born lucky" I reply. "I get wounded but you're better looking, you can't have everything" and we would practically come to tears laughing over the always repeated personal joke.

God help me if I ever even hint aloud how I looked up to him as my personal ideal comrade I would of liked to be.

So when I heard he died, I cried and felt very vulnerable. I felt his death as such a loss that I cannot talk about him without tears coming to my eyes, so I feel your loss of Larry, as he too was part of me. This poem is a personal one. I hope it conveys how I feel. Use it as you see fit.

Love,
Manny (Sam Nahman) Harriman

ON THE DEATH OF MY COMRADE
LARRY CANE 1912–1976
(Poem written at Madrid, Spain, September 1977)

I cried
When I heard
You died Larry

The tears flowed
while rage
racked my insides

How could you die Larry
Not you
Not yet
We are almost there

Only yesterday
When the Ebro erupted
black earth—darkened red
exploding in Spanish hills

While death whistled
a chilling morning song

You held my hand Larry
scared that I was
and calmly with a smile
said don't worry, Sammy
we'll see Spain's warming sun again
How could you die Larry
Not you
Not yet
We are almost there

The rising sun is
already warming my face
Oh, how I would love
to see your face again
ablaze
In Spain's new full sun.

NOTE ON EDITORIAL PRACTICES

THE WORLD WAR II correspondence of Lawrence Cane to Grace Singer Cane totals just over 300 letters. In addition, five letters that Cane wrote to other family members are known to exist. All of these original letters are in the possession of Lawrence Cane's son, David Cane. The 186 letters that appear in this volume are transcribed as they were written. Letters that were not included in this volume were omitted because they contained details that distracted from the main story or were repetitive of previous material. Similarly, selected portions of some letters were also deleted. The latter deletions are indicated in the text by ellipses. Very rarely, obvious spelling errors have been corrected. No additional modification of spelling or grammar was made. Remarkably, all of these letters represent first drafts and essentially none of the original letters contain words that were crossed out. Only one letter, Cane's V-Mail of June 10, 1944, sent immediately after the D-Day landings, bears any marks of the Army censor. Official Army documents are reproduced verbatim in the Appendixes. We have provided explanatory footnotes to identify key persons, places, and events.

1

Basic Training: Geiger Field, Spokane, Washington
August 28–November 8, 1942

Co. B., 1229th Reception Center
Fort Dix, New Jersey
28 August 1942 (postmarked)

Darling Grace;

I'm in the Army now—really! It's almost 9 P.M. and I've been going ever since I got here 2 P.M.

Uniform, equipment, shots in the arms, walk here, stop, stand, keep moving, sit down, eat, hurry up, slow down—whew!

I don't have enough time to write a decent letter. I will first chance I get.

All my love, Larry

Co. B., 1229th Reception Center
Fort Dix, New Jersey
28 August 1942

Dearest Grace,

I'm snatching a couple of minutes after noonday chow to write. Here's hoping I'm not interrupted by the goddamn whistle. Every time I try to do anything, the whistle blows, and I've got to run like a madman to line up with the rest of the men.

Well, (very briefly) here's what's happened to me so far:—

When I waved goodbye to you from the foot of the stairs in the station, we entered the train. We waited there about twenty minutes and then pulled out.

All along the line up to New Brunswick N.J. people waved to us. At Newark we took another batch, and at New Brunswick we were treated a real moving-picture farewell to the boys from that town.

The whole town was jammed on the station platform and the streets below. The local scout troop and the high school band was there. The mayor was there and all the mommas and poppas and sisters and brothers and sweethearts and wives and kids. There wasn't any rah-rah stuff, not much cheering—just waving and quiet smiles with a catch-in-the-throat and tears-in-the-eyes. I was deeply moved.

We arrived at Fort Dix at 2 P.M., were lined up and marched off to eat (good sense that).

After that we were lined up again and marched to a barracks for injections and clothing.

First thing there, we stripped naked and had the old short arm inspection.[1] Then, still naked, in single-file, we passed by three medicos. One smallpox vaccination, two shots in the right arm for anti-tetanus.

Oops there goes the whistle—

Two hours later:— Just got interviewed, took out $10,000 insurance, finished window-washing detail.[2]

To get back to yesterday and the injections. After we got the injections (some of the boys felt momentarily sick and had to sit down) (I was O.K.) we, still naked, were measured for clothes and shoes.

Then slam-bang, the stuff was thrown at us. Everything from soup to nuts—really impossible to describe adequately. It's like being thrown into a machine a civilian and being ground out (with lots of rough edges) a soldier.

This morning, I took my I.Q. and mechanical adaptability tests. Judging from the general results, I did pretty well.

---

[1] Short arm inspection is military slang for the medical examination of a man's genitals.

[2] The National Service Life Insurance (NSLI) program was created on October 8, 1940 to manage the insurance needs of World War II service personnel. Over 22 million NSLI policies were issued from 1940 until the program was closed to new issues on April 25, 1951. The maximum face amount of a policy was $10,000.

Crap, another interruption.—

5:30 P.M.—after dinner.

Finally, I can finish. The rest of the evening is my own.

You can get the idea of the kind of hurry-up existence this is by what's happened to this letter.

My first impressions of this man's Army? Well, at first everything seems confused, and still is to most of the other new fellows. But, I could quickly see that there's a tremendous efficiency to all this hustle and bustle. There's thousands of men pouring in and out of here all day long—and they're coming in and going out on schedule—An enormous job. It's like cramming wash into a laundry bag. Most of the stuff gets in, and what's left hanging over the edges is just shoved in with a little extra attention. It's the same with us, most of us get through the first few days O.K., those that don't are just shoved along.

It's a far cry from our wonderful but raggedy-assed International Brigade in Spain. You ought to see the two pairs of beautiful, sturdy shoes they give us—and compare them a little sadly with the rope-soled canvas shoes of a few years ago.

The food's good. It's wholesome and there's plenty of it. No garbanzos here.

There're two things I've seen I didn't like though. The first, is the segregation of Negro troops.[3] It hits you in the puss the minute you step off the train. From the day they enter it seems they keep them in their own companies + their own areas. They can circulate freely, though (Which, of course, doesn't alter matters).

The second is something that doesn't happen, which should begin as soon as men get into the Army. Nobody has told us what this war is about and why we have to win it.

We got a welcome speech from a chaplain and his most notable contribution to building morale and fighting spirit was ". . . we have been challenged."

Another lieutenant read us the Articles of War, describing penalties for everything from venereal diseases to shooting crap. But,

---

[3] The armed services remained segregated throughout World War II. Nonetheless, black Americans demonstrated strong support for the war effort, maintaining that they were fighting a Double V campaign that included victory over fascism abroad and victory over Jim Crow laws at home. Segregation in the armed services was ended by the 1948 executive order of President Harry S. Truman.

not a word about fascism, about Hitler, about Japanese militarism. Or, do I expect too much? . . .

Darling, I've been saving this for the end of the letter:—

When I get some time to myself like now and in bed last night, I miss you so much I get all choked up.

Last night I couldn't sleep well. It's a far cry from a hard army cot to a soft bed where I can reach out and hold my Gracie in my arms, and smell your hair in my nostrils, and kiss you on the back of your neck.

Darling, I love you and miss you. Write to me.

All yours, Larry

Co. I, 3rd Battalion
922nd Engineers Reg't (Av'n)
Geiger Field, Spokane, Washington
3 September 1942

Dearest Gracie;

Read that address and weep. I couldn't be much farther away from you and still be in the country.

It took us four days of grueling travel on a troop train to get out here. We couldn't get off the train, couldn't mail any letters en route. That's why you haven't heard from me the last few days. (I sent you a telegram this morning!)

Darling, you'll probably be as miserable and depressed as I am to see where I've landed.

Although I'm only a few miles outside of Spokane, it might just as well be the middle of the Pacific. The prospects for seeing each other before a long time has elapsed, is very slim. . . .

Geiger Field is an airbase near Spokane, Washington. From the looks of things it's pretty new, and lacks a lot of facilities.

The outfit I'm in is also new, with officers who have just been transferred here from all over the country.

Our basic training will start this Monday, Sept 7. It will include infantry drill, handling of rifle, machine gun, small arms, and anti-aircraft weapons as well as digging gun emplacements and the varied forms of construction work. Most of it will be old stuff for me. Kind of a review.

The sergeant is going to blow his damn whistle again in a few minutes, so I'm going to finish this letter in time to catch tonight's plane.

Darling, I love you. My thoughts are with you constantly. Please don't worry about me. Give my regards to everybody, and a special hug for Sara Jane.[4]

More to-morrow,

All my love, Larry

———

Co. I, 3rd Battalion
922nd Engineers Reg't (Av'n)
Geiger Field, Spokane, Washington
4 September 1942

Hello Grace Darling;

. . . Here it is just a week in the Army and it seems like I haven't seen you for a year.

We were interviewed by our company commander today. When I told him my background, he said that was fine. But, we'll see what happens. Up to now, I've been getting the dirty end of the stick.

By that I mean being stuck in this branch of the service. I really think I should be some place else. If not the armored force, then certainly the infantry.

But, there I go, beefing again.

I've made up my mind to make the best of a distasteful situation. If the opportunity to get out to another branch presents itself, I'll try to grab it. If not, and I'm stuck here—well I'll do my darnedest to be a good man. . . .

About the men out here. I find them just about the same as I did in Ft. Dix, and I have the same feeling about inadequate handling of the problems of chauvinism and confusion about the war.

---

[4] Sara Jane Miller was the four-year-old daughter of Marjorie Singer Miller, the older sister of Grace Cane. She was a favorite niece of Lawrence Cane.

This may be a people's army, but Christ it has a long way to go. . . .

Last night, I dreamed about you. It was a beautiful and tender dream, and through it all I was sad because I realized how long it will be before I can hold you and kiss you again.

So long for today sweetheart.

All my love and all my kisses. Larry

—————

Co. I, 3rd Battalion
922nd Engineers Reg't (Av'n)
Geiger Field, Spokane, Washington
6 September 1942

Grace Darling;

Today is my first day off since I'm in the Army. There's no reveille out here Sundays and no inspections—which means if you have no fatigues like K.P. then you've got the day to yourself.

So, this morning, I got up for 7 A.M. breakfast, came back, and went to sleep again. I got up at 10 A.M. and went out and played some touch football with fellows from my company. It is now 11 A.M. (2 P.M. your time), and I'm writing this letter to you. . . .

The only difference between me and most of the other men around here, is that they're continually beefing about being in the Army. In my own quiet way, I try to convince them that there's a war on, and that their own necks are at stake. I try to show them they're part of America too, and that they can't expect somebody else to do all their fighting for them.

Some of them already know I've been in Spain. While they respect my opinion, they think I'm just some kind of a soldier-of-fortune. But, that's all right, I aim to be one of the best soldiers in camp—they'll listen to me all right.

What this Army really needs is an educational system which would indoctrinate the men—officers as well—with a true spirit of fighting democracy.

One thing I'm glad to say is that most of the men know Hitler is the main enemy, and they're agreed that a Western Front is the way to beat him. But they're too preoccupied with their own personal problems—with being so far from home and loved ones, with being uprooted from the normal course of civilian life.

I think that after we get into the routine of things that feeling of homesickness and discomfort won't be so keen. I think most of them will accept the responsibility of being soldiers and assume an attitude of . . . "Well, there's a job to be done. Let's destroy these bastards and get it over with. . . ."

A lot will depend, of course, on the direction our government takes. If we open a Western Front, the morale will be O.K. But, if we fart around like we seem to be doing yet (as far as a new front is concerned), well things won't be so good, either back home or in the Army.

Well, darling, I guess I'll shut up for now. Last night, I passed one of the barracks and I heard our song float out into the night air. "You made me love you . . . ", welling out under the stars.[5] I yearned for you so much, I nearly cried.

So long, sweet, be a good girl.

Your loving, Larry

―――――――

Co. I, 3rd Battalion
922nd Engineers Reg't (Av'n)
Geiger Field, Spokane, Washington
8 September 1942

Grace Honey;

I've got some news for you. They're sending me to the N.C.O. school. That's the school for non-commissioned officers. I attended my first class last night. That's the reason I didn't write to you yesterday—no time to myself.

The course runs for four or five weeks, after which time I take an exam. If I show up well in training and get a high mark on the exams, I'm pretty sure to become a sergeant in a little more than a month. Not bad for a newcomer. . . .

---

[5] The favorite song of Lawrence and Grace Cane was Harry James' wartime hit, "You Made Me Love You."

I've found out that if I get into the air-borne engineers, I'll probably get shipped back east for training—somewheres in Virginia. That would be swell for us, we could see each other pretty often so long as I'm in the country. If I stay out here, from the looks of things, we'll have to wait till the war's over. So, you can understand why I'm so anxious to be transferred.

Gosh, honey, I haven't received a letter from you yet. I hope to hell I get one soon. I'm very anxious to hear from you. If you only knew how much I yearn for you, how hungry I am to see you, and hear you, and hold you, I think you'd bawl. . . .

All yours, Larry

Co. I, 3rd Battalion
922nd Eng. Reg't (Av'n)
Geiger Field, Spokane, Washington
10 September 1942

Grace, My Darling;

I got your letter sent to Ft. Dix, and your three-in-one letter, and the pictures, and the clippings. Sweetheart, if you only knew how happy they made me. I was as excited as a child. . . .

I was called down to battalion headquarters today. The battalion commander asked me if I would lecture to the N.C.O. school on some of my experiences in Spain. Of course, I accepted.

I understand the Colonel of the Regiment and most of the commissioned officers will be there to listen to me. The event takes place next Tuesday. I hope I do O.K. . . .

Your ever loving, Larry

Co. I, 3rd Battalion
922nd Eng. Reg't (Av'n)
Geiger Field, Spokane, Washington
11 September 1942

My Sweetheart;

Just got back from my first hike. It wasn't bad—nothing to what's coming. We're taking basic infantry training now. Standard stuff and duck soup for me. . . .

I don't know about that subscription to P.M. yet.[6] You see, I haven't had my interview about a transfer yet.

I was tempted to talk to the battalion commander about it (when we had the talk about the lecture)—in Spain I wouldn't have hesitated. But, here it would be going over the head of my company commander. That would be a sure way of lousing myself up with him, and I'd probably be certain not to get what I want. I want to know just where I stand before you send me any kind of subscription. Thanks for the thought.

One of the methods of training employed by the Army is the showing of moving pictures. In the last couple of days, we've seen some really splendid ones on venereal diseases and first aid in training and for wounds received in battle. Their use is of course restricted to the Army, but if they could be shown in every high school in the country they would certainly save a lot of grief and eliminate a lot of useless pain and suffering. . . .

I'm trying to put my thoughts together for that little lecture on Tuesday. The officers around here seem to be watching me closely. Every once in awhile they suddenly order me to take charge of my squad or platoon to put them through drill or calisthenics. Yesterday, my lieutenant asked me privately what I thought about his instructions on the general problem of skirmishing (This is advancing under fire). I'm watching my step, + keeping my mouth shut—I'm not tooting my horn about my past experiences. If I get anywhere, I want it to be unquestionably on merit alone. If I stay in this outfit, I'll undoubtedly be placed in

---

[6] *PM* was an inventive, but short-lived New York tabloid newspaper that from 1940 to 1948 championed the causes of minorities, workers, the downtrodden, and the disfranchised. Its writers included an extraordinary group of men and women from I.F. Stone to Margaret Bourke-White to Dr. Seuss.

the weapons company. That's the outfit that does the fighting with this branch of engineers. . . .

When mail-call rolls around, I dash up to company headquarters, and hang on every name that's called. Cane! Cane! Did he say Cane? . . . Christ, gimme that letter. Then I tear it open eagerly and devour the news from my wonderful wife. . . .

So long for today, sweet.

All my love, Larry

Co. I, 3rd Battalion
922nd Eng. Reg't (Av'n)
Geiger Field, Spokane, Washington
12 September 1942

My Dearest;

. . . There's a political discussion raging in the back of the barracks. About ten fellows are blowing off steam about the international situation and the war. Some of it is pretty good—and some of it is so naive I have to smile to myself. The general trend is healthy, though. Most of them seem to think that we're Americans goddamit, and when we get over there we'll fix that Hitler's wagon. Offensive-minded is the word—and that's a good spirit to have for men who are in an Army that's being built for offensive operations. Not one guy has expressed appeaser sentiments.

There's a storm brewing, Bub. A storm that's going to blow fascism from the face of the earth. . . .

By the way, let me explain in more detail just what my lecture to the N.C.O. school and officers will consist of.

The class for the evening (Tuesday Sept. 15th) will deal with the question of personal security in battle. Some officer will lecture on the main fundamentals as dealt with in the basic field manual. Then I am to get up and go into the problem more extensively telling personal experiences to illustrate each point. I have been allowed a half hour to cover the subject briefly. And then there is to be a question and answer period for as long as the men have questions.

There's what I call a real opportunity for getting in some education. Of course, any political questions will have to be handled with tact. No one has told me that, but I'm sure that would be correct in such a situation.

The bugle has just sounded retreat. I'll have more time to write to-morrow. Darling, I love you, adore you, miss you, send you my adoration in these measly written lines, and ache for the day when I can love you again for real and for the rest of our lives.

Your loving, Larry

Co. I, 3rd Battalion
922nd Eng. Reg't (Av'n)
Geiger Field, Spokane, Washington
15 September 1942

My Dearest;

I've been trying to get this letter off for the last two days. I've just come from class. The lights in the barracks are out, and I'm now sitting in the latrine where the lights are kept on all night. Not a very romantic place, but dammit it's the only place I can get to finish this letter.

I just finished my talk and it was a great success—no kidding. The men had all kinds of eager questions, and enjoyed it immensely. They gave me a swell round of applause when it was over. Even the officers congratulated me and told me it was very enjoyable and informative. I'm very gratified at the outcome. . . .

Darling, I want you to send me our marriage license. I'm going to file for an allotment so that you can get fifty bucks a month from the Gov't.

What'll happen is, I'll get the license. Then I'll make out my dependency claim. The Army will take a photostatic copy of the license, clip it to my application and send the whole business to Washington. As soon as they've taken the photostat, I'll mail the license back to you.

On Nov. 1, your first payment will be seventy-eight dollars. After that $50.00 the first of each month. You didn't count on it, but, honey you're going to get it. I guess it will come in mighty handy.[7]

My quarantine ends this week, and I'm going to try to get a pass on Saturday night to see what Spokane looks like. I'll try to get my uniform pressed up so I can take a picture for you. If I can't get it done this Sat. night, I'll do it as soon as I can. . . .

I'd have to be a Walt Whitman to begin to do my feelings justice. I love you the length and breadth and sweep of this land. From the flatlands and red earth of New Jersey through the grimy coal towns of the Alleghenies and the belching, glowing blast furnaces and chimneys of western Pennsylvania, over the corn fields of Ohio and Indiana and Illinois and Iowa, through the golden and the mellow wheatlands of Minnesota and South Dakota, around the Bad Lands of North Dakota climbing up, up over the continental divide of Montana with her purple snow-capped Rockies, through the winding fir-timbered Snake River country of the Bitter Root mountains down, down into the Cascade Range and over to the broad, beaming Pacific. All that and much more expressed in three little words. I love you. . . .

Loving You, Larry

———————

Co. I, 3rd Battalion
922nd Eng. Reg't (Av'n)
Geiger Field, Spokane, Washington
16 September 1942

Dear Baby;

Say, I'm doing pretty well out here. I've been appointed acting staff sergeant. That means I'm in charge of a platoon of men. I

———

[7] In June 1942 Congress enacted the Servicemen's Dependents Allowance Act to provide family allowances for dependents of enlisted men in all branches of the armed services. Each family allowance was determined by a contribution from the federal government plus a voluntary allotment authorized by the enlisted man. The government allowance was fixed at the monthly rate of $28.00 for a spouse, $12.00 for the first child, and $10.00 for each additional child, up to $60.00. The enlisted man could, if he so chose, also allot $22.00 from his monthly pay. Allotment checks, modest as they were, often provided critical financial support to family members of enlisted men.

run it, the lieutenant gets the credit. That's about the size of it. The non-coms run the lower units of any army.

Every time we get field instructions I'm called on to explain a few things to the company. I tell them stories, experiences, importance of this or that, and a few educational hints about the war.

The whole battalion knows about the guy from Spain. When I walk down the company street or the regimental area, I can hear guys whispering sometimes "See that guy, well . . . bzz . . . bzz." I seem to get along pretty well with the fellows, as far as I can tell.

Maybe I'm spoiling my chances for a transfer because the co. commander may not want me to leave, but I guess my job is to do the best I can. After all, darling, us guys got a tradition to uphold. The best, the most advanced, the most self-sacrificing among the people. . . .

So long beautiful beauty. Don't worry so much about the war. We'll get a new front—and we'll wipe fascism from the face of the earth. And the time isn't far away.

I love you. I love you. I love you. Larry

Co. I, 3rd Battalion
922nd Eng. Reg't (Av'n)
Geiger Field, Spokane, Washington
21 September 1942

Hello Honey;

I took care of your allotment today. On Nov. 1st you'll get $50.00, and the same every month thereafter. I thought I'd be able to wrangle a little more for you the first month, but they take out a couple of months insurance from the first pay and there won't be enough left over for a full allotment. I'll send you a money order for ten bucks or so at the end of this month.

I had a long heart to heart talk with my company commander today about my desire to transfer to a different branch of the service. He told me he has a very high regard for me and would like me to stay in the outfit. But, since I want to transfer, he's going to talk to the Colonel of the Regiment first chance he gets. He said he doubted whether I could get the transfer, but if I do have to stay he wants me to apply for Officers Training after I get my sergeancy officially. He said he'd be very glad to recommend me. That's a pretty good setup. It means that if I do get transferred, I'll probably be a staff sergeant (confirmed official) by the time it goes through—which in turn means I'll probably be able to keep the rating wherever they send me. If I stay, I'll be a staff sergeant and recommended for OTS.[8]

Let the chips fall now, I'm not going to worry about it any more. . . .

The whistle just blew, sweet. If I end this now it'll make tonight's plane out of the field. So long, my love. I love you.

Your, Larry

———————

Co. I, 3rd Battalion
922nd Eng. Reg't (Av'n)
Geiger Field, Spokane, Washington
23 September 1942

My Dearest;

. . . I've mentioned it before, but it's become part of the routine in my company. Any time there's a lecture by the company commander or any of the lieutenants, I'm called on to add to the discussions and illustrate from experience. And I'm glad to contribute. Sometimes I feel a little funny being put on the spot that

---

[8] OTS stood for Officer Training School. The official name of the officer training schools was Officer Candidate School or OCS. However, servicemen frequently referred to OCS as OTS. When the Army began mobilization in 1940 there were only 14,000 professional officers on active duty. As mobilization continued, the officer shortage became more pressing, reaching near-critical proportion during the summer of 1942. In response to this shortage, enrollments in Officer Candidate Schools, which had been established in July 1941, dramatically increased. These new officer training programs were usually 90 days in length and graduates of these programs were called "90-day wonders." By the end of 1943 approximately 300,000 officers had graduated from OCS, outnumbering regular Army officers by a ratio or 40 to 1.

way, but the fellows like it—so, who am I to deny the masses? (Getting high falutin'). . . .

[T]here was a beautiful sunset just a little while ago. That's one thing that can't be beat out here—the sunrises and sunsets.

I've seen them in Spain with their delicate pastel shades and I thought they were matchless. But, out here the colors are wilder and more passionate. They're just like America. Wild, breathtaking, brilliant and spirited. . . .

Last night, at the non-com school during a lecture on jungle warfare an officer gave us the best piece of straight-from-the-shoulder good old American hoss sense about the war I've heard since I came into the Army. I was delighted. He referred to me at one part and said, "If any of you men have any doubts about what our enemy is like and what we must do + go through to win, ask Private Cane—he can tell you." This guy is an old-timer, up from the ranks.

The jist of his talk was—"You're being fashioned and trained as professional killers. The thing that justifies this is the kind of war we are fighting. We are fighting for our homes, our families, + our independence as a nation. We are fighting the worst barbarians in the history of the world. Show them no mercy. Nazis are not to be argued with or treated fairly. Kill them. We are going to go forward. Forget about waiting for the enemy. We are going to go into Europe and Asia and Africa and ferret the rats out and kill them. There will be no Marquis of Queensbury rules about this business. Your job is destroy and kill fascists and fascism for the future of civilization."

Not bad, eh?

About my needs. Darling, the only thing I need is you. I don't need money or stamps or stuff . . . I'm well fixed. (Well, anyway, I can get along O.K.) . . .

Goodnight, my darling, goodnight. I gather you in my arms and kiss your brow. Sh-h-h. Go to sleep, Gracie. S-s-h-h-h. I love you.

Larry

Co. I, 3rd Battalion
922nd Eng. Reg't (Av'n)
Geiger Field, Spokane, Washington
28 September 1942

Hello Dearest;

Here I am in my special writing room (you know where). I almost had a chance to write to you this afternoon. But, just as I sat down we got orders to stand by to move out to fight a forest fire. We were on the alert until it was time to go to N.C.O. school. . . .

I heard a radio dispatch which said the Nazis are retreating from Stalingrad.[9] God, I hope it's true. What a stand!

Whenever a man or a people fight fiercely and gloriously in the future—it will be said that he or they fight like Russians. Wait and see.

I'm running close to bed-check time, sweetheart. I'll close up now, con todo mi corazon. I love you, my darling.

Your, Larry

Co. I, 3rd Battalion
922nd Eng. Reg't (Av'n)
Geiger Field, Spokane, Washington
2 October 1942

Hello My Darling;

Yesterday this time I was biting my fingernails, waiting for our call to go through.

It was really unsatisfactory, wasn't it? Over so soon, and we didn't know where the hell to start.

But, I'm happy because I did hear your voice (a little sleepy, but my Gracie).

---

[9] Stalingrad, located on the Volga River some 1,500 miles east of Berlin, was the scene of the decisive battle during the winter of 1942–43 in which the German advance into the Soviet Union was halted. Not until late January 1943 did the Germans finally surrender.

I got your letter, telling me how you're taking hold of yourself. You're absolutely right.

Don't waste time mooning for me, darling. Love me, want me, think about me—but take it like our Russian sisters. . . .

Today, the N.C.O.s fired the M1 (Garand) rifle for the first time. We weren't shooting for official score. But I ended with fourth highest shooting score, and an average, which, if it had been official, would have qualified me for sharpshooter.

That's not bad considering I haven't fired for four years, and that a lot of these Westerners out here were born with rifles.

My company commander and another from another company asked me to see them tonight. They want to chew the fat about Spain and speak to me about OCS.

We'll see what happens. . . .

Your loving and faithful Larry

Co. I, 3rd Battalion
922nd Eng. Reg't (Av'n)
Geiger Field, Spokane, Washington
3 October 1942

Hello Darling;

Have I got a choice bit of news for you!

Remember, I told you last night about my appointment with my company commander? Well, the upshot of the conversation was that he wants me to go to the engineers officers training school.

He told me he is going to try to have me accepted <u>before</u> my basic training period is over. He said I was an exceptional man, would make a fine officer and felt that I really ought to go to OTS as soon as possible. Wow! Pardon the blushes.

He was pretty swell about it and said he was going to work on it immediately. Told me the Officers course in the Engineers was the toughest in the Army, but he thought I could breeze through it.

And, darling, here's the best part of all—the Engineers School is in Ft. Belvoir, Va., only about six hours from N.Y.C!

So keep your fingers crossed. . . .

By the way, I came out top man in the N.C.O school. Grade 96.05 %

See where Roosevelt thinks that Willkie is "theoretically" right about a Second Front now.[10] Says he thinks we should have it, but can't open one at this time. Phooey! If we keep on waiting, there'll be a lot of truth to Hitler's ravings about preparations— the bastard *will* be prepared. Beating him then is going to be a horrible, grinding, bloodbath. . . .

With a hug and a kiss and a heartful of love,

I'm yours, Larry

Co. I, 3rd Battalion
922nd Eng. Reg't (Av'n)
Geiger Field, Spokane, Washington
5 October 1942

Dearest Gracie;

Hello monkey. Haven't seen a letter from you for three days. You're not forgetting about me are you? . . .

Know what I did this afternoon? We got a shipment of .50 caliber anti-aircraft machine guns.

When a gun comes from the factory, it's packed in thick, impossible coat of grease (known as cosmaline). In order to put the gun in working condition, the grease must be washed off thoroughly and every single nut, bolt, + pin of that gun given a light coat of oil. And, honey is that a job!

Never seen a gun like that make before. Co. commander asked me if I knew enough about the gun to take her down. I said sure

---

[10] Wendell L. Willkie (1892–1944) was the Republican nominee for president in 1940 when Franklin D. Roosevelt (1882–1945), running for an unprecedented third term, easily won the election. In 1941–42 Willkie served as Roosevelt's special emissary and traveled to England, the Middle East, China, and the Soviet Union.

and took a detail of men. We got her down finally, and cleaned her + reassembled her. Do I look and feel like a grease monkey right now!

But, honest, I certainly enjoyed that work. There's nothing I like about Army life more than taking guns apart, and seeing what makes them tick. . . .

Buenos noches, for now, sweetheart.

I love you, mi mujer y novia.

Larry

━━━━━

Co. I, 3rd Battalion
922nd Eng. Reg't (Av'n)
Geiger Field, Spokane, Washington
10 October 1942

My Darling;

Got back from maneuvers about 1 A.M. this morning after a grueling 20-mile night march through the mountains. Full field pack and equipment.

We spent three days skirmishing through the hills. I feel like a mountain goat.

On the way back, my platoon was assigned the job of leading the whole battalion back to camp. We traveled over unfamiliar terrain by map and compass (also stars) and got 'em all back safe and sound (Well, some of them had plenty blisters).

Do you want to know what happened when I got back?

I fell asleep immediately and dreamt I was loving you. Darling, you must have felt that one way back in New York. Was it wet! Amazing ain't it? After that march, too. . . .

Your loving, Larry

Co. I, 3rd Battalion
922nd Eng Reg't (Av'n)
Geiger Field, Spokane, Washington
12 October 1942

Gracie Darling;

. . . So you're going to be a U.S.O. hostess on Friday nights, eh? Well darling I won't make any cracks. But remember, you belong to daddy—not only your heart but all of you. And don't you dare get too sociable—it brings on complications even with the "nicest" boys. . . .

Well, we got a new instructor today. A young shavetail who tried to impress us with his toughness was really giving the class the works. He got around to asking questions about the machine-guns—scared a few of the boys into giving fumbling answers, and then raked them over the coals.

I happened to glance out of the window while he was "impressing" us and he must have thought I wasn't paying attention. Here's what happened:—

"You there, looking out of the window!"

"Yes sir?"

"Get up and tell us what you know about the .30 cal. Browning water-cooled machine-gun."

The class went quiet in delighted anticipation. I got up and calmly began, "The .30 cal. Browning water-cooled machine-gun is gas-operated, belt-fed, and water-cooled as its name implies. It weighs . . . etc. . . . etc. . . ," and then followed a twenty minute lecture on machine gunnery.

Darling, you should have seen the poor guy's face. First his mouth opened gradually, then his jaw dropped + he stared in amazement, then his face turned red. The class enjoyed it immensely.

Finally, he couldn't take it any longer, so he interrupted and asked,

"What would you do if you ran out of water?"

"I'd piss in it, sir."

The class and the instructor couldn't believe their ears. I was just being impish because the answer in the manual to that one is you'd use the water in the condenser can that comes with the gun.

"What did you say?"

Solemn as an owl, I repeated, "I'd piss in it, sir." Well, the class roared, and even the instructor grinned. He called it quits then.

The rest of the class was politely conducted. . . .

Darling, that's enough of this chop-chop. I love you sweetheart mine. I'll sign off till tomorrow and see you tonight in my dreams.

Your own, Larry

Co. I, 3rd Battalion
922nd Eng Reg't (Av'n)
Geiger Field, Spokane, Washington
17 October 1942

Hello Baby;

. . . You ought to see my formal application for O.T.S. In the space for battle experience, there wasn't enough room. I had to take it into the margin. The Corporal taking the application started to bug his eyes out and wanted to know where the hell ever I was at.

My Co. commander is writing to Ft. Jay on Governor's Island for a transcript of my physical exam. I may not have to take another physical. Just a thorough going over by the O.C.S. board.

Now listen, Bub, I haven't got a letter from you for three days running. Come on now—Poppa is anxious. Get on the ball and start grinding 'em out.

I'll close with all my love, and a bear hug.

Your, Larry

Co. I, 3rd Battalion
922nd Eng Reg't (Av'n)
Geiger Field, Spokane, Washington
19 October 1942

Hello My Daaarling,

I'm sitting in the Soldier's Service Center in Spokane writing this letter while I wait for a couple of boys to go back to the camp.

I had a wonderful trip to the Grand Coulee Dam yesterday.

We went on a specially conducted tour of the insides and saw how a dam works.

Darling, the magnitude of this job appalls the imagination. To think that man has arrived at the point where he can create such an immensely intricate edifice, and still wastes time killing his fellow-beings just doesn't make sense.

Some day he'll just concentrate on conquering nature and not human beings and nations.

Grand Coulee is but a whisper compared to the wonderful world we're fighting for.

Man will conquer and harness not only the energies of swift-flowing rivers. He'll harness the source of all energy—the sun. He'll control floods and drought. He'll eliminate disease. He'll travel not only above the earth and beneath the sea but new horizons will lead out into space. And he will blot out of existence the scourge of civilizations—poverty.

We'll never see it—but we will see a good start made in that direction. We'll help grind Hitlerism into the dust—and maybe we'll see a new democracy for wider millions of people.

We'll become part of the heritage which future generations will build on.

I feel like I'm standing on a mountain-top hand-in-hand with you. Behind us is the history of man, beneath our feet is the bloody mud of the present, and out there in the future is the tomorrow of our dreams. Hold my hand tightly, darling. Grip my arm and put your head on my shoulder. Out there are the generations we have stored in our loins.

See what I mean, sweetheart.

To get back to a more lowly plain—

I just saw a parade passing through the streets for the Community Chest of Spokane—and what do you think? There was a hammer and sickle flowing in the night breeze. You heard me. It was carried by the standard bearer of a mounted group dressed in Cossack uniform. They represented, so I was told by a nice old lady "Our gallant Russian allies!" . . .

Your own, Larry

Co. I, 3rd Battalion
922nd Eng Reg't (Av'n)
Geiger Field, Spokane, Washington
20 October 1942

Hello Bub;

My OTS papers have been signed, sealed and delivered. They're on their way to the Board. I understand school is to open (that is, the new class) in about a month. That means I should get a decision within a couple of weeks.

I'm wishing very hard. . . .

I love you, sweetheart. No matter what happens, or where I go, you'll be in every beat of my heart. You're there for me forever—part of the fire that runs in my blood—the fire that burns with hatred for oppression and love for the people.

The Pine Camp [radio] program is now ripping wide open. The tune is "Praise the Lord and Pass the Ammunition."[11]

Swell stuff!

I haven't much else to say right now, Bub. I just want to register a wee complaint. Maybe it isn't your fault but dammit I've just got one letter from you in the last five days. If you knew how

---

[11] The popular wartime song, "Praise the Lord and Pass the Ammunition," was written by Frank Loesser in 1942. The song told the story of how Navy Chaplain Howell Forgy at Pearl Harbor supposedly manned one of his ship's gun turrets after the gunner was hit, saying, "Praise the Lord and pass the ammunition." In actuality, Forgy, stationed aboard the *U.S.S. New Orleans* during the attack, urged the men on board with the words, "Praise the Lord and pass the ammunition."

I look forward to mail call and that precious envelope from you, you'd really do something about it.

Gimme a break darling.

Your loving, Larry

===

Co. I, 3rd Battalion
922nd Eng Reg't (Av'n)
Geiger Field, Spokane, Washington
21 October 1942

Dearest Baby;

. . . We got some Mexicans + Indians came up from Texas and Utah today. Some of them sent as replacements to my platoon. You should have seen the faces of the Mex kids light up when I spoke to them in Spanish.

They said they're very glad to be with us, and hope they stay. I hope they do. They're farmers. And after you teach a farmer left from right, he makes a damn good soldier. He'll make a better one when they tell him what Hitler means to do with his land and his country.

Say, aren't those babies at Stalingrad doing a job? When I think of what that kind of fighting means in blood, + suffering, + heroism it gives me goose-pimples.

When we get the chance to do our stuff we'll turn in a good performance too, in all parts of the world.

Going to see "Wake Island" tonight.[12]

So long adorable.

Your, Larry

===

---

[12] *Wake Island,* the 1942 Frank Capra (1897–1991) film, was the first of the great war films produced upon America's entry into the war. It depicted the heroic defense of the strategic Pacific stronghold.

Co. I, 3rd Battalion
922nd Eng Reg't (Av'n)
Geiger Field, Spokane, Washington
23 October 1942

My Darling;

Had my interview this morning. It was over in fifteen minutes—which was quite a surprise to me because the other fellows all spent about a half-hour before the Board.

They were very nice and friendly. All they asked were a few brief questions about my background and education. Then they asked me to tell them about Spain—from the technical, military angle (No politics or anything. Not even, "Are you a communist?"). Of course, I was right at home.

A couple of questions were really funny. The medical officer on the Board asked, "Do you drink?"

I said, "No sir."

"Never?"

"Oh yes sir. A couple of beers once in awhile."

"Where does port wine originate from?"

"Beg pardon, sir?"

"Where does port wine come from?"

"I don't know sir."

"Well then, what's the difference between bourbon + scotch."

"I'm sorry sir, I don't know."

They were all grinning at this.

They asked me what I thought should be the qualities of a good officer.

Among the things I mentioned strongly were courage + intelligence.

One officer said, "I've known lots of men with courage who couldn't make good officers."

I quipped back with, "They couldn't have been very intelligent sir."

They grinned at that too.

All in all it wasn't bad. Of course, I still don't know how I made out. So you and I will just have to keep on wishing. . . .

I love you. Larry

Co. I, 3rd Battalion
922nd Eng Reg't (Av'n)
Geiger Field, Spokane, Washington
24 October 1942

My Dearest Baby;

. . . That's a fine bunch of boys I've got there. They're all as anxious to see that I get OCS as I am. They keep wishing me the best and every half-hour another one comes over to find out how things are going.

And let me tell you darling. In the two months I've been with them, they've learned what we're fighting for. Honest, sweetheart, they're raring to go. They've gotten over their original homesickness (not that they've forgotten) to the extent that it doesn't interfere with their thinking and soldiering. They want a new front opened in Europe. They eat up the war news, and they really admire the Russian stand.

With good leadership, these men are going to make wonderful fighters. And they're just a small iota of a very large organization of men just like themselves.

Maybe they haven't got much book-larnin', maybe their table manners aren't so good, maybe some of them are slow to catch on. But they're honest and generous and wise-cracking guys. They're America and they're ready to go. The People Yes. . . .

Your own, Larry

———

Co. I, 3rd Battalion
922nd Eng Reg't (Av'n)
Geiger Field, Spokane, Washington
26 October 1942

Hello Sweetheart;

Don't laugh, I'm about to become an author. Honest, I'm not kidding.

Today, the executive officer of the battalion (second in command) called me into his office and said:

"Ahem, Corporal, you know you may not be with us very long. If higher channels O.K. it, you will be going to OCS."

I didn't say anything. I wondered whatinhell was up.

"Now, Corporal, the board that interviewed you found your remarks very interesting. They have recommended that you be requested to write an article on infantry weapons used in Spain, and compare their efficiency with our own weapons. You will make any observations that you wish concerning suggestions for changes in our weapons or in their use in combat."

You could have knocked me over with a feather. He went on:

"This article will be mimeographed for distribution to the officers of the battalion. If it's good we will publish it in the Geiger Field Journal."

How do you like that? Me, another Veteran Commander. Some stuff!

I guess I better do a good job. The hell of it is, I'll just be writing from memory, and I won't be able to get as technical as such an article really should be.

Anyway, this little request confirms what I believed to be true. I've passed the Board and the physical exam with flying colors. Everything hinges on Washington. And, with some of the boys getting breaks, I've got a damn good chance. . . .

Say, hon, I have been thinking about the Western Front. Today, I had a conversation with a guy out here who's a lawyer in civilian life. He is just a Corporal here, but quite influential outside.

He has friends in the State Dept. And he told me some things that have been a suspicion in the back of my mind for a long time. It fits in with the picture that's been forming.

Know what I think, baby? There would have been a Western Front long ago—but the Clivedens are still powerful in England and their American cousins here are still finagling for a negotiated peace.[13]

All the talk about not being ready is a lot of crap.

Listen darling, everything is ready—Our production, our army + navy, the psychology of our people.

---

[13] The Clivedens were a group of wealthy Hitler appeasers who spent many weekends together at Cliveden, the estate of Vincent Astor and his wife, Lady Astor. They were given the name Clivedens by Claude Cockburn, a war correspondent in Spain when Larry was there.

Some way, somehow, these bastards have to be ferreted out and America must howl for Hitler's blood.

If some strategy could be organized to bring this about—if, perhaps, Roosevelt and all his circle (statesmen, radio chains, newspapers, etc.) would come to the people with the dire peril that confronts us, and point to those responsible for delay—they'd run for cover and this war would be over that much sooner. With us the victors!

Is anything being done along those lines? Does the Song Sheet, or some of the fair-haired boys ever say anything about it?[14]

If they don't, I feel emphatically that a grave mistake is being committed.

Say, here I've been rambling on without telling you how much I love you and how much I miss you and how much I yearn to be with you. Baby, you're 3200 miles away from me physically, but you're coming closer. Next week will tell the tale. I hope with all my soul it'll be a happy one for us. . . .

Well, lights are due to go out soon, beautiful. Tomorrow's another day. I LOVE YOU.

Yours, Larry

Co. I, 3rd Battalion
922nd Eng Reg't (Av'n)
Geiger Field, Spokane, Washington
30 October 1942

My Darling;

How's my Sunnyside auxiliary of the U.S. Army Engineers doing?

Here's a song that was written by our Battalion Chaplain. Sung to the tune of "Hinky-Dinky Parlee-Vous."

---

[14] The "Song Sheet" was a reference to the *Daily Worker*, the newspaper of the Communist Party-USA. The "fair-haired boys" was a reference to the bigwigs of the Communist Party-USA.

I

We are the boys that get there first and build the fields
We blast 'em out and smooth 'em down for bombers wheels
Repair and Camouflage 'em too
Defend 'em if the foe gets through
Aviation Engineers.

II

Its up to us to know our stuff from A to Z
No job's too small, no job's too tough to keep us free
While we do our duty without a peep
Our Sergeant sits on his big fat jeep
Aviation Engineers.

III

Who get's the credit for all that's done + all the cheers
The pilots + gunners + radio men + bombardiers
But we're pretty nice guys to have around
When the glory boys want to set 'em down
Aviation Engineers.

IV

What would the Air Corps do with[out] Engineers?
How could the war be won without Engineers?
We'll lick the Japs + Nazis too
We'll camouflage 'em black + blue
Aviation Engineers.

Like it? We do. It's got the stuff. Especially when a large body
of men sing it out.

Songs are a reflection of the morale and mettle of a people
during war. Out of the hazy first-period of this war with its crappy
rah-rah songs which were merely a sign of the confusion that
existed throughout the nation, are coming ballads that speak the
mind of America. Cocky, fighting songs that are full of wise-
cracks characteristic of our people. They're songs that say we are

ready to fight and ready to win, and they show who the enemy is.

I love you darling. Keep pitching. Larry

========

Co. I, 3rd Battalion
922nd Eng Reg't (Av'n)
Geiger Field, Spokane, Washington
2 November 1942

My Darling;

Sit down. Take it easy. Now—
I'VE BEEN ACCEPTED FOR O.C.S.
Happy? Um-yum, so am I.

When I'll leave is still debatable. Whether it will be this week or next or the week after, I still don't know. But don't you dare get anyone else to hang those drapes—I want to do that job all myself. Stop worrying about the hooks.

Darling, I don't think I'll be able to stay ten days with you. If I get five I'll be lucky. . . .

Now that I'm going to Officers School, they probably won't confirm my sergeancy. But don't worry in three months or so I'll be a shavetail, and there'll be plenty of dough to get along on. Know what a 2nd Looie gets? (If he's married).

$150—base pay
60—rental allotment
45—rations
15—incidentals
$270—per month

Think we can get along O.K.?
So do I.
Well, back to dreaming about you sweetheart. I'll be seein' ya.

All my love. Larry

2

Officer Candidate School and Military Intelligence Training: Fort Belvoir, Virginia and Camp Ritchie, Maryland
November 9, 1942–July 31, 1943

Fort Belvoir, Virginia
13 November 1942

My Darling Gracie;

Look what I've been forced to do. My bags haven't arrived yet, so I've got to improvise. This is a menu folder. What I'm going to do about underwear, socks, clothes, etc.—I still don't know. I'm so dirty my drawers are on the verge of crawling off into a corner somewhere and dying of shame.

I can't write much on this kind of stationery, sweetheart. But, this is a place I couldn't even dream of before for discipline and strictness. Everything we do is on the double (which means on the run in civilian talk). And I mean everything—study, eat, wash, write, move your bowels, drill, etc. And do they keep us at attention! Some morning soon I expect to wake up at reveille and find that I went to sleep standing at attention like an Egyptian mummy.

This is absolutely the toughest officers' school in the Army, both physically and mentally. It's going to take everything I've got to get through, past experience to the contrary notwithstanding.

They say they get easier on us in a couple of weeks. I suspect they don't get easier—we just get used to it!

Don't worry if you don't get mail every day, my baby. We're on the go 16 hours out of every 24—not much time to write.

I'll see you soon, sweetheart. I'm about 3000 miles closer to you now—can you feel it? . . .

All my love, Larry

═══════

Fort Belvoir, Virginia
15 November 1942

Hello My Baby;

This is Sunday. Do you think we've got the day off? Not on your life.

We've been out doing the manual of arms all morning, and before that we had an inspection.

After looking over the schedule for the next two weeks, I've come to the conclusion that it is humanly impossible to complete all the reading assignments. You could, I guess, if they gave you a month to prepare for a week's work—but in 12 study hours a week? Never!

Darling, you could never pass in this joint. Everything must be as exact and precise as a lathe turning out stuff to the ten-thousandth of an inch. I bet there'll be no living with me when I'm finished here.

The officers have microscopic eyes. Anything $1/16$ of an inch out of line merits restrictions, a calling down, and the wrath of God.

A speck of dust, a quiver of the eyelids, and an officer is on your neck—insulting you like an army manual come to life.

For instance, take some things we do around here. When you walk, it must be at attention—and I mean attention! No talking, looking right or left, or swinging the arms with a break at the elbow or more than 6″ to the front 3″ to the rear. That applies whenever we're outside the barracks. Makes us look like mechanical men.

When you talk it must be right out of the manual.

When you eat you get 10 minutes! The food is splendid, but I haven't had time to taste it yet.

When we go from one place to another we "double-time."

And so on ad infinitum.

But, really, this place will probably be fine for me. If I make good, I'll learn a great deal, I'll be in swell physical condition, and I'll really be on my toes.

Everything is geared to high speed for 16 hrs a day. I guess they figure if you break down under it, you're not capable of being an officer.

Well, thousands have been able to do it. I expect I'm as good as the next guy, so I'm in there pitching.

Darling, I'll be seeing you soon. Our first weekend will be all our own. No relatives, no friends, no interruptions. Just the two of us, sweetheart—

Your own, Larry

Fort Belvoir, Virginia
19 November 1942

Darling;

No time to write, no time to breathe. Every second crammed with scurrying around, formations, classes, drill, study, problems, tactical maneuvers, lectures—Good Christ, I feel like I've been caught in the middle of a tornado and I'm whirling around. And math, oh mama! Math for demolitions, math for mapping, math for musketry, math, math, math.

Any poor slug of a soldier who doesn't have a good background in mathematics is lost.

Aside from a lot of petty crap and misery that's heaped on your head around here, this is probably the best officers school in the country. The subjects taught are invaluable—I wish they gave us more time to absorb the stuff.

You know, darling, usually when someone says he has no time to write, that's the crap. But, here, it's the absolute truth. Darling, it's incredible—but there is not <u>one minute</u> to spare here.

This letter has been written over a period of <u>3 days</u> in odd snatches.

About the weekends—I'll never know until Saturdays whether

I can get in. They have a demerit system here. More than 6 per week. + you get extra duty on the weekend. So far I'm doing all right. I don't know whether passes will be permitted this week-end, though.

Hang around for a call this Sat. If you don't get one by 1 P.M. I won't be home this weekend. It's lousy, darling, I know. But that's the best we can do.

So long for now.

I love you and miss you terribly.

Your, Larry

———————

Fort Belvoir, Virginia
2 December 1942

My Darling;

I've been dying to write to you since I got back. I wanted to tell you how happy you made me and how wonderful it was to love you again.

Yes, sweetheart you put your finger right on the spot in the letter I got today—Seeing each other again <u>has</u> tempered the loneliness.

You know, Gracie, you <u>have</u> changed a bit. You're more self-confident. There's something firmer and quieter about you.

The way you felt when you said goodbye is just a reflection of that. You don't have to be amazed at yourself, my darling, you <u>are</u> a good soldier.

I'm proud and happy that my wife is such a great guy and that she loves me so much. . . .

Something that I've been aching to see ever since I got into the Army has happened. Today we saw the first of a series of seven films entitled "What are we fighting for?"[1] Traces the post war

———

[1] Cane was referring to the enormously popular documentary series, "Why We Fight," produced by Frank Capra, with the Signal Service Photographic detachment, between 1942 and 1945. These documentaries were instrumental in conveying the U.S. servicemen's role in the war and the responsibility of the public to support the war effort.

world up to the present war, shows the development of fascism, and compares the life in fascist countries with our own. One of the things the film brings out is that labor unions were destroyed in every fascist country, + that American labor has the right and must continue to have the right to organize.

A fine picture. And a good bunch of people to show it to—future officers. . . .

I love you.

Your own, Larry

––––––––––

Fort Belvoir, Virginia
7 December 1942

Dear Wife:

. . . How are you love? I'm still fighting the whirlpool rapids at this place and making headway.

We've started on our leadership assignments.

Let me explain that before I go on. From here on to graduation day, everything that we do is regulated and run by the students themselves. Of course, the officers are still over us and classes are conducted by officer instructors.

But all practical work, like company drill + scouting, river-crossing, bridge-building, machine-gunnery, assault of fortified positions, demolition, map problems, etc. etc. etc. are run by men appointed for each day.

For every assignment you get a mark which takes in many factors all adding up to—What kind of an officer are you.

Part of the officer's job is to worry you and pest you, to try to confuse and intimidate you, to see if you can remain calm and think clearly in a trying situation.

Well, Bub, they don't bother me a bit. I think I've done pretty well so far in my assignments.

Yesterday, the company commander tried to trap me while I was giving a drill in the manual of arms to my platoon. He barked at me about a movement that was being executed—asked me if I thought it was being done correctly. I said "Yessir." Then he turned to the platoon + asked them. Half of them said I was wrong. He turned to me and yelled "Well, what do you think now." And I barked right back, "Sir, I don't give a damn. I'm still right." He looked at me a minute, then said "That's right, you are." . . .

I love you with all my soul—my wife, my sweetheart, my woman.

Your, Larry

=====

Fort Belvoir, Virginia
4 January 1943

Hello My Sweetheart;

I got your welcome package and I thank you from the bottom of those bottomless drawers.

Darling, I'd have to have an ass like Fatima the dancing lady to fill those things.

I guess I can fix it up, though. All I have to do is stick them in the quartermaster's laundry, and I'm sure to get someone else's shorts back.

Thank mother too. The gloves and the socks and the under-shirts are really swell.

Tomorrow night's the night—a <u>thirty</u> mile forced march through thickets, mountain trails, <u>along railroad tracks</u>, through knee-deep mud, through streams, etc, etc. We'll make camp in pitch dark—and then break it. It promises to be a real lalapa-loozer.

Oh yes, all we've got to lug is rifle, bayonet, full-field pack, gas mask, canteen, cartridge belts, and sundry other paraphernalia—a mere 60 lbs or so.

I got a faint suspicion I'm going to be kind of tired on Wednesday.

It's all in the grind, though. I guess most of us will come through it O.K.

They've sure put our class through the meat grinder. Outside of a little extra riding from the officers these past few days, I'm doing O.K. so far.

All I can figure, is this new company commander wants to see if I can take a lot of crap, and has probably instructed them to give me the works.

That's the way I see it. My marks are still good. And, if I may say so, I still rate pretty high in all leadership assignments I've been given.

Of course, I may be naïve.

Well darling, so much for now. I love you now and always.

Your own, Larry

Fort Belvoir, Virginia
9 January 1943

Beloved;

You must have wondered why I didn't call you Saturday night—Probably thought something's wrong.

Well, it is.

I've come down with a case of grippe.

Just my gawddam luck. I'll be stuck here in the hospital now for a week or ten days.

When I come out, I'll be set back to the next class—which means I'll graduate a couple of weeks later.

There's nothing to worry about, darling. Just an ordinary run of the mill case of grippe.

But it is exasperating. Seems everything I ever do has tough going involved in it some way.

Hard way Cane that's me—something always getting screwed up.

I'll spend my stay here cussing and stewing in my own steam.

Ain't it a helluva note, sweetheart?

I was wondering whether or not to let you know. I figured you'd have to have an explanation for Saturday and also for an extended stay at this joint.

Anyway, I know you'll be a good girl and not worry. So help

me, darling, all I've got is the grippe, and I'll be up and around again in a few days.

Your loving, Larry

—————

Fort Belvoir, Virginia
20 January 1943

Hello My Wonderful Wife;

Getting better by the day and more expectant about my leave by the hour.

There's nothing speculative about it either, Bub. The Medical Corps now insists on a fifteen day leave for all cases of grippe, flu, etc. The reason is too many serious rebounds when men are returned to active duty immediately after having such sicknesses.

Good idea, isn't it?

I can move around now and leave my ward to go to eat in the general mess hall, and read books over in the Red Cross recreation hall, and go to the movies, so this place doesn't oppress me quite as much.

I can get to a phone too. So wait for my call Saturday night, love.

I should be coming home next week. Whee! Two weeks with my Gracie!

Darling, aren't those Russians the stuff? They take so much and then they strike back and crush Nazis. What people!

Just think, the thing that makes them that way is the same belief that you and I have. The belief in a better world, a finer and cleaner world, a place where people like you and me can make a wonderful life together without worrying about insecurity and war.

We'll have that world, Bub. Anyway we'll hold hands and watch our grandchildren enjoy it.

And, don't you forget it, sweet. We're going to have grandchildren—lots of them.

Bye for today my wife, mistress, and woman. I kiss the strawberry on the back of your neck, the little mole on your shoulder blade, and your round little belly.

I love you, adore you.

Your, Larry

======

Fort Belvoir, Virginia
10 February 1943

Sweetheart;

. . . The headlines say the Rooshians are flanking Kharkov.[2] Those babies are really going, aren't they? If they take that place, they'll be in a position to swoop down towards the Crimea—and if they pull an envelopment like that—it'll be a blow that will stagger Germany.

Here at the school, some of the instructors are remarking about the possibilities of an early joint United Nations invasion of Europe. Soon, soon, I hope.

Our company Day Room now sports a tremendous color chart of the weapons and tactics and uniforms of the Russian Army. The remarks contain the highest praise.

Bub, that'll be all for today. Wait for my call Saturday.

I love you con todo mi corazon. Larry

======

Fort Belvoir, Virginia
15 February 1943

Hello Sweet;

Today the sun was out—but it was murderously cold.

Jeez, no luck with the weather down here. If it doesn't rain, it snows. If it doesn't snow, it freezes. If it doesn't freeze it rains—just a vicious circle.

---

[2] Kharkov was a Russian industrial city in eastern Ukraine. The city was the scene of very heavy fighting. It changed hands four times and was finally liberated on August 23, 1943.

We had a fine exhibition on the assault of a fortified position this afternoon—shooting flame-throwers and throwing TNT all over the place.

We've got a Captain from the Chinese Army attached to the class. He's a little gink who's studying organization and mechanization of the U.S. Army.

I got into a conversation with him and the men gathered around us. You should have heard the wonderful way he told us about the New China, and why it is necessary for people to consider nation above self. It was really what some of these guys who are praying for cushy jobs needed to have to somebody tell them.

Is it as cold up in N.Y. as it is here?

Hell. I bet Washington would never have settled in Virginia if his cousin hadn't given him Mt. Vernon.

The guy who wrote "Carry Me Back to Old Virginny" must have had stones in his head.

So to bed for now, sweetheart.

I'll see you and love you in my dreams.

Your, Larry

Fort Belvoir, Virginia

22 February 1943

Hello Bub;

Washington's Birthday + this little man has had a busy day.

Besides everything else I had another complete physical—That makes the fourth since I've come into the Army. Everything was O.K., of course.

Just a few minutes ago, I signed my discharge papers. Technically I'm not in the Army any more. That's a little legal formality an enlisted man has to go through before getting a commission.

I'll get new identification tags and a new serial no. when I graduate. And by the way, there'll have to be a damn good excuse to get me out now. All the major courses are finished, and this next week is something of a gravy trail.

When I went over to the hospital for the physical, I ran into

Ben Sills—one of the boys from the West Coast. He's been here two weeks and his old wound started to bother him. So the poor guy needs an operation now. That'll probably mean he'll be released from the school. It's too bad. He's one of the best guys to come home. . . .[3]

Did you see in the papers where the engineers have been thrown in the line in Tunisia? They're taking part in the counter attacks which seem to be slowing up Rommel.[4]

G'night now, Bub. Sleep tight and dream of me as I do of you.

Your loving, Larry

Fort Belvoir, Virginia
28 February 1943

Darling;

How do you like that? Me, military intelligence.

I haven't the slightest idea what it's all about yet. The only thing I've been able to find out is that the place I'm going to is some kind of school for Military Intelligence officers.

What kind of intelligence work I'm going to do, what the setup is, is a complete mystery to me.

Everyone at the school thinks its a wonderful assignment.

As far as I'm concerned, I'll have to see before I think it's wonderful. It can really be interesting, or it can be a million other things. . . .

By the way, being assigned to G2 [intelligence] must mean I've been very thoroughly investigated. They probably know most of the big things that have happened to me since I was born.

They must have decided I was a young man of sterling character, or something. Hot stuff!

---

[3] Ben Sills fought with the Lincoln Battalion during the Spanish Civil War.

[4] Following the Allied invasion of North Africa on November 9, 1942, Germany occupied Tunisia, making much of the country a battlefield for the Northwest Africa Campaign until the surrender of the Axis forces in May 1943. Field Marshall Erwin Rommel (1891–1944), one of the best-known and most capable German generals, led the attack against the British and American forces in North Africa.

I'll call you Wednesday, darling. And see you soon, and give you my love in person.

Your very own, Larry

—————

Camp Ritchie, Maryland
10 March 1943

Hello Darling;

Arrived safely and spent the day signing papers + making out forms.

I don't think I'm going to like this place very much. We're salted away in these hills, and civilization seems to be a thousand miles away.

School starts officially on Saturday. I hear the schedule calls for seven days of straight school, then one day off—seven on one off, etc. This is to go on for two months.

With the connections to N.Y. being what they are, I think you'll have to visit with me for awhile.

As soon as I can, I'm going to see what can be arranged about lodging. Seems like that's going to be somewhat tough too.

I still don't know what the hell this is all about, really. Just know we're to get a course in intelligence methods.

Tomorrow, I'm going to get a language interview and, you'll be glad to hear this, a dental examination.

I slept a bit on the train, but I'm all fagged out now.

I'm going to turn in now.

I love you with all my heart and all my soul.

Your, Larry

—————

Camp Ritchie, Maryland
11 March 1943

My Dearest Gracie;

It's pouring rain out here and this place is a sea of oozy, sticky mud.

Was interviewed in <u>four</u> languages today—English, French, Spanish, + German.

Have finally learned a bit more about what I'm here for.

There'll be no romantic nonsense of special missions, etc. for your husband. Looks like I'm doomed to become a full-fledged member of the Brass Hat Department.

I'll be doing staff-work with combat intelligence, either in a division, corps, or Army headquarters.

I'm afraid I won't get to be with line troops in this war.

I'll probably spend my time on reconnaissance jobs + poring over maps and aerial photos.

The interviewer that assigned me said I probably will be invaluable with my training, experience, + background. Ho-hum. Maybe.

Me a staff officer. Ugh!

We got issued some books that we'll have to use. Imagine when I opened the Field Manual on the organization of the German Army and found it to be in German! A reprint of the latest field manual issued by the German Army itself.

I was half-afraid to open the manual on the Japanese Army. I thought the damn thing might be in Japanese. But it wasn't.

I sure see why they want us to know foreign languages.

Some of the stuff promises to be extremely interesting. I should be a pretty well-informed military man by the end of this course. . . .

My wife, my wife. I love you so much.

Goodnight, sweet.

Your adoring, Larry

Camp Ritchie, Maryland
12 March 1943

My Darling;

. . . Today, we had our introductory talks.

It seems from now on, as far as what goes on here is concerned, I'll have to confine myself to the state of the weather.

There is something else that I must tell you now so that you will understand if, perchance, you don't hear from me for sometime.

This is something of a jumping-off place.

I'm scheduled for a couple of months of schooling, but sometimes men leave before they are completely finished with the course.

I'm not kidding or being romantic now, sweet. Usually the next stop from here is the battlefield.

When, how, + where we go is something we don't know—and when we do, we can't tell. That's to insure getting there.

Now that you understand that little bit of sobering business, let me tell you what I've been planning to do about us, as long as I am still here.

In the first place, this is a hell of a hole for a woman.

I've located a little hotel about 2 miles from here which is supposed to be kind of nice—at $15.00 per week + no cooking facilities. . . .

You might as well be a little more comfortable in your loneliness. Out here you'd be so damned cooped up you'd feel you were in jail.

At home, you have your work, your friends, your family—and me from time to time.

Here you have absolutely nothing—and me from time to time.

I honestly think you'd be better off home. Somehow, I'd feel I was a selfish bastard if I insisted on dragging you out here.

That's about all now, darling.

Con todo mi amor, Larry

Camp Ritchie, Maryland
21 March 1943

My Darling;

So my Gracie is going to be a lathe operator!
I still can't get over it.
I can just see you standing there, in dungarees maybe,—turning out parts; picking one up and putting a micrometer on it once in awhile; then wiping the oil off your hands with a dirty rag and running some more pieces off.
A far, far cry from the Gracie I met a little more than four and a half years ago.
I think it's wonderful, sweetheart. . . .
I'm bursting with pride for you.
You may not like it—it may be tiring—it certainly will not be like anything you've ever done. The people you'll meet will not be a Mrs. Castles or a Mrs. Aldrich—they'll be a lot simpler, + a whole lot less phoney.
You're going to work with the people you've only met or read about before. There'll be stinkers like everywhere else. But, by + large, they'll be friendly and generous—and maybe you'll really see for yourself why they're the ones who carry the future.
Good luck, darling. The Canes are really establishing a fighting tradition. . . .
Well, "Keep 'Em Rolling" has a new meaning for me now. It'll be my wife breaking her back over a whirring chuck—my wife and the millions of other working stiffs back home.

I love you, querida mia. Larry

———————

Camp Ritchie, Maryland
22 March 1943

Sweetheart;

It's 6:30 P.M. now. You've been in what's probably a clattering nuthouse for a couple of hours already.
Feels strange and bewildering, doesn't it? You're probably

wondering if you can make a go of it, aren't you? Maybe you're even a bit afraid of the machine in front of you.

Well, honey don't let it get you. Don't be afraid and don't worry about how you'll turn out.

You'll be O.K.

Just takes a little practice and experience. After awhile you'll be able to do your job in your sleep—it'll be that easy.

You might even become bored stiff with going through the same operations time after time.

If you do become weary at times just remember, there's a direct line from you to the front to Hitler's bloody heart.

You want to know what to do, how to act?

How can I tell you more than just to be your own wonderful self.

Do your job well—a good worker is respected for that by everyone.

Be a bit reserved—but not a cold fish. Be friendly, but not too friendly or intimate with the men in the shop. Take it from me, it's bound to be misinterpreted if you are.

Fight the War in the Union. . . .

Never get careless at your machine—observe the safety rules. They're probably plastered all over the plant, so you'll know what they are right away. Other than that—just tie right in and give it hell.

I'm going out on a night compass problem, so I won't get much sleep tonight.

While I'm out in the hills, I'll be thinking of the wife I love so much, of the long, hard pull ahead of us, and of the family we hope to have someday.

Goodnight my love.

Your own, Larry

Camp Ritchie, Maryland
28 March 1943

Hello Darling;

It was nice being home. Wasn't it?

When I got back, we got into Camp about 1 A.M. and we had a night problem last night—so that wasn't so nice. Kinda rough. . . .

Say—listen to this.

I'm trying to get myself put into a special section that's been organized here—A class in advanced terrain intelligence. Has to do with reconnaissance work, maps, etc.

Well, while I'm at the section office talking things over with some of the instructors, my map instructor calls me aside and asks me if I'd like to stay at Ritchie for awhile and <u>TEACH</u>!

Holy Cow, you could have knocked me over. I told him, for Chrissakes I didn't want to stay here any longer than I had to, and that I wanted to get out into the field.

Well, the upshot of the matter is that he has already recommended me (this is before he even asked me) to the major who heads the Terrain Intelligence section.

Good Lord, I don't want to stay in this joint and be a teacher.

I told him very emphatically how I felt. Now I hope that they give me a break and don't order me to stay after graduation, against my wishes.

Darling, please hope very hard that I don't get stuck.

It's very flattering to know that I'm respected that much. But, that's not the kind of reward I'm looking for.

That's all the dirt for now.

I love you mucho mucho.

Your, Larry

Camp Ritchie, Maryland
23 April 1943

Hello Darling;

Got back from the two-day problem safe + sound.

It was really a dilly.

As luck would have it, it poured the first night, and we were drenched.

I didn't really get dried out until yesterday when we got back.

But, I kind of liked the problem, because it proved to me I can still take it. We did about 45 miles through very rugged mountain country in two days, we had no sleep to speak of, and very little food.

I was afraid I was getting soft at this place. We have a lot of classroom work and very little physical exercise.

Poppa can be a rough boy when he has to.

The men here are really burned up about the execution of the men who bombed Tokyo.[5] I guess the same is generally true about the rest of the army and civilian population.

Have you noticed the intensification of comment in the press about Japan lately?

Seems to me, the executions coming at this time are just part of the desperate game the Axis is playing to confuse us, break our concentration on invasion of Europe, create wide public demand for pressing of the war against Japan.

Why else should the Japs pick this time, a year after the event, to execute the men?

But, just like Pearl Harbor and a few other events, I think the Axis is miscalculating about America. They'll get a lot of shouting and demands from reactionaries to blast Tokyo.

True we'll get sore as hell, but we'll still invade (I think so even more now, because of some promising signs here).

---

[5] In April 1942 sixteen Army bombers aboard the U.S. aircraft carrier *Hornet* launched the first bombing raid against Japan. This was the famous Doolittle Raid, named after the bombing commander, Lt. Col. James H. (Jimmie) Doolittle (1896–1993). Because of bad weather and the longer than expected flight, fifteen of the planes crash landed in China. Of the seventy-five fliers who crashed in China, eight were captured by the Japanese; three were executed as "criminals" the following year.

The only thing that will happen will be we'll fight harder, and take <u>less</u> prisoners.

There isn't a red-blooded man in America who isn't saying "The dirty sons of bitches," and wishing he could put a bayonet through a few of these lice.

I bought a trench coat finally, Bub. Spent $22.00 on it.

It's got a detachable inner lining and looks pretty snappy.

The tailor has it to shorten the sleeves and the length.

Boy, will I look the dashing lieutenant when it's ready.[6]

I'll be home Monday night, love. I don't know the train, so I'll meet you home.

How's your back, sweetheart? Get it in good shape, it's due for another beating.

I love you, love you.

Your, Larry

————

Camp Ritchie, Maryland
1 May 1943

Hello Darling;

May Day Greetings![7]

It's a helluva world and a sadly battered civilization the sun shines on this day. But, there's victory ahead. . . .

Just heard a news flash that the Government is taking over the mines.

I think that's a good move.

If they take over the mines and set up a decent price stabiliza-

---

[6] Officers in the U.S. Army were responsible for purchasing their own uniforms.

[7] The international working-class holiday, May Day, originated in pagan Europe. The modern celebration of May Day as a working-class holiday evolved from the struggles for the eight-hour work day in 1886. May 1, 1886 saw national strikes in the United States and Canada for an eight-hour work day. In Haymarket Square in Chicago, police attacked striking workers, killing six. In Paris in 1889, the International Working Men's Association (the First International) declared May 1 an international working-class holiday in commemoration of the Haymarket Martyrs. The red flag became the symbol of the blood of those who had died in the fight for worker's rights.

tion and control system, it'll not only solve the mine situation for the time being but also help the rest of the country as far as living standards go.

Lewis is being roundly cursed in the Army.[8] I think all of America feels the same way.

He's a very unpopular man right now.

I heartily agree with all of America.

There's one thing that bothers me. His actions are a black eye to all of organized Labor. He's tearing down much of the good will and respect that's been established by Labor. It's going to take a long time to win it back. . . .

I love you, Bubby. Here's a May Day kiss.

Your, Larry

———————

Camp Ritchie, Maryland
8 May 1943

Look, darling, the first lilac [lilac enclosed] of the season.

I love you, Larry

———————

Camp Ritchie, Maryland
10 May 1943

Darling;

I'm thoroughly disgusted at the moment.

My fears about staying here for some time have been realized.

Seems that no one in my class is being shipped at the moment.

What they seem to be doing is establishing an officers' pool. And while we're here, we'll be kept busy doing post graduate work, teaching classes, giving basic training to enlisted men, and going through a hardening-up process ourselves.

---

[8] John L. Lewis (1880–1969) was head of the United Mine Workers (UMW). In 1943 striking UMW coal miners, especially in West Virginia, were thought to be unpatriotic. Federal troops were eventually used to open up the mines.

Some of us will go right over—others will be assigned to units in the U.S.

Right now, we're in the lap of the War Department. Future assignment is up to them, and it can be a matter of days, weeks, or months.

There won't be any leaves for most of us, and I probably won't be one of the fortunate ones.

There's just one thing that's better. From now on we'll be getting the weekends off.

So, at least, we can be together Sat. nights and Sundays. . . .

I love you, Larry

========

Camp Ritchie, Maryland
18 May 1943

My Darling;

How can I express the happiness that is in me for the six wonderful days I spent with you?

Words are so meager—at least my words are.

All I can say is "my cup runneth over."

The first thing that happened to me when I got back this morning—I was called in for an interview by another Major about staying here as an instructor.

My answer was the same as it will always be, NO!

I'm hoping desperately that they'll forget about it now and stop bothering me.

My place isn't here—buried in the Blue Ridge Mountains giving boring lectures on some damn fool subject like staff duties.

My job's at the front, where men will be shaping the world's destiny with guns.

It's what I know best and what I want to do.

No matter how much anyone insists on the importance of training men + officers for battle, as far as I'm concerned that's somebody else's job.

I belong at el frente.

Your voice letters were waiting for me.[9] Where to find a victrola so I can run them off? . . .

> Con mucho, mucho love
>
> Your, Larry

=====

> Camp Ritchie, Maryland
> 23 May 1943

Grace Darling;

. . . Just read the newspapers about the dissolution of the C. I.[10] Save the resolution for me to read.

It's part of the big things that are brewing.

I hope, my darling, that when the explosion takes place, you'll be able to say proudly—"My husband is there."

If I run to form—I will be there. I always manage to be at the rough spots somehow.

> I love you, my wonderful wife. Larry

=====

> Camp Ritchie, Maryland
> 9 June 1943

Darling;

A bit of interesting news.

On the 21st of this month I'm going to lecture the post-graduate group on the "military geography" of Spain.

---

[9] For a small fee, letter writers could record voice letters on 78 RPM records for loved ones and friends. Recording booths were located at designated defense industries, USO facilities, and other public buildings.

[10] C.I. stood for the Communist (Third) International (also known as the Comintern), a federation of Communist Parties all over the world founded in 1921 and directed by Moscow. Diplomats, especially in the United States and Britain, did not trust the group. As a gesture of good faith, Stalin disbanded the Third International in 1943. The first two Communist Internationals were founded before World War I.

The event will take place in the Post Theater, and I'll have at my disposal several tremendous colored maps.

For preparation of the lecture, some highly confidential information will be placed in my hands—stuff that the British Admiralty has been compiling.

The scope of the lecture will be very broad, as any discussion of military geography must be.

So, I think there are going to be some eyes opened (I hope).

So much for that. . . .

About all I do now is go through the motions, and live for the weekends when I can get home and be with you.

See you Saturday, honey.

All yours, Larry

Fort Belvoir, Virginia
28 June 1943

Darling;

Arrived safely this afternoon.

The thing that first strikes you about this place is its neatness + order.

It's G.I. from the word "Go."

I've been assigned to an outfit that's just entering the really serious (i.e. tough) phase of its basic training.

Looks like I'm going to be quite busy.

Matter of fact—looks like I'm going to pull O.D. (Officer of the Day) for the 4th of July weekend.

Oh well, I've had it easy for too long.

My roommate's a native Virginian. Seems a nice sort of guy. But, as usual, decision reserved.

I love you to distraction + I miss you like all hell already.

Your, Larry

Fort Belvoir, Virginia
29 June 1943

Sweet;

This afternoon I start with a bang.

The boys are scheduled to build foxholes + then let tanks run over them (with them inside.)

After that there's a hike and a night bivouac.

Tomorrow night and all day Thursday and Sat. nite and all day Sunday I'm O.D.

What a program. Oy veh!

I'm really back in the Army with a vengeance.

Still in the process of getting acclimated. Looks like all work and very little play.

Darling, the weather is putrid.

If you think N.Y. is bad, wait'll you experience this place.

It's hot and sticky so that you're oozing sweat all the time.

I seriously doubt the advisability of your living in a climate like this.

You'd probably be sick all the time.

Everybody in Camp takes salt tablets to prevent heat prostration.

Let me know if you'd like to come down the weekend of the 10th. If so, I'll make reservations at the Officers' Club for a room.

I hope I'm not scheduled to be on duty that weekend.

More tomorrow—

All of me, Larry

Fort Belvoir, Virginia
4 July 1943

Sweetheart;

I'm really disgusted for fair this time.

ME, in an Engineer DUMP TRUCK Co! Probably spend the rest of the war hauling manure across the swamps of Louisiana.

I don't know the first goddam thing about a truck, never drove one, can just about tell the hood from the ass end, and they give me such an assignment.

Well, if that's how they treat men who know something about combat, and who are anxious to fight—the hell with them.

I've always been a conscientious soldier and officer, darling. But, this beats anything I've heard for a long time.

They'll get no sterling performance from me from now on.

I'm feeling rotten, honey.

Please excuse me for cutting this short. The rest of this letter would only continue beefing if I made it longer.

The only bright spot I have in my heart and soul right now is my love for you.

Your own, Larry

═══════

Fort Belvoir, Virginia
5 July 1943

Darling;

Well, I started my new school today.

Some fun!

Been running around like crazy getting moved over, getting papers signed, going through miles of red tape. And me fuming inside all the time. The weather didn't help me any either. It's hot, and sticky.

Looks like I'm stuck on the crap list from where I sit. What do you think darling.

God, how I've wanted to be with you and talk to you the last couple of days.

I can't talk to anyone around here. They think I'm nuts to want combat. They say, "What's wrong with an Engineer Dump Truck Co? It's easy work and there's not much danger."

What can you say to people like that?

The way I look at it, I've got about a month to wangle out of this assignment. That's all I'll be thinking about as far as the Army is concerned.

I'll find out who I can see and try my damnedest to talk him into doing something for me.

About this weekend, sweetheart.

I'm going to call for a reservation for a room tomorrow.

We'll only be together Saturday evening + all day Sunday, so you'll have to leave N.Y. about 11 A.M. Sat., and leave here Sunday evening.

But, I'll write complete directions to you in tomorrow's letter. Bye now.

All my love as ever, Larry

———————

Fort Belvoir, Virginia
6 July 1943

Hello Bub;

Gosh everything seems to be snafued for me the past few days.

I couldn't get a room for us here on the post for this weekend. They're all booked up.

So, instead of you coming down here, I'll come home this weekend.

We'll have more time together because I don't have to get back until 6:30 Monday morning.

Expect me home between 10–12 P.M. Saturday nite.

I'm already beginning to maneuver to get out of this deal.

Tonight I'm writing a letter to my old Major at Camp Ritchie. See what he can do for me.

A drowning man grasps at straws. and if the bastards don't let me get into a combat unit, I'd rather spend my time teaching at Ritchie (If I can get it now) to supervising the hauling of garbage in the swamps of Louisiana.

If I ever do get back to Ritchie, darling you're packing up and coming to live with me quick like a bunny. You'll have that summer vacation you're longing for allright.

I know you must have written me, but like everything else my mail must be screwed up, because I haven't received a letter from you these past few days.

Oh well, I'm sure I'll get one by tomorrow.

Goodnight now. I love you. Larry

———————

Fort Belvoir, Virginia
12 July 1943

Hello Honey;

Got your wire and sent the registered letter canceling our lease as of July 31st.

I think the best thing for us to do is leave for Louisiana on the 1st of August, regardless of what time I'm supposed to report there officially. Then, if I do get a few days off, we can use them to get acclimated and get a place to live.

Now, pay attention honey—I'm going to tell you how we're going to travel to Louisiana—pullman—for practically nothing.

I'm going to put in a request for Gov't transportation at the Quartermaster's. Which means they'll give me a slip which I'll exchange for a first class train fare on the R.R. Then I'll pay for a lower berth on a pullman—about $7.00

At the same time I'll buy a first-class ticket for you—about $60.00.

That means I'll pay out in cash for fare about $70.00. That'll be easy because I'll have the money.

Now, after we get to Claiborne, I turn in my duplicate copy of the Gov't transportation slip, + within 5 days, I'll receive about $62.50 from the finance department (or, 5¢ a mile).

So we'll ride in style, even if we are riding to hell.

I'll put in for reservations as soon as I can this week.

Oh, and by the way, I don't have to pay any tax on my pullman because I'm traveling under Army orders. And the first-class ticket entitles you to sleep in my pullman.

There's nothing new about my situation. Haven't heard from the Major. Haven't even received your mail yet.

I feel kind of hopeless about anything happening.

Guess I'll just have to resign myself to my fate. It'll be hell just to read about how we're winning the war.

The only bright thing about it is that you're coming to live with me.

Gosh, I'm happy we decided to do that.

It'll make life a great deal more bearable for both of us.

I love you, sweet. Larry

========

Fort Belvoir, Virginia
19 July 1943

Darling;

. . . Funny, the world's on fire, I'm in an army that's building to a great climax, and I'm bored stiff.

Guess that's because I'm not in the main current, just sort of in the back wash.

España was never like this.

I can't say that I thoroughly enjoyed myself then—there's nothing very enjoyable about combat.

But, at least I was filled with a consciousness that I was contributing to human progress. I was proud that I was a member of that pitifully small band of men who were the conscience of the world.

Here, dammit, I feel like they've put me behind bars—and given me some kind of warden's job. Respectable but safely tucked away.

Oh hell, I wish I could get a break and get some action.

I know it'll mean separation for a long time, sweetheart. And, I know you'll live in constant fear.

But, don't you want to be able to tell our kids how their daddy helped to rid the world of the worst monsters in history?

Sure you do.

Till tomorrow. All my love, Larry

========

Fort Belvoir, Virginia
27 July 1943

Darling;

The day for the start of the long trek draws closer.

We'll probably have some inconveniences to put up with when we get down there, but it'll be swell being together again.

Claiborne is going to be made an all-Negro Camp by the end of the summer. Which will probably mean that some of the congested living conditions in Alexandria will be lightened somewhat.

It's a helluva thing to have to say, but we're going to be living in a part of the country where white chauvinism will blow in our faces like a bad breath continuously.

How are you, sweetheart? . . .

I've nothing left to say, except that I love you and that there's something new and wonderful and tender in my love,

Until I call you Friday night.—

Your ever loving, Larry[11]

---

[11] Here the letters to Grace end until January 1944. From August 1943 until January 1944, Lawrence Cane was stationed at Camp Claiborne, Louisiana where he commanded a supply company of black troops of the 582nd Engineer Dump Truck Co. During this period he was joined by Grace, and the two lived in an apartment near the base. In January 1944 Cane's company received orders to go to England. Grace moved back to New York and Lawrence Cane traveled north with the 582nd to Camp Shanks, New York in preparation for deployment overseas.

3

Preparing for the
D-Day Invasion: England
January 25–June 5, 1944

582nd Engr. Dump Truck Co.
Camp Claiborne, Louisiana
25 January 1944

Darling;

As I write this you're probably about one hour out of St. Louis on the way home.

I won't attempt to describe how I feel—my words are miserably inadequate.

I love you, my wife and my comrade, and all I want out of life is to be able to face it with you beside me always.

Nothing new happened today except that we're swamped under a Niagara of endless administrative details in preparation for the big event. . . .

You didn't get sick on the train did you, darling? Please take good care of yourself—I hope so deeply for both of us that everything turns out O.K. and that we both get our fondest wish.

We should—don't you think? We've broken so many wishbones over it. And even when I won, I always wished that you'd get what you wanted.

You'll find enclosed, a tiny violet. I picked it up this morning right outside my hut.

I don't believe in omens. But, I felt you were speaking to me from the train and saying good morning—and telling me not to worry. So, I picked it up gently and carried it carefully folded away until now.

Here it is—It's how you said good morning to me Jan. 25, 1944.

Don't be angry with me, sweet, if I don't go on, and on.

I'll write more tomorrow.

I'll love you always, Larry

=====

582nd Engr. Dump Truck Co.
APO 9497, NY, NY
[on troop train to Camp Shanks, NY]
31 January 1944

Darling;

At last, I can sit down and actually write you a letter. My God, how we had to work these last few days!

Since you left I've had practically no sleep at all—until last night. That goes for all of us.

But now we're on a train—the train. (that accounts for the ragged script.) We got a swell break on the train deal. We're riding pullman—the first time most of our boys have traveled that way.[1]

I was appointed quartermaster for the entire troop train.

We're traveling with a white outfit on the same train—they in one section, we in another. In good old Army fashion we have separate messes and separate cars.

It's my job to see that the troops are supplied with all food + rations during the trip.

So, I've managed to get the mess sergeants together anyway— They get together about their menus, exchange ideas, and each thinks the other is a pretty good guy. (Not very much, but it's something.)

We left camp in high spirits—everyone, officers as well as men, expressing the fervent wish that we never see the goddam place again.

Incidentally, our outfit left with the reputation of being one of

---

[1] "Riding pullman" is a reference to the Pullman sleeping car, invented by George Pullman in 1857. The sleeping car changed from day to night use by swinging down the upper berths and folding the seats to make them into lower berths. Heavy curtains were drawn over each berth in order to provide privacy for sleeping passengers.

the best colored outfits ever to come out of the camp. That's what the general himself said. . . .

I love you.

Your, Larry

━━━━━━━

582nd Engr. Dump Truck Co.
APO 230, NY, NY
Somewhere in England
21 February 1944

Darling;

I'm sending this V-mail[2] note hoping that it will reach you before my first letter.

At least you will know if it gets to you more quickly that I'm O.K.

Note my change of address.

I couldn't get in touch with you any faster way.

I'm not writing much in this since it's all in the letter. You'll be surprised at its length.

Don't worry about me. I'm in the best of health.

My love and regards to all.

Your own, Larry

━━━━━━━

582nd Engr. Dump Truck Co.
APO 230, NY, NY
Somewhere in England
21 February 1944

Hello Darling;

At last I can sit down and write you from my new address.

The trip across was uneventful and marked chiefly by rough

---

[2] See footnote 22 in Introduction.

weather, crowded living quarters, and a perpetual poker game in my cabin.

I lived in a room which was originally constructed for two people, but which accommodated twelve second lieutenants of assorted shapes and sizes.

This BMT-Canal-St-during-the-rush-hour-effect [New York subway] was achieved by the ingenious arrangement of three-tiered bunks.

Getting in and out of our happy little dungeon was a feat worthy of a circus performer.

As a matter of fact, my unique method of getting into my cot at night, which was on top of course, earned me the nickname of "Zambini the Human Cannonball."

I used to vault from the floor right into the bunk to the accompaniment of a loud fanfare of circus music, cheers, catcalls, and ringmaster announcements from my fellow sardines.

The poker game cost me exactly two-dollars and eighty-five cents. Not bad, considering the fun I got out of it. It was less a game than a wisecracking-bee.

I didn't get seasick at all. But, then I never did before.

Lots of the men aboard certainly became limp, green rags the moment the boat began to roll.

My first vision of England was one worthy only of the pen or brush of a great artist. All I can say is that it was beautiful. I was speechless and deeply moved by the delicate pastel shades and the wonderful coastline. I kept wishing you were at my side so we could hold hands and just drink in its beauty.

My impressions of England are just preliminary, but what I have seen so far I like immensely.

The first thing we got when we got off the boat was a speech of welcome which told us briefly and unequivocally why we were here. There was no monkey business about it. Everything right on the line. We're here to invade the continent.

To me, the most thrilling remarks and those which practically floored the gentlemen from the South, were deliberate and blunt orders that in this theater there will be no racial discrimination whatsoever.

And, darling, it means just that. Any open demonstration of

racial prejudice—even a remark—is a serious offense liable to a court-martial.

The people of England—the children, men, and women—are friendly and hospitable to our Negro soldiers.

Our boys are amazed, delighted, elated over their new status. Complete social equality, something undreamed-of for most of them. Their morale has gone up 500%.

As a result of these conditions, colored soldiers are making a splendid record in this part of the world.

The young womanhood and manhood of England are in uniform. And the women—they do everything. We don't even begin to approach their organization for the war effort.

That's probably because this is really a country at war. At night England is black, black as the inside of my pocket. The people are calm and cheerful. After four years, war seems to be accepted almost as the normal mode of life.

But the country bristles with troops, planes, and arms. They are tucked away in the neat countryside waiting, training, girding for the day—Our Day.

As for my own present situation, I am quite pleased with our setup. We are billeted in a little town—and amusingly enough my outfit owns half the place.

To be more exact, the most prominent buildings in town were requisitioned by the Government for use by the military, and they are in our custody.

So, we as officers, and large local landholders, are now prominent citizens of the community. We shall be expected to tea shortly by various members of the local royalty. . . .

As for our job, it looks like I'm going to like it.

So much for me—

How are you, darling? How do you feel? How is that little bit of both of us inside you getting along?

I've been biting my fingernails mentally over what the doctor would say. Do you need an operation?

Are you getting your allotment? Did you receive your crates from Louisiana? Have you bothered any more about getting an apartment with Lucie?

I've got a million anxieties about you.

Gracie, my sweet, underneath everything—in my secret heart,

I hope and yearn that this will be over soon and that I can return to you safe and sound.

My God, how I miss you.

Please write to me, sweet. It'll be some time before I get your letters. But keep them coming. You'll never know how much I hang on the mail.

Give my love to Mother and Sara Jane and Marge and to my Mom + Pop and all the rest.

I love you, Larry

582nd Engr. Dump Truck Co.
APO 230, NY, NY
Somewhere in England
24 February 1944

Hello Darling;

I've become something of a roving ambassador-at-large these last few days.

As I've told you before, getting settled means travel over a good portion of England for me.

I don't mind it at all because I'm certainly seeing the place.

There are plenty of evidences of war around—physical. Very few towns of any size have missed their share of bombs.

There is plenty of evidence also that Britons were prepared to fight to the death and put into practice Churchill's promise to fight "on the beaches, in the fields, in the streets. . . ." during the Blitz period.[3]

Every road leading into each town has its roadblock, its anti-tank obstacles, its mined approaches, its barbed wire, its pillboxes.

These have all been neatly placed on the sides of the roads now.

[3] The Blitz was the name given to the concentrated bombing of London from September 1940 through May 1941. Cane was referring to a famous speech that Prime Minister Winston S. Churchill (1874–1965) gave in the House of Commons on May 13, 1940, when many thought a German invasion was imminent. Churchill's actual words were, "[W]e shall fight on the beaches, we shall fight on the landing grounds, we shall fight in the fields and in the streets, we shall fight in the hills; we shall never surrender."

But they're ready for instant use—I guess that won't be necessary though. Heinie is the boy that will have to worry.

One of the things that's caused a great deal of amusement:—

During the Blitz, all road signs, street marks, town signs, etc. were torn down as an additional precaution against parachutists.

Since maps of any kind are difficult to get, and since the average Englishman is a kind of stay-at-home and rarely knows anything about places ten miles from his own town, I've been having quite a time getting directions from the natives. (Doesn't tie in with being a colonial power, does it?)

Usually, they run something like this—"you want to get to—? Frightfully easy. You just take a left turn beyond that large tree. Proceed three hundred yards, then take a right turn. Go another hundred and fifty yards and turn left by the white house. Then turn around and go right, then left, then right, then two lefts and there you are."

And they always end up with "You simply cawnt miss it old boy."

Of course at first, naive and gullible furriner that I am, I followed the directions and invariably found myself hopelessly lost.

Now, when I'm puzzled about where to go, even if I see a horde of Englishmen I say the hell with it, wet my finger, hold it up in the air, close my eyes and take off.

As you travel the highways and towns of England the vehicles that predominate most are U.S. Army trucks, bicycles, and baby carriages—with baby carriages far and away the most abundant.

I do believe the birth-rate must have gone up at least a thousand percent.

I guess these English lads don't waste any time with their wives when they get home on leave.

When I got in today, there were two V-mail letters waiting for me.

My heart skipped a beat hoping they were from you. But when I opened them they were from the Vets[4] + Ruthie Wellman. . . .

By the way, I managed to finagle a bicycle for each officer in the company. They're due to arrive tomorrow. When they come we're going to be real landed gentry—real estate, our own mov-

---

[4] Vets is a reference to the veterans of the Spanish Civil War.

ies, library, recreation hall, carpenter's shop, mechanic's shop, parking space, bicycles, tea with the upper clawses, our own px— pip, pip and cheerio old dear.

Darling, I wish I'd receive some mail from you. I know it can't be helped, but I miss you so much and keep worrying about the same things. . . .

Your loving, Larry

━━━━━━━

582nd Engr. Dump Truck Co.
APO 230, NY, NY
Somewhere in England
27 February 1944

Darling Wife;

. . . I had an interesting experience the other night.

Every Friday the local post of the British Legion (same as the American Legion) runs a dance.

Of course, our boys jammed the hall.

At first, they were rather shy about asking the girls to dance.

In spite of the fact that we had told them that the English did not have the same attitude toward mixed association, they still could not quite believe it.

When the first pioneer hesitatingly asked a girl to dance, they watched him with wonderment. When the girl accepted without any self-consciousness or embarrassment, they waited for the heavens to fall.

When nothing happened they took courage.

The evening was, for them, a memorable occasion. They had some difficulty getting used to British dance steps, but they did quite well before the dance was over.

When Sam and I got in, I sounded him out.

The poor guy said he was shocked.

I told him he better get used to it. And so had a lot of others. Because tens of thousands of Negroes will come home with a lot of new ideas when this is over. . . .

We're so far apart, darling, and so much history has to be written before we get together again.

Good night, Gracie. Here's a kiss.

Your loving, Larry

———————

582nd Engr. Dump Truck Co.
APO 230, NY, NY
Somewhere in England
6 March 1944

Dearest;

I've changed my mind about your sending me packages. Every once in awhile, if you've got any extra change, please send me some candy. You know, the kind I like best—Nestle's with almonds. Any gooey stuff with cream centers.

I thought I'd be able to do with the ration we're allowed, but it seems like I'll never get to eat it myself.

You see, the rationing on things like that is very severe over here. Civilians can hardly get sweets—especially in the small villages.

Every night, when we open our PX all the little boys and girls in the town line up + watch the sale of candy + chewing gum with longing eyes.

They're much too polite, the poor things, to ask us outright for some of our precious purchases—but they stand around like well-mannered puppies at a dinner table.

And, hell, I just buy my week's allowance and go outside and divide it up.

I never could resist kids and puppy dogs.

I've been getting a look at some historical sites—England's just lousy with them.

In our own little village there's a church that was built during the Norman conquest—with a fairly recent added wing—about 500 years old!

About a mile out of town there's an old ruined Roman bridge with the abutments and piers still standing.

A few miles away there's a tower where the first English translation of the Bible was made.

Last Sunday I went to a town called Bath, where the Romans built baths over the natural mineral springs, over 2000 years ago.

And, darling, I took a bath in the same tub so many Roman conquerors wallowed in.

The water was quite warm. It wells up out of the ground at a temperature of 120 Fahrenheit.

They must have been neat people, them Romans. There wasn't even a ring around the tub.

Just outside the city stands Bath Abbey. A dismal looking, dirty, weather-beaten pile of Gothic architecture—covered with green mold, ivy, and the accumulated bird dung of 1000 years.

I stood off to the side and watched the sun shine through the stained glass windows—painfully and painstakingly pieced and colored by so many forgotten monks in the Middle Ages.

I heard the bells pealing, and calling a few aged and devout people to mass.

Couldn't help being a little awed at the thought that to this repulsive-looking monument to the Almighty had come generations to pour out their hearts. Countless people through the ages to pray for a little better lot.

What a goddam waste of human love! . . .

The one thing that stands out about England above everything else—more than their funny little trains and freight cars, more than their diminutive automobiles, more than their tidy farms—is age and tradition.

Everything is old and solid looking. History just shrieks at you everywhere you turn.

And the British know it and are quietly proud of their surroundings. They bring their children up to be proud of it. That's why they can sing "There'll Always be an England." They really believe it. . . .[5]

---

[5] "There'll Always be an England" was a popular British wartime song written by Ross Parker and Hugh Charles.

I hunger for you so. If I could only be with you, so I could touch you, talk to you, smell your hair, love you.

Gracie, Gracie you're my very life's blood.

I love you, Larry

582nd Engr. Dump Truck Co.
APO 230, NY, NY
Somewhere in England
20 March 1944

Hello Darling;

Seems like the Army thinks I need some more education, so I'm now attending another school.

It's only for a week, thank goodness.

The school is located at a large English manor house, with beautiful grounds.

The place is buried away in a quiet, pastoral setting. If it wasn't for the subject we're studying you'd never think there was a war on.

Everything is hush-hush, of course. It's one of those places Jerry is probably very much interested in. No, it's not Cp. Ritchie stuff. . . .

Darling, how's your tummy? And how's little "Joe"?

My God! How I wish you and I could be together. Even just for a little while.

Sometimes the hunger for you and the loneliness sweeps me so intensely, I can hardly stand it.

I take out your pictures, and re-read your letters, and just yearn.

The toughest part of this war for me is being away from you.

Hon, you take good care of yourself, won't you. No meetings and stuff, until the baby comes and you're strong again.

And, don't go tramping around too much looking for an apartment.

Well, I've got to be a good boy now and attend to my lessons.

Good night, my love.

Say hello to everyone for me.

I love you, Larry

582nd Engr. Dump Truck Co.
APO 230, NY, NY
Somewhere in England
26 March 1944

Darling;

Today was the most beautiful day we've had since I've come to England.

The sky was blue and cloudless, the air warm and sweetsmelling—whispering promises of pulsing life as it brushed across the fields.

I picked you a little bouquet of flowers—primroses and violets. I breathed their delicate scent deeply as I picked each one—and each one was a kiss from me to you. . . .

Darling, I'm so envious of you. How I wish I could have been with you to share the happiness of that moment. The baby moved!

There's so much I'm missing.

To be able to look at you adoringly, to hold you in my arms and dream and plan, to be anxious about every movement you make, to pet you and comfort you—Ye Gods! And here I am getting ready for the grim Battle of the Century.

Maybe our kid will be able to grow up in a better world. Anyway, I'll be in there pitching for you and for "Joe." . . .

The war news from here is pretty much the same.

We hear the bombers going over every night to drop their load on the home of Nazidom—and they're really getting plenty of crap dumped on them.

But, the news from the Russian front continues to amaze everyone. Everywhere here, in the Army, you ask about what's happening by saying, "Where are the Rooshians today?"[6]

If we give those babies another couple of months, like as not we'll wake up and find them on the other side of the Channel, telling us to come on over, it's safe now.

Nothing more to write for now, hon.

---

[6] By the spring of 1944 the Soviet Army had taken the offensive, breaking through to Leningrad, ejecting the Germans from Ukraine, and initiating a new offensive in Crimea.

Just one thing, are you getting your 200 bucks each month?
I love you Gracie mine.

Your, Larry

========

582nd Engr. Dump Truck Co.
APO 230, NY, NY
Somewhere in England
30 March 1944

Hello Darling;

We finally received our radio and victrola from Special Services.

Do you know the first record I played?

That's right—"You made me love you."—Harry James.

For a few moments there wasn't any War, and Army; no long, tough months ahead. There was only you + me.

God, I felt so lonely when the record was finished! . . .

The men, incidentally, are in love with radio + the records. They stay up after taps, blare the thing during meals, and have a jam session with Savoy Ballroom gyrations whenever they get a chance.[7]

I think if you were to offer each one a carload of diamonds in exchange for those swing recordings, you'd be left with a lot of diamonds on your hands.

We've managed to scrape, and scrounge, and steal a lot of books and athletic equipment too.

As should be expected, the books are gathering dust. A lot of these poor guys can't read or write very well. But, baseball, football, basketball, volleyball, boxing and running are getting their full share of attention.

---

[7] The Savoy Ballroom opened its doors on December 14, 1926 and closed in 1958. The Savoy was a two-story ballroom which spanned the whole block of 140th Street to 141st on Lenox Avenue in Harlem, New York. The Savoy could and very often would hold up to 4,000 people, with about 15 percent being white. Leading black and white musicians performed at the Savoy, and the ballroom claimed the best dancers in the nation.

I told you we run our own PX. Now we've opened our own barber shop for the men.

We've got two wonder-mechanics in the Company, They can do anything—fix a motor, wire electric lights, lay bricks, do carpentry, plumbing—now they've gone in to the barber business.

They built their own revolving barber chair out of packing boxes and scrap metal. It's really hot stuff.

I've got them working on a little invention I designed. We're going to use our air compressor to make ice-cream.

Just a little of that Yankee ingenuity you always read about. . . .

I love you. Larry

P.S. Oh, those Rooshians! Those wonderful Rooshians!

———————

582nd Engr. Dump Truck Co.
APO 230, NY, NY
Somewhere in England
12 April 1944

Grace Darling;

. . . I've been gone three days on a job—a rugged convoy job which took us down to the Channel.

I stood on a hill and looked over to where I knew France was. Couldn't help thinking, How soon?

I'm back in our sleepy little town now—and I'm one sleepy little head.

There's been no sleep for this wicked one for three days. . . .

There's something that's been puzzling me—

I read the salient points about the Soldier Vote bill in Yank magazine.[8]

Tell me—can I vote?

I know damn well that Southern States will probably prevent voting by soldiers—so they can keep on preventing Negroes from voting.

---

[8] The Army magazine, Yank, was widely read by enlisted men and junior grade officers during World War II.

But, does New York State permit a federal ballot? If so, do I have to ask permission to vote? And who the hell do I write to? And how soon does my request have to be in?

The Republicans seem to be dusting off some moldy-looking prospects to put on sale for election this year.

Win the war—But watch the Peace, eh?

I'm pretty sure, from the way things look over here, that by the time November rolls around we'll have our Second Front. And more than that, Nazism will be on the brink of the precipice—at least.

You notice I don't say we'll end the Nazis this year—maybe yes, maybe no—but if we don't, I'll say we'll be damn near it.

I think the situation will be too much for the Republicans to take over, no matter how much they say they're for winning the war + the peace.

All I can see is FDR. He gets my vote this year if it takes 6,000 miles of red tape to get it in. . . .

I love you. Larry

—————

582nd Engr. Dump Truck Co.
APO 230, NY, NY
Somewhere in England
18 April 1944

Darling;

. . . Feels awfully strange being a prospective Poppa at long distance. I hope I'll have the good fortune to return home soon and be a real Pop. As for your back, darling, it'll be a pleasure to rub it.

So Mark's finally in. Poor boy—Keesler Field in the summer time.[9] He'll probably get his basic flight training by taking a spin on some of those mosquitoes they've got down there.

I confidently believe that we'll be through over here before he

---

[9] This is a reference to Grace's younger brother, Marcus Singer. In 1943, at age 17, Marcus left college and, with his mother's permission, enlisted in the Army Air Forces. He was stationed at Keesler Field in Biloxi, Mississippi.

gets his chance to fly combat. It'll take a lot of doing—but we're agonna do it.

The Japs will take a bit longer—but not as long as some people think.

About that C.C.N.Y. [City College New York] reunion, the first I heard about it was your letter. I wouldn't have been able to get there even if I knew it was taking place.

Hon, don't worry if my mail gets a little irregular. Might even be a couple of weeks at a stretch without hearing from me.

You just keep on writing steadily to me as ever.

I love you darling.

Your, Larry

582nd Engr. Dump Truck Co.
APO 230, NY, NY
Somewhere in England
1 May 1944

Grace Darling;

This is the first time in over a week and a half I've had a chance to write to you.[10]

We're tired and dusty, and I'm a bearded desperado—but I'm writing before another minute is out.

There must be a lot of mail from you piled up for me somewhere—I haven't been able to get any mail for a couple of weeks either.

Darling, look at the date above. This year it comes on the eve of tremendous events. The last sands are running out of the hour glass.

How's "Joe"? And you, hon, are you feeling O.K.? I'm hungry for news. After getting mail regularly—two weeks without seems like a year.

---

[10] Cane is, of course, referring to the final preparations for the June 6, 1944 D-Day invasion of Normandy.

Just to make sure you get my birthday greetings to you in time, I'm starting with this letter. HAPPY BIRTHDAY DARLING.

I love you, Larry

582nd Engr. Dump Truck Co.
APO 230, NY, NY
Somewhere in England
3 May 1944

Grace Darling;

I hope you haven't been worried by the sudden gap in my letters. We've been terrifically busy recently. What we've been doing and where we've been is, of course, impossible for me to describe—you'll understand.

Suffice it to say, we're now enjoying a breathing spell, and that gives me a chance to try to catch up on my letter-writing to you. None of us have been able to receive any mail for the past couple of weeks, and darling I ached to hear from you. . . .

I had a hilarious few minutes a couple of weeks ago when I opened a package from the Service Men's Committee of the Liquidometer shop.

After unraveling reams of paper and chunks of sawdust stuffing I unearthed a bottle of Vitamin B tablets. Of all the nutty things to send me! Reminds me of the box of soap I got in Spain when I was in the Sierra Pandols.[11]

By the way, you'll be amazed to hear who I've made friend of.

We're in a combat engineer group, and the Protestant <u>chaplain</u> and I are great friends. As a matter of fact, he's plugging as only a chaplain can in his own quiet, unobtrusive way to get me transferred to one of the combat engineer battalions in the outfit.

Whether anything will come of it I don't know, + I've arrived

---

[11] In the Sierra Pandols in Spain during the brutally hot summer of 1938, the Mac-Paps were holding a rocky position where the water had to be brought up at night by mule. One day, a package arrived from a group of supporters in the States. Hoping for chocolate or cigarettes, Cane opened it to find only bars of soap inside.

at the point where I don't get excited over promises any more. . . .

Know what he told me? He thinks I'm more religious in my own attitude and life, in spite of the fact that I profess a disbelief in religion, than most men he has ever known.

He should know—oy, veh!

He's a nice guy, though. I honestly like him. . . .

Give my love to Mother + Sara Jane and every one else at home.

Here's a kiss, darling.

All my love, Larry

582nd Engr. Dump Truck Co.
APO 230, NY, NY
Somewhere in England
10 May 1944

My Darling;

The past few days have been very busy ones—we've been roaring up and down the highways + byways of England. We roll 'em day + night in this outfit. . . .

As you probably have surmised, I too have changed my abode here. We're no longer in the sleepy little town we were first billeted in. We are now in the Channel region—living out in the open. . . .

About the Soldier Vote—I was well taken care of. First you, then the Vets, . . . then the CIO [Congress of Industrial Organization]. My request for a ballot is well on its way—and I've also taken care of all New Yorkers in my company.

You ask why I don't write on both sides of the paper. Well, officers' mail is spot-checked by Base Censors and if anything is included that shouldn't be there, they *cut*, not blot, it out. If there's anything on the other side, that gets cut out too. So a censored letter that has writing on both sides is really butchered. . . .

About "Joe's" name. If he's a him, how about David Earl—after the "Earl"?[12] If she's a her, I like Laurie Ann.

Gee, darling, I'd like to see you now. There's so much more of you to love. I get so lonely for you. . . .

To you, darling, my heart and all of me.

Your, Larry

———————

582nd Engr. Dump Truck Co.
APO 230, NY, NY
Somewhere in England
26 May 1944

Sweetheart;

Today was an eventful day. We had real honest-to-goodness fried eggs for breakfast.

Over here in the ETO (European Theater of Operations) that's quite an event. And along with it, we had oranges—nice juicy American seedless oranges.

You know what the old soldier says when the chow gets extra good—"Something's up."

This afternoon we even had the famous U.S. Army band from Washington visit us and give us a concert.

They played a few marches and military songs which included the Russian "Meadowland." In addition they entertained with a whole lot of "Gershwinia."

Chief diversion during the concert was provided by a herd of cows, led by a frisky young bull, which was fascinated by the blare and clang.

Time after time they closed in on the band and joined in the music with fervent moos.

Each time they came close, the guards would chase them away.

The picture of stern young guards armed with rifle, bayonet, and tommy gun shooing cows in the interest of things esthetic was too much for even the bandmaster. After wiping hysterical

---

[12] The "Earl" was a reference to Earl Browder (1891–1975), the General Secretary of the Communist Party of the USA from 1929 to 1944.

tears of laughter from his eyes he was moved to render, "Bury Me Not on the Lone Prairie."—which he claimed was one of the few cowboy songs extant that wasn't written in Brooklyn.

All in all, the day's been pretty good.

The only hitch was that the mailman didn't bring me one of those blue envelopes from you that always makes my heart skip a beat. . . .

There's work to do now—so I'll knock off.

I love you. Larry

582nd Engr. Dump Truck Co.
APO 230, NY, NY
Somewhere in England
28 May 1944

Hello Sweetheart;

. . . Today is a beautiful day. Warm delicious cool breezes every few seconds, blue skies—and lazy as hell.

The men are lying around—snoozing, writing letters, taking sunbaths. Here + there one with enough energy to overcome Spring fever is washing socks in a bucket.

Every once in a while a plane circles around—just a reminder that there's a war on. Otherwise, from all outside appearances this could be a senior Boy Scout camp.

Nothing to indicate the appalling maelstrom we are going to let loose when the time comes.

Of course, if you were to go down in the woods a few hundred yards away, your eyes would probably bug out, if you didn't expect to see what was there. . . .

I love you and miss you and every night I lie in bed and think about you. I dream of the day when we can be together again—and hope that I'll have the good fortune to live in peace with you and "Joe" and the "Joes" to come.

Te quiero mucho. Larry

582nd Engr. Dump Truck Co.
APO 230, NY, NY
Somewhere in England
31 May 1944

My Darling;

Yesterday was Decoration Day.[13] It was hot here, and we had lots of work to do. We were wringing wet before the day was half over.

I kept thinking about the decoration days I used to spend so long ago in my boyhood. There'd be a gang of us from the Scout Patrol go on an overnight hike up in the mountains. One year it would be the Ramapos; another, up Bear Mt. somewhere; another, along the Sunset Trail.[14]

We'd always find a stream or pool, or lake somewhere. We'd tear our clothes off and race each other—last one in was a jerk. We'd hit the water with a splash, and come up screaming and gasping with delight at the shock of the clear mountain water.

First swim of the year, it was—And a glorious one at that.

It's been a long time since camping trips—And this year—well. . . . Someday, maybe I'll be able to tell you about it. Someday, perhaps, I'll sit "Joe" in my lap and tell him the story of the crushing of Nazism. Of how, in appalling struggle, mankind took another step upward.

And speaking about Joe—Darling, you amazed me in your last letter. Imagine you weighing 118¼ lbs.—and just in your sixth month. You must be beginning to look like a little butter ball. They'll have to roll you to the hospital when the time comes.

If I could only put my arms around you and feel you just once. That profile view of yourself that you drew makes me wonder if my arms would be long enough to reach all the way around.

I want to take this opportunity to wish you a very happy wedding anniversary—and tell you that you're the most wonderful wife a man ever had. I want you to think of me on June 16th as being at your side and whispering in your ear that I love you.

---

[13] Decoration Day, now known as Memorial Day, evolved during the 1860s when people gathered to honor the Civil War dead by decorating the graves of Union and Confederate soldiers with flowers. Memorial Day is now an occasion that honors all those who have died in service to the nation.

[14] These are references to popular hiking areas in New York state.

Four years, darling—four hectic years for the entire world. We were always so busy the first couple of years—and the last two there's been the Army. But loving you, and being loved by you whether we've been together or apart has given me the greatest happiness any man could ever want.

My greatest desire now is that Providence will be kind to me and permit me to spend our fifth anniversary together again, safe and sound.

So long, my love, don't worry about me.

I love you. Larry

MAP 1

Planned D-Day landing zones for the U.S. First Army, June 6, 1944. the actual landings on Utah Beach occurred about 2,000 yards further south than planned. Lawrence Cane landed on Utah Beach between H+20 and H+30 min with the Combat Engineers assigned to carry out the assault demolition work. (Based on Map II, The Final Overlord Plan, in Gordon A. Harrison, *Cross-Channel Attack* [Washington, D.C.: Government Printing Office, 1951].)

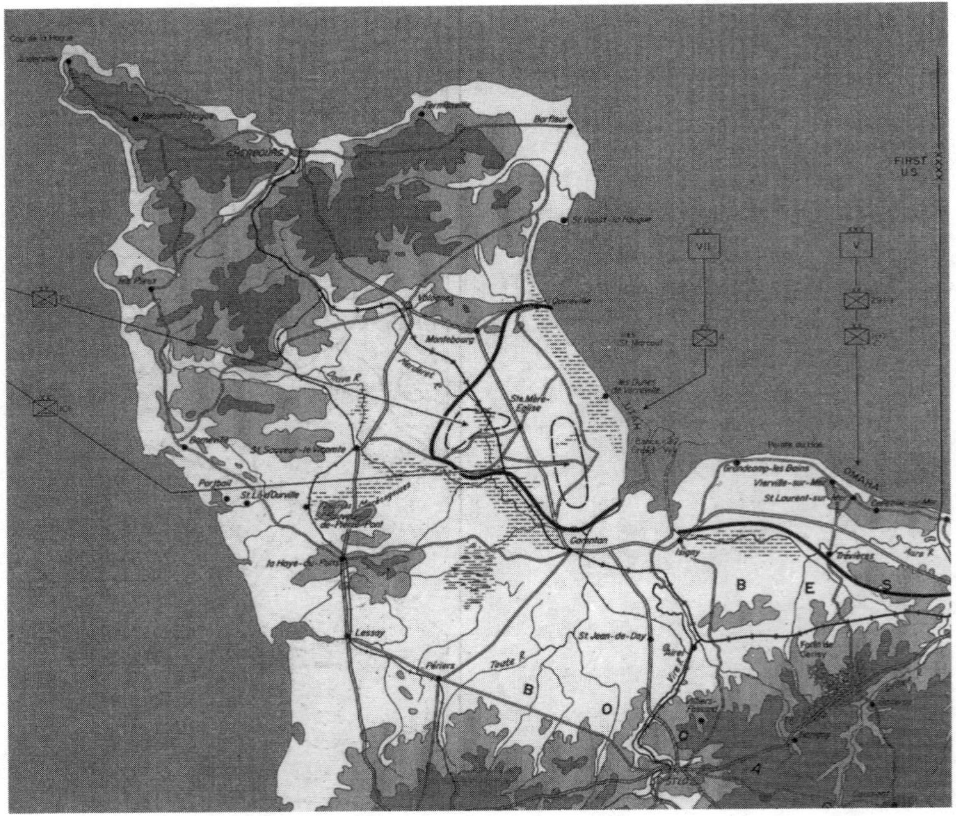

4

The D-Day Invasion and Beyond: Fighting in France and Belgium
June 6–September 14, 1944

582nd Engr. Dump Truck Co.
APO 230, NY, NY
Somewhere in France
10 June 1944

My Darling,

I know you must be at your wits end by now, for not hearing from me.

I landed in France on D-day with combat engineers in the assault wave.[1] Helped storm through the beach defenses and am still at the front (Everything is front line area here right now anyway).

My outfit has been [*censored*] so you know I'm just where I want to be. Although I'm still officially in my old company, actually I'm on detached service with the [*censored*]

And, darling, we are raising hell.

Last night, I had charge [*censored*] while our outfit ferried the [*censored*].

You can tell our kids that daddy got plenty of Nazis.

I love you, darling. Please don't worry about me.

My love to everyone. A big letter to follow when I get a chance to get a breather.

Your own, Larry

---

[1] When Americans awakened on the morning of June 6, 1944 to the news of the long-awaited D-Day invasion, Cane's father, Abraham Cohen, remarked, "I don't know where Lawrence is or what he is doing, but if he is not on one of those beaches, he is probably somewhere writing letters of protest." (Grace Cane as told to David E. Cane.)

582nd Engr. Dump Truck Co.
APO 230, NY, NY
Somewhere in France
11 June 1944

Gracie Darling;

I wrote my first V-mail note to you yesterday. I'm sorry I couldn't sit down and write any sooner, because I know you've probably been worried. But I'm still alive and well and hoping that I'll remain that way.

You remember my anxiety about getting into some real action—about being up front where people like us should always be? Well, darling, I should never have worried about it. Somehow, I always get to where the fighting is hottest.

As I mentioned to you in my note, I landed in France on D-day, 6 June, 1944, with the combat engineers in the assault wave. I was in on the storming of the beach fortifications and since then have been right up in the thick of it with the parachute troops.

While we were back in England, my company was assigned as the trucking outfit for the Engineer Combat Group[2] that was picked to do the assault engineer work in our section of the invasion bridgehead. Of course, since landing you know what kind of jobs I've been going out on.

A couple of nights ago, we ferried paratroops across a river and I was placed in command of all heavy machine-guns assigned to provide overhead fire for the crossing.[3] It was a ticklish job because I had to set the positions up after dark, and estimate by compass bearings the fields of fire to be covered in the crossing area. It had to be just right, or we would have been firing into our own troops.

---

[2] 1106th Engineer Combat Group.

[3] Cane is referring to the ferrying of paratroops from the 101st Airborne over the Douve River, near the hamlet of Brevands, east of Carentan, by the 49th Engineer Combat Battalion, commencing at 0100 hours on June 10, 1944. A provisional machine gun company drawn from Company B of the 237th Engineer Combat Battalion equipped with .50 caliber machine guns was used to increase the density of fire prior to the crossing. See History, 1106th Engineer Combat Group, 9–10 June 1944, National Archives at College Park, Maryland, World War II Operations Reports, Record Group 407, Box 19304.

The job came off O.K., and as a result of the crossing we were able to link up with the other American bridgehead below us.[4]

We are making what I think is satisfactory progress. Jerry is tenacious and he is not being routed yet. But we are smashing him back and piling the stuff in behind us.

What's going on at other places, I do not know. You've probably been able to get more information about that than I have.

But the day we stormed the beaches, and dropped from the skies to open this long-hoped-for Front, Jerry was through, and he damn well knows it.

He'll take some beating yet—and there's probably a lot of rough stuff ahead of us. But, in the light of history it won't be very long.

Not the least of my memories of this job will be the crossing of the Channel in those damned LCT's.[5] God Almighty, what a miserable ride that was! I have been tossed around in boats before, but this goddam cruise took the cake. I got seasick for the first time in my life, and I wasn't the only one.

Well so much for now my Darling. I've got your picture out and I miss you so much I feel like crying. Please take care of yourself, and don't worry about me. At least, not too much.

Give "Joe" a pat for me—and when you go to sleep tonight tell the little one that daddy hopes to be back soon.

I love you.

Your, Larry

---

[4] This is a reference to the link up of the bridgeheads at Utah Beach, where he landed, and Omaha Beach.
[5] The LCT was a Landing Craft Tank that brought troops, weapons, and vehicles to invasion beaches. A larger version of this vessel was the LST or Landing Ship Tank. For a first-hand account of the departure from England and crossing of the Channel by Cane's LCT #2331, see Appendix C, the Diary of Lt. George A. Worth.

582nd Engr. Dump Truck Co.
APO 230, NY, NY
Somewhere in France
12 June 1944

Darling;

Catching a few moments to say hello again. We are still moving forward. We just took an important town this morning. After it fell, the French civilians streamed up out of their cellars and caves and gave us wine and cider and their fervent blessings.

The first chance I get I'll try to describe this operation as I saw it. It's been absolutely stupendous.

My boys have come through wonderfully. I'm proud as punch of them. As a matter of fact, the whole American Expeditionary Force in France is a terrific outfit.

I miss you and love you beyond your imagining.

I haven't received any mail for weeks, and I sure would like to begin receiving letters again.

Take care of yourself and our Joe.

Con todo mi corazon, Larry

582nd Engr. Dump Truck Co.
APO 230, NY, NY
Somewhere in France
13 June 1944

Darling Mine;

Yesterday, I had an experience I shall never forget.

We captured an important town,[6] and as the last shots were being fired and the last snipers being sent where they belong, we

---

[6] The town Cane is referring to is Carentan on the Douve River. Its capture allowed American troops to consolidate their position and provided the starting place for the difficult hedgerow fighting in Normandy which ultimately led to the breakthrough at St. Lo. The 1106th Engineer Combat Group was engaged in building bridges and clearing mines in this region.

moved in to throw a bridge across a stream to replace the one that Jerry had blown up a few hours before.

As we arrived at the bridge site, which was on the outskirts of town, an old woman crept out of a pile of rubble that had formerly been her home. She was followed by a deformed and ragged old man and three dirty, snotty-nosed little children. Two girls, one boy.

The old lady carried something close to her breast and painfully struggled up the debris until she stood at the highest part of the mound. Then gently and proudly she shook what she had in her hands, and out fluttered the tri-color of France.

The old lady was crying when she fastened the flag with a couple of bricks. "Vive la France," she said brokenly. "Vive la liberation de —," she cried naming the town we had captured. And the little kids and the old man all repeated "Vive la France. Vive l'Amerique."

Then the old lady ran into her cellar and came out with apple-cider. She was sorry, she said that this was not the . . . "Pays du vin, seulement des pommes."

I called her "mère" and she called me "Mon petit." And when the old man asked me some questions which were nobody's business but our own to know, and I told him so, she said "Bien répondu, mon petit."

She asked if I was married and I said yes and showed her your picture and she exclaimed that you were "très jolie." And when I told her you were "enceinte" she called on the Bon Dieu to bless both of us and our baby. And when I went away she kissed my hands.

Goddam, isn't that worth fighting for?

But not all civilians here are like that.

Jerry has been dropping parachutists behind our lines who dress in civilian clothes. There are also the "collaborateurs" to contend with.

They act as snipers, spies, and saboteurs.

Naturally, we are not very merciful with these fancy people when we catch them.

So far I have seen no evidence of the French underground. Perhaps, as we work farther inland and reach the larger cities we shall hear from them. Anyway, if we don't I'll feel disappointed as hell. I've always believed so implicitly that the French people would grasp this opportunity to reassert their fierce traditions of liberty, and that the wild, blood-tingling call of "Aux armes, citoyens" of the Marseillaise would once again resound throughout France.

Or am I an incurable romantic?

One thing about the fighting here so far. It's practically been straight infantry and artillery on both sides. And as far as the air is concerned—we own the skies. Jerry doesn't dare come out until after dark—and then our ack-ack plays hell with him. If he had more stuff, I believe he would have shown it already, because the place to stop an invasion is on the beach—and we're a good deal away from the beaches now.

Behind us there comes a steady flood of materiel and men. Since we have no ports yet—we brought our own. Pre-fabricated, floating docks that were floated here from England, and alongside of which big troop transports and cargo ships tie-up and unload.[7] Artillery, tanks, men, delousing stations, ordnance shops, infantry, tanks, more artillery, an endless flow.

And overhead serenely, guarding it all, roars our air force.

I believe that when enough comes in you're going to read about much more spectacular advances on our part. We are going to smother Jerry under a sheet of flame and fire. We'll crush him and grind him to a bloody pulp underneath the weight of the stuff we'll bring to bear against him.

And, dammit, the sooner the better.

I am writing this in a foxhole and it's raining. That accounts for some of the blurs you see on these pages.

How's my darling these days? Do you miss me as much as I miss you? Or is that possible?

Good lord, I ache for the day when we can be together again. I'll kiss you from your toes to the top of your head and bite your ears for good measure. I'll love you until you yell Uncle.

Take care of yourself, darling. Be good, and take it easy. Pat our "Joe" for me.

---

[7] The floating docks that Cane is referring to were artificial harbors built by the Allied forces during the Normandy invasion. These artificial harbors were known as mulberries.

I love you.

Your, Larry

====

582nd Engr. Dump Truck Co.
APO 230, NY, NY
Somewhere in France
15 June 1944

Darling;

Tomorrow will be four years that we're married.

Happy Anniversary, darling!

Let's hope that by next year things will be different, and that we can really enjoy our anniversary together.

Our outfit has been paid a very high compliment. The general has said that never in the history of the U.S. Army has a Negro outfit achieved such a reputation for efficiency and courage under fire.

There is even rumor of a Presidential citation for us.

Perhaps, in spite of all my squawking and dissatisfaction with my lot, I have contributed in a small way to making the company what it is.

Things are pretty much the same. We keep pushing ahead, foot by foot. Painful + slow, but sure. Jerry resists bitterly. Behind us, in a never-ending stream come more men and materiel. The day will come when Jerry's orderly retreat will become a rout, and I do not believe that it is very far off. Maybe I'm too optimistic, but I think so.

Anniversary greeting from my foxhole again, darling.

I love you. Larry

====

582nd Engr. Dump Truck Co.
APO 230, NY, NY
Somewhere in France
16 June 1944

Darling Mine;

Today is anniversary day for us, and I ache for you. Being so far away makes me feel so blue.

Here I am in a damned foxhole which is my residence, and I keep thinking of my wife and the baby that's coming and my real home across the ocean.

I love you, Gracie. It's such a great pity that we can't be together today.

We've had some amusing experiences while foraging for food. You can be amused, you know, even here, if you take time out to look at it the right way.

We're living on canned rations just now, and naturally we constantly try to supplement them with fresh food.

I went out on a little reconnaissance yesterday and tried to buy a cow.

Being careful about the property rights of the peasants, I thought we'd better not appropriate any of the livestock roaming around.

One farmer wanted 18,000 francs for an old beatup cow. The franc being pegged at 2 cents, that would make it $360.00.

I told him that I could damn near buy the Empire State building for that kind of money back home. He shrugged his shoulders and told me that everything in France was "très cher" these days.

I continued my search and stopped a farmer along the road. Pointing to some cattle and horses grazing in a field, I asked him whose they were. He replied that they belonged to the Germans, who had "requisitioned" them from the farmers.

Last night, we had plenty of beefsteak.

In addition we found a store of wines, including champagne, plenty of eggs and chickens, and got some black bread. So we had quite a feast.

As far as my work is concerned, I'm back with my company now, and we run a fairly uneventful (right now, anyway) trucking business for the rest of the outfits in our group.

Yesterday, we received our first newspapers since landing—copies of the Stars + Stripes three days old.[8] For the first time we got some news about the rest of the bridgehead area, and learned something about how the world received the news of the invasion.

It must have been a tremendous day for America. I guess if prayers could win for us, we're practically in the barn right now.

We have received no mail yet.

Please give my love to everyone, darling. And to you, sweetheart—all my longing all my heart.

Your own, Larry

582nd Engr. Dump Truck Co.
APO 230, NY, NY
Somewhere in France
18 June 1944

Darling;

Today is Father's Day. And, as a prospective Poppa, it behooves me to say a few words.

I hope when this damn war is over, that our kids won't have to go through the same thing. I believe that before too long, we'll be in a position to see that peace will be guaranteed for a long time.

I hope the opportunity will be well-used.

Right now, of course, we're still coming in—hand over hand, practically. But, the time is not far off when we'll really begin to stretch our legs. Then, watch us roll.

I pray that the heritage I'm helping to build for our "Joe" will not be an empty one.

Things with me are pretty much the same. You know, of course, that I'm back with my company. After the beaches and

---

[8] *The Stars and Stripes,* a newspaper published by and for U.S. soldiers, first appeared in April 1942. During World War II it aimed its stories at the G.I. in the foxhole.

the first few days of assault jobs, they probably figured I'd done my job.

So they've got me trucking again. If that's the way they want it, so be it. I got in some damn good licks, anyway.

I love you, sweetheart. Here's a great big kiss.

Your, Larry

582nd Engr. Dump Truck Co.
APO 230, NY, NY
Somewhere in France
19 June 1944

Darling;

Just started to receive mail from you.

Got a letter dated the 1st of June and a V-mail from the second.

Good to hear from you and know that you're getting along O.K.

There must be a gob of mail you wrote before those dates that hasn't come to me yet. Probably floating around in England somewhere.

One thing I had to do that breaks my heart—I had to burn your letters after reading them. You know up to now, I saved every letter I ever received from you. C'est la guerre. . . .

I love you as always, darling. Please don't worry about me.

Your, Larry

582nd Engr. Dump Truck Co.
APO 230, NY, NY
Somewhere in France
22 June 1944

Darling Mine;

. . . Here in Normandy, we've made some good progress in the past few days—but you know all that and this'll just be old stuff by the time you get this letter.

As we streamed along the roads in pursuit of the "Herrenvolk" we were greeted by the first real bursts of enthusiasm since landing. Prior to this, in the country around the beaches, the people seemed afraid, or at least restrained.

And well they might be. These Normandy peasants are such poor, wretched folk. Really crushed by the invader. Their sons and young men either prisoners of war, or working in German factories. Their daughters in German whorehouses in the large cities, or leading a bedraggled existence on the farms whose fields lie fallow. And their children. Poor, undernourished, pale, with big blue eyes.— Here the people "ont les yeux bleus."

It'll take some time to wipe out the effects of German paternal care.

Right now we're outside the city you read about in the newspapers on the above date.[9]

At the moment the air force is having a field day bombing and strafing with practically no opposition except ack-ack that I can see.

Of course, it'll be different on the ground. Jerry'll be there for the doughboys to slug. But, I believe we'll have the place a good deal before you get this letter.

So much for that.

You don't know how proud and happy it makes me feel to hear that you're feeling O.K. and that "Joe" is doing so well. Gosh, it's going on seven months now, isn't it? Pretty soon, we'll be poppa + momma. Bet some of our old friends were frankly envious of you.

Me too, darling. I wish so much that I could be with you.

I love you so much.

Your, Larry

---

[9] After securing the beachhead in Normandy, the VII Corps attacked north in order to capture the key port city of Cherbourg. The final assault began on June 22. After six days of hand-to-hand fighting, the Germans surrendered. Unfortunately, the harbor itself was so badly damaged that it could not be used for weeks.

582nd Engr. Dump Truck Co.
APO 230, NY, NY
Somewhere in France
24 June 1944

Darling;

Received quite a batch of mail from you today, including your anniversary greetings. You were wondering where I was on D-day. I guess you know now.

I was right where I had always hoped and dreamed I would be—in the thick of it.

If I live through this—along with the fact that I fought in Spain, I shall be proud that I was with the first troops that stormed the beaches of France. With the assault teams that pulled out the mines, blasted the sea walls, blew up the obstacles, cut through the barbed wire, smashed the pillboxes, and then built the bridges and repaired the roads through the inundated areas.

After that, for awhile, we operated with the paratroops, and I was in on some good jobs there too.

Since then, of course, you know that I was sent back to my company. Right now, we are running a fairly unexciting front-line trucking service.—Hauling mines, explosives, bridges, wounded, ammunition, rations, and any damn thing else they have a notion to use us for—even Nazi prisoners of war.

We've been to everyplace (practically) that you've read about in the newspapers.

So, you can see that I am not very dissatisfied with my job.

Day before yesterday, I had another wonderful experience.

I was cruising along in my good jeep Sara Jane, on a reconnaissance mission, and stopped to ask some civilians a few questions.

It turned out that the civilians were <u>Spaniards</u>.

They were former members of the Spanish Republican Army, who had been incarcerated by the French after the fall of the Republic, and then had been inherited by the Germans after the fall of France.

For the past few years, they and thousands upon thousands of others, had been used as slave labor by the German Army to build the fortifications we are now busily engaged in demolishing—occupants and all.

These particular men had hidden in the woods when the Germans retreated from the area, and were now ensconced in a nearby chateau which had formerly been a German headquarters. They were enjoying a strange new experience—freedom after five years of slavery.

You can just about imagine the kind of get together we had. One of them even knew a boy I had in my company in Spain.

Then I got down to brass tacks and asked them about fortifications and positions. After about two hours, I had a wealth of information about the area which I later brought directly to the G-2 [intelligence division] of our Corps.

The information is, of course, something that cannot be discussed, but I believe it is playing a part in the job immediately at hand.[10]

So you see, truth is still stranger than fiction.

Tell my Pop for that he's got me wrong, I really do write once in awhile. And as for mail to the U.S. before D-day, it was all held up.

There were thousands in the Army, particularly officers, who knew that our next "exercise" was the real thing. We had to know—because the details of every assault job had to be memorized, maps scanned, aerial photos and intelligence reports studied, and the job organized.

It was inevitable that some words would slip through, in spite of rigid censorship, if they allowed the mail to get back home before the actual invasion began.

So that's why there was no mail for awhile.

Bub, from now on, mail should come in to you pretty regularly.

We're not quite so fortunate, because we keep moving all the time—And you'll never know how sweet it feels to be able to chase the hated Nazis.

One word is engraved in my heart when we go after those

---

[10] The information gained from the former Spanish prisoners dealt with tunnels and fortifications at the Fort du Roule, a massive citadel that dominated the harbor of Cherbourg. The capture of Cherbourg gave the Allies control of an actual port and completed the sweep of the Cotentin peninsula. This set the stage for the push to the south and the eventual breakout from the Normandy bocage country.

bastards, "REVENGE." For Spain and my maimed and dead comrades, for my people, the Jews, for the destruction, the devastation, the suffering of all the peoples of the world. It's a terrible thing to say, perhaps, but I am full of hate and my soul cries with the Russians, "DEATH TO THE GERMANS. DEATH TO THE NAZI DESPOILERS."

That's all for now, darling. I'm a helluva husband to be raving on like this without telling you how much I love you, and how much I long to be with you. Bub, you know I do. And, I'm impatient for the day when we can put the guns away, and I can come back to you and "Joe."

Te quiero mucho, mujer mia.

Your own, Larry

———

582nd Engr. Dump Truck Co.
APO 230, NY, NY
Somewhere in France
26 June 1944

My Darling;

Yesterday was quite a day for me. I received an armful of mail, including your Fathers' Day greetings and a lot of back letters. . . .

I also had my first bath since leaving England. A marvelous hot shower that was left intact by the Germans in their hasty advance to the rear.

You can just about imagine how dirty I was. But, there's one thing that I'm thankful for. So far, we haven't been bothered by lice.

When I went to Spain, I was crummy a week after I got there, and the damn things were with me for two years after that.

Here's hoping the cooties stay out of my drawers.

There's been some bitter fighting around here, as you've no doubt read, but we've got the situation well in hand now, and it's only a matter of a little time before we clear up this front.

Of course, after this battle, there'll be more to come—hard ones too, no doubt. But, we'll get there O.K., I'm sure.

Your news from home makes such swell reading, darling. And mail is still the greatest morale-builder of all.

Folks back home wait for mail pretty anxiously, I know. But here, men wait for mail call with desperate eagerness. And when none comes, a man feels pretty miserable. . . .

Please take good care of yourself, darling. And, don't worry too much about me. So far, I'm in good health and spirits. The only thing that bothers me is that I wish so damn hard that I could be home with you.

I hope the day isn't too far off, when my wish can come true. I love you, Gracie.

Your, Larry

582nd Engr. Dump Truck Co.
APO 230, NY, NY
Somewhere in France
28 June 1944

Darling;

Things are quiet in this sector right now. For the first time since D-day, we hear no guns. But, I guess that will soon change—and the strange quiet will give way once more to the normalcy of the crack + rumble of artillery and the angry clatter of the machine-guns.

What an amazing conglomeration of peoples the Germans had on this front! They had Poles, Czechs, Italians, and Russians (yes, Georgians), and of course their own élite "Herrenvolk."

Among their prisoners who worked as slaves were French, Spanish, Tunisians, and Russians (even Russian women—who have real tales of horror to tell).

And this is a noose that they have tied around their own necks—a noose that will one day strangle them. . . .

By the way, the taking of Cherbourg was a fine job. From what I could see, I think we'll have that port going full blast in a few days.

Funny that I should see it almost exactly seven years after I first came there. It's quite changed. Besides the devastation—it's shocking how four years of Nazi occupation have changed the face + appearance of the people.

There isn't much else to write now, darling. Nothing more, except to tell you I love you and long for you and hope that everything will go well with you.

Te quiero. Or perhaps it would be better at this time to say, "Je t'aime, ma femme."

Your own, Larry

582nd Engr. Dump Truck Co.
APO 230, NY, NY
Somewhere in France
3 July 1944

Darling Mine;

It's been raining steadily here for over a week now. So you can just about imagine how we're living, and how much I'm enjoying this mess.

Ugh—rain!

Yesterday I had to go on an errand that carried me through most of the bridgehead area. I'm telling you—we're here to stay!

One of the most interesting sights to me was the reaction of a group of about 2,000 Jerry prisoners, waiting to be transported to the PW [prisoner of war] enclosures.

As they watched the unending convoys, they looked completely stupefied! Couldn't believe their own eyes! Where had this enormous weight of materiel mushroomed from?

Hitler has those guys hypnotized.

The errand that I went on had to do with the offer of command of another Dump Truck Company in another Corps. A promotion to Captaincy went along with it.

Darling, I hope you won't think I acted foolishly, but I refused, and did so emphatically enough for them to accept my refusal.

You see sweetheart, I've had the good fortune to be in <u>the</u>

crack combat engineer group in France.[11] We've established a brilliant reputation, and I'm proud to be in it.

Furthermore, I'm on the verge of a transfer to the best battalion in the outfit.[12]

This is what I hoped and dreamed for so long—if I gave it up now just because I could become a Captain, I'd feel the same as if I'd sold out to a boss for a substantial raise.

Anyway, I wouldn't feel clean inside.

Besides, as far as the Service is concerned, you know as well as I do that I could probably do a better job in any capacity in a combat battalion than I could as the commander of a Dump Truck Company.

So, hon, you pat our little "Joe" and whisper that Daddy is probably nuts, but that you'll both string along with him.

There isn't much else to write.

Oh yes—there is an Underground here, sweetheart, and as we progress, their work grows more important and their contributions more impressive.

Je t'aime, ma femme. Beaucoup kisses.

Your, Larry

238th Engr. Combat Bn.
APO 230, NY, NY
Somewhere in France
5 July 1944

Darling;

Yesterday was the Fourth of July. I can't say that we had a safe and sane fourth here, but we certainly celebrated it with a great big bang—lots of bangs.

It was an auspicious day for me personally because my transfer finally came through.

Yes, darling, I am now in a combat engineer battalion. My new address is:

---

[11] The 1106th Engineer Combat Group.
[12] The 238th Engineer Combat Battalion.

Lt. Lawrence Cane 0–1110976
238th Engr. Combat Bn., APO 230
c/o Postmaster, New York, N.Y.

Much as I wanted to leave my old outfit, when the time came to say goodbye, I felt kinda funny. I had been with them so long, I'd become attached to them more than I had realized.

The new battalion that I'm in, is, of course, not a Negro outfit. So, I guess I'll have to learn all over again how to get along with white soldiers.

I finally made it—I hope it turns out O.K. . . .

Enclosed, hon, you'll find the first copy of the Stars + Stripes printed in France. Not very pretentious, but it's an historic issue. It means we'll get news daily now.

Give my love to our "Joe." I miss you so much.

I love you Gracie.

Your, Larry

=========

238th Engr. Combat Bn.
APO 230, NY, NY
Somewhere in France
6 July 1944

Hello Darling;

Busy getting acclimated to my new surroundings. Believe me, it's quite a change.

Right now I'm in one of the line companies and in command of a heavy weapons platoon. The job's right up my alley, and you <u>know</u> I'm feeling pretty good about the deal.

Every once in awhile I have to pinch myself to see if I'm just dreaming. . . .

One of the Vets, in writing to the "Volunteer," said, "The wheel turns, and one by one the vets drop into their appointed places. . . ." I guess that applied to me too.[13]

---

[13] During the Spanish Civil War, the International Brigades produced several periodicals, including *Volunteer for Liberty,* for the mostly English-speaking 15th

Over here, we're still making advances, although they're slow and painful. Our main preoccupation right now seems to be building up our bridgehead. Naturally, since we're still confined to a comparatively small area, Jerry can, with the forces at his disposal, make things difficult for us.

But, it shouldn't be too long, a month, maybe two—unless I'm overly optimistic—before we really start to roll. We'll fan out into France proper then, and we'll tear the guts out of the German Army here.

We'll be racing the Russians to Berlin then. Personally, I hope they get there first. They have some very good ideas about what to do with Nazis and the Nazi State.

Every time we have a bull session here, we're uniformly amazed at the swift progress of the Red Army. Those Rooshians are astounding people.

Take it from me, it's going to be a mighty difficult thing to spread lies about the Soviet Union in America after this war is over. The Red Army has won the respect and admiration of everyone in the Army. . . .

Take good care of yourself, darling—the two of you.

Your, Larry

———

Brigade. Sixty-three issues were published between May 24, 1936 and November 7, 1938. In 1939 the Veterans of the Abraham Lincoln Brigade began issuing *Volunteer for Liberty* in New York. This four-page publication appeared every other month and carried articles on the organization's official positions, disseminated information about Spain and Spanish affairs, and provided personal information about veterans. After World War II the publication appeared more irregularly and during the 1950s changed its name to *The Volunteer*. By the year 2003 *The Volunteer* was still being published regularly, not only in hard copy, but also on the Veterans of the Abraham Lincoln Brigade website at http://www.alba-valb.org.

238th Engr. Combat Bn.
APO 230, NY, NY
Somewhere in France
15 July 1944

My Darling;

Yesterday was the "quatorze juillet"—France's Fourth of July.[14] It was celebrated by continuing our slow, dogged push. We go at a snail's pace, we fight for every foot.

But in the line against us are Hitler's best élite troops—That is, the best that are left to him. There are the S.S. and Parachute Troops—and the Panzers. Germans, these. No backward elements of the conquered peoples.[15]

When these are mauled sufficiently, I believe our weight will begin to tell with more effect. Like a rolling snowball, we will gather momentum—our gains will be much more satisfactory.

I say satisfactory. I mean satisfactory to me. Supreme Headquarters may be content with the progress. But, I'm impatient. With all other American G.I.'s I want this damn victory to come fast—so we can get the hell out of here and live normal lives.

We don't expect it to be easy. Nobody here has any illusions any more. We're prepared to take our losses, no matter the cost. But, dammit, we want no long drawn out affairs.

Enclosed you will find the emblems that will go down in history as the symbol of barbarism and maniacal depravity. They were taken off the overseas cap of an S.S. man.

Here's something that you may not have read in the papers—or if you have, didn't quite believe.

I have seen boys of 14, 15, 16 years old in the S.S. Panzer—Grenadiers. Children who should be home playing marbles over here being killed, and dealing out death.

They come right out of the Hitler Jugend. They know nothing

---

[14] The Fourteenth of July, Bastille Day, commemorates the storming of the Bastille by angry citizens during the French Revolution on July 14, 1789. The storming of the Bastille became a symbol that power no longer resided in the king but in the people.

[15] SS (Schutzstaffel) Troops represented the elite of German society, both in physical abilities and political beliefs. The SS Troops to whom Cane is referring is Das Reich, the 2nd SS Panzer Division.

but Nazism. As long as their older, tougher non-coms are there to lead them—they fight fanatically. Their non-coms eliminated, they are lost.

And these are not isolated cases.

From what I have seen and heard from German prisoners themselves, there is a very high percentage of adolescent youths now in every crack German infantry division.

Hitler is scraping the bottom of the barrel. He is committing national suicide.

Frankly, I don't believe the Germans have very much left.

I hope so much that I will have the good fortune to see their complete defeat soon—sooner than I had dared hoped for before the invasion.

Because, there's just one thing I hope + dream of above all else, and that's to come back home to my Grace safe + sound.

I love you, darling.

Your, Larry

238th Engr. Combat Bn.
APO 230, NY, NY
Somewhere in France
16 July 1944

Grace Darling;

At long last, your letters started to arrive again. A batch of them came in yesterday. Considering that they had to pass through my old outfit before getting to me, they got here pretty fast. The latest was dated 30 June.

I'm glad that you're finally aware I'm in France. And I'm more than glad you're receiving my letters so regularly.

You ask how I can write so frequently. Well, hon, we're strictly engineers now. They only used us for assault work during the first few hectic days.

Now we're busy clearing mines + booby traps, improving and

maintaining roads, building bridges, etc.[16] We get a chance to move back + sleep at least once every 24 hours. So, before turning in, I write to you.

Don't worry too much about me darling. Just keep concentrating on "Joe."

I love you terribly.

Your, Larry

———

238th Engr. Combat Bn.
APO 230, NY, NY
Somewhere in France
18 July 1944

Hello Darling;

. . . Today is the eighth anniversary of the start of the Spanish Civil War. I hope that the job, begun then, hasn't much longer to go before completion.

The world has been a long time smashing Hitler. This year should see it finished.

How I hope I'll see that day, and be able to come back home to you!

Gee, I wish I could see you now. You must be cute as the devil with your tummy sticking way out.

You tell that "Joe" of ours to stop kicking you like that. What kind of bringing up is he getting—hitting his mother that way?

After raining almost continuously since D-day, the weather man gave us a break yesterday—it was nice all day. Today it's alternating between clouds + sunshine—but there's no rain.

I hope we get a stretch of real good summer weather—we'll raise plenty hell if we do.

Since Cherbourg, we've been fighting our way through swampy, flooded areas. And between the muck, the rain, the mosquitoes, + Jerry it hasn't been any fun.

---

[16] In mid-July, Company C, of which Cane was a member, built the second Bailey bridge across the Tribehou Causeway and removed three minefields for the 552nd Field Artillery.

We're just about out of that region now, and maybe we can get going a little faster. Especially if we get a break in the weather.

The sooner the better.

Try not to worry too much, darling. I know it's hard, but try anyway.

Remember, I love you terribly.

Your, Larry

———

238th Engr. Combat Bn.
APO 230, NY, NY
Somewhere in France
21 July 1944

My Darling;

Things go along in much the same manner.

It's been raining, as usual, and we've been pretty busy. Matter of fact, if you don't hear from me for a few days, don't worry.

I just won't have time. . . .

We've heard rumors of internal dissension in Germany. How true they are, we can't tell.[17]

I fervently hope that they're not just a propaganda stunt—and that Germany is really cracking up.

How I hope to see that day!

Darling, I know how you must feel about my safety, and that no matter how much you try—there's always a tight little gnawing ball of fear.

I can't tell you to forget it—that's probably impossible. But, I can tell you to concentrate on the baby, and try very hard not to think of me in danger. . . .

Remember, darling, no matter where I am or what I'm doing—I'm always with you.

---

[17] Cane is referring to the fact that on July 20, 1944, several politicians and senior active-duty and retired officers attempted to assassinate Hitler at a conference in Rastenburg, Germany. Hitler survived with minor injuries. About 200 accused plotters were executed and several thousand were sent to concentration camps.

MAP 2

Breakout from Normandy.
During Operation Cobra, July
25–29, 1944, the U.S. VII
Corps attacked just west of
St. Lo. The 1st Platoon of
Company C of the 238th Engineer Combat Battalion was
assigned to the advance guard
of Combat Command B of
the 2nd Armored Division.
Passing through Notre–Dame-
de-Cenilly by July 27, the
point of the armored column
reached St. Denis-le-Gast the
next day and Lengronne by
July 29. (Based on Map VII,
Enlarging the Breach, in
Martin Blumensen, *Breakout
and Pursuit* [Washington,
D.C.: Government Printing
Office, 1961].) See Appendixes D and E.

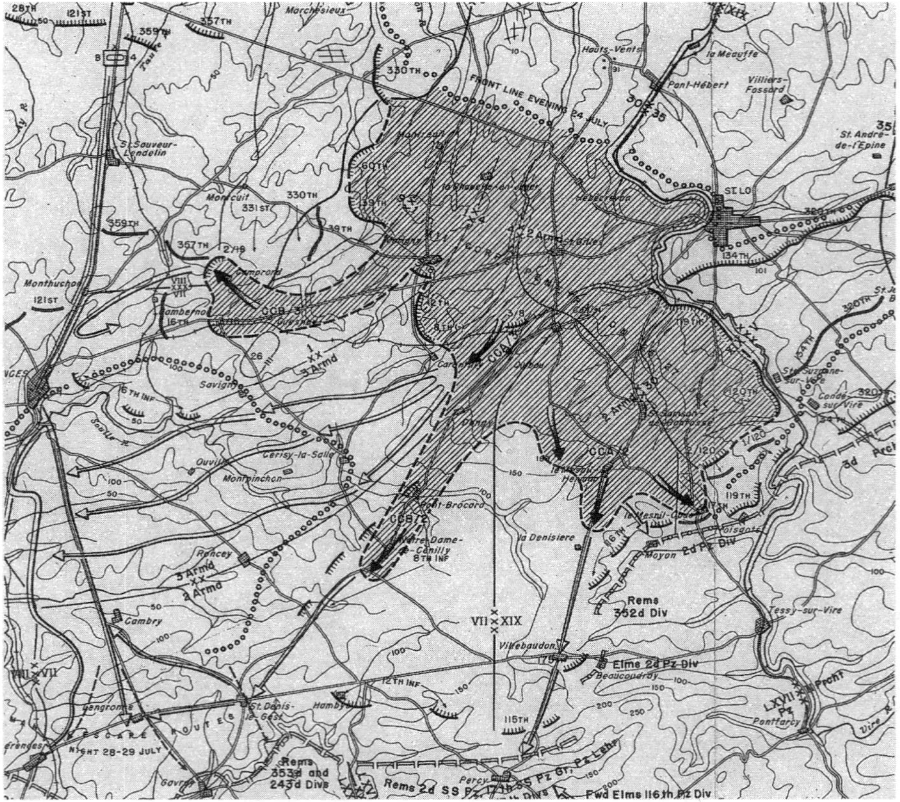

I love you.

Your, Larry

―――――

238th Engr. Combat Bn.
APO 230, NY, NY
Somewhere in France
31 July 1944[18]

Hello Darling;

Still in there punching.

I'll bet America has been devouring the news these past few days.

We've been beating the crap out of the Krauts. We're moving fast and furious and I hope to God we can keep it up until the day we can end this.

The faster we can move, the sooner that'll be.

I'm damn proud to be with the combat engineers. They sure work and fight us till we're slaphappy, but we sure do a job.

Darling, I'm just able to snatch these few lines off because I don't have time for a longer letter.

Enclosed you'll find a German decoration that's given to men who spent the Winter of '41–'43 in Russia.

Please take care of yourself + "Joe" honey.

I love you terribly.

Your, Larry

―――――

―――――

[18] This letter was written on the day following the action near St. Lo for which Cane was eventually awarded the Silver Star for heroism in battle. As part of the Operation Cobra breakout of the Normandy beachhead, Company C of the 238th Engineer Combat Battalion was in direct support of Combat Command B of the 2nd Armored Division, with Cane's 1st Platoon, commanded by Lt. John B. Wong, at the point.

238th Engr. Combat Bn.
APO 230, NY, NY
Somewhere in France
2 August 1944

My Darling;

Yesterday was a happy day for me. I received a big batch of back mail which you had sent to my old company, and also four letters which you had mailed to my new outfit. . . .

By the way, don't bust your buttons—but I've been recommended for the Silver Star for "conspicuous bravery" in action.[19] And the unit I'm with is receiving an Army battle citation.

Looks like I'm going to wear a lot of ribbons one of these days, if I ever get a chance to wear a blouse again.

I love you and miss you terribly. Take good care of yourself, darling.

Your own, Larry

238th Engr. Combat Bn.
APO 230, NY, NY
Somewhere in France
8 August 1944

Gracie Darling;

. . . We've got Jerry moving back now. I believe we'll be in Paris before too long. And, when Paris falls to us this time, the end of the Nazis will not be far off.

---

[19] The Silver Star is the third highest decoration given for combat by the U.S. Army. It denotes extraordinary gallantry under fire. In France, on the night of July 29–30, 1944, during the massive American breakout from St. Lo, elements of the 2nd Armored Division were in danger of being encircled and destroyed. Cane performed a personal reconnaissance under extremely heavy fire and led these vehicles to safety. For this and other actions during the breakout, he was awarded the Silver Star. Cane's Silver Star citation and affidavit are included in Appendixes D and E. Cane describes the ceremony when he received the Silver Star in his letter of 11 November 1944. See Mark Bando, *Breakout at Normandy: The 2nd Armored Division in the Land of the Dead* (Osceola, Wisc.: MBI Publishing Co., 1999), p. 83.

The other night, I sat in a command post dugout and listened on the radio to the call of the French provisional government to the people of Brittany (Brest Peninsula).

"Frenchmen of Brittany, the hour of liberation has struck." "The forces of the interior have already received their combat orders and are engaging the enemy." "Workers—occupy the factories—make each one a fortress. Do not let the hated invader destroy the machines." "Farmers—attack retreating German columns. Cut them to pieces." "Frenchmen of all classes—no quarter to the enemy."

These were some of the phrases that came ringing through the air waves, to the accompaniment of the thud and rumble of artillery all around us.

Talk about getting goosepimples, I sure had 'em!

As the German Army retreat gathers in momentum, so will these rousing calls to arms become more widespread. Revolt will spread like a prairie fire through France + the rest of Europe.

The once all-conquering German legions will end up a panic-stricken, disorderly mob. For them there will be no way out, no escape. They will be too far from home. They will die like mad dogs, or become Allied prisoners for their own protection.

It is already beginning + I have seen it with my own eyes.

The only thing I hope all the time, is that it all happens three times faster than it actually will.

Because, darling, there's just one thing I'm praying for, and that's to be able to come back home to you safe + sound. . . .

I love you beaucoup, beaucoup.

Your, Larry

———

238th Engr. Combat Bn.
APO 230, NY, NY
Somewhere in France
10 August 1944

Hello Darling;

The push continues, but they've got us in a rear area working on roads for the time being. We don't mind much, though.

We've been working and fighting pretty hard lately, and the rest is welcome.

After pushing ahead until you're practically blind with fatigue, you kind of think maybe somebody else should fight the war for awhile.

Last night, I had a funny experience.

About one o'clock in the morning, one of the men woke me and told me that I was wanted urgently at the command post.

Well, I cussed a bit (I had been dreaming of home + my Gracie) but dutifully I got up out of my luxurious foxhole apartment and stumbled through the darkness to the CP.

Inside was a middle-aged French peasant and his teen-aged daughter.

Their tale was a confusing story of having awakened in the night to find a strange man moving about the house. They had asked who it was and lit a candle, but the light had been knocked down by the man, who kept repeating in broken French "bonjour m'sieur" and "Kamerad, Kamerad."

They had run out of the house and gone to look for soldiers to investigate the situation, had run into our outposts, and were taken in for questioning.

Incidentally, they said they had left three women and about seven children behind in the house.

The whole story sounded crazy, and we suspected a trap of some kind.

Anyway, I got together a patrol and took the man + his daughter along.

When we got to the house, which was silhouetted in the moonlight, I deployed my men, put the Frenchman in front of me and a sergeant and tiptoed up to the house.

Keyed for anything, we opened the door, pushed the Frenchman in front of us and poured inside.

Using a flashlight we saw sprawled on the floor one very drunk G.I.

Goddam!

We arrested him, received the enthusiastic thanks of the Frenchman and his crowded family circle, and I went back to my foxhole to sleep. . . .

Take care of yourself darling.

I love you. Larry

========

238th Engr. Combat Bn.
APO 230, NY, NY
Somewhere in France
12 August 1944

Darling Mine;

For the first time since we came up on the beaches—we're getting something of a rest. How long it'll last, I don't know.

It's just my unit, of course. The drive still continues.

We're bivouacked just outside a little town that hasn't even been touched by the war. And what's even better, there's a swell lake nearby—and, God it's been wonderful to go swimming again.

The people around here just can't do enough for us. They're crazy about the Americans.

Yesterday evening, a couple of other officers and myself went on a trip through the hills to see what we could pick up in the way of eggs, chicken, and liquor.

At every lonely cluster of farmhouses we stopped, we were received with eager hospitality.

The little old Frenchwomen, in giving us some eggs said, "I gave a son to the Army of the Resistance, the least I can do now is to give the liberators of my people a few eggs."

It's quiet here too—We can hardly hear the artillery. And when we do it is just dull thudding, which is miles away.

The only thing we can see of the war right here is <u>our</u> planes droning overhead all day long. They've been soaring over majestically since early morning today. There must be something big up.

Of course, at night, Jerry takes over and runs his fighter-bombers all over the skies.

But, we don't mind them too much. Here's hoping they don't drop any mail around here.

I guess it's allright to tell you now—

I was in on the big break-through. I was with a platoon of engineers assigned to the advance guard of one of the armored columns.[20]

My men rode the tanks, while I rode a bounding jeep.

It was during the advance that pocketed a lot of Jerries that I pulled the job which got me the recommendation for the Silver Star.

The Jerries were trying to break out, and temporarily cut off the advance guard of tanks.

There were a lot of tanks + equipment that were in danger of falling into enemy hands.

So, I volunteered to get them out.

With some luck, I managed to take about a hundred armored vehicles, including thirty medium tanks, through enemy held territory. . . .

[Your own, Larry]

———

238th Engr. Combat Bn.
APO 230, NY, NY
Somewhere in France
13 August 1944

Hello Darling;

Today is such an unbelievable day for us.

It's a beautiful Sunday morning. The churchbells in the little town near us are calling the people to mass. And they're coming down the roads in family groups—scrubbed and cleaned, wearing their very best.

As they pass our bivouac area they wave and smile to us. The little girls blow us kisses, the little boys proudly give us the V for Victory sign.

---

[20] Cane is referring to the important role that he and 1st Platoon, Company C played during Operation Cobra. For a description of Cane's role in this action, see the Introduction, pp. xxvi–xxvii, as well as Appendixes D and E.

Our boys are washing, shaving, preparing to go to church, writing letters, washing drawers, or just plain snoring.

You stand up for a minute to look around you at the beauty of the countryside.

All around you are apple and pear orchards, heavily laden with fruit which will ripen shortly. There are wheatfields everywhere. The wheat has been cut + shocked, in the neat, inimitable style that characterizes the French peasant. The golden shocks look like they've been dressed right for inspection.

You muse for a brief moment. There'll be no French wheat for German bread this winter. If the wheat's in here, it's also in the rest of France.

You wonder if the French have purposely delayed thrashing the wheat so that the Germans couldn't carry it away.

If it stands still shocked, it's very difficult to handle—would require a hell of a lot of transportation which the Boches do not have. And if they want to destroy it, they have to burn each shock separately—not as easy to do as setting a match to a field and letting it burn like a prairie fire, if the wheat is uncut.

Oh, those goddam Boches! What's that old saying—"Whom the Gods would destroy, they first make mad."

They're mad allright, and we are destroying them.

All morning our planes have been roaring over—flying east into the sun.

Ten flights of thirty-six B-26's—Billy Mitchells[21]—already.

And still they come.

Jesus Christ! you say to yourself. How will those bastards stand that stuff? It isn't only today. We roar over and deliver blinding, crashing death to them every day like that.

And from your experience, you know that those who are not being killed are being terrorized, are surely becoming demoralized, and are having pounded into the marrow of their bones and the chilled corners of their hearts the knowledge that they have

---

[21] The B-26 was an American medium-range bomber known as the "Marauder." It was actually a close relative of another widely used medium-range bomber, the B-25 Mitchell. The latter aircraft was named after Col. William C. "Billy" Mitchell (1879–1936) who in the 1920s had been a vigorous and controversial—and, as it turned out, farsighted—advocate of the future military role of air power.

lost the war. That before them stands not the glorious hypnotic dreams of their paranoiac Fuehrer—But Death!

For a long time, I have hoped and dreamed that I would live to see the day when fascism would be destroyed. There have been many disappointments, as you well know, darling. But, I've always had a tendency to be over-optimistic. I wished so hard, sometimes my wishes became confused with reality. I and you too (a lot of others also), used to have a tendency of stretching our interpretation of events. The pot of gold never was very far away—and so we had some bitter disappointments.

But now, I tell you, the monster is staggering—he's bleeding from many wounds. Already he even has internal hemorrhages.

Just think for a moment, doesn't every lesson you've ever learned from history say that our triumph is near?

I tell you, I am convinced to my very soul that the German Army will be finished before the year is out, <u>at the very latest.</u>

But enough of this.

There's one thing about this rest area—makes me think even more intensely about my Gracie, and little "Joe," and the home that's waiting for me.

Oh my darling, if I could only hold you in my arms and kiss your lips, your eyes—if I could breathe deep the perfume of your hair—if I could just kid you about your tummy—if I could just whisper I love you.

Good God, how I miss you!

There's so much suffering and misery connected with war.

For me the worst thing is terrible loneliness and longing—the heartrending yearning that I have for you.

We have so much time to make up for.

I love you so much, darling.

Take good care of yourself.

Your own, Larry

238th Engr. Combat Bn.
APO 230, NY, NY
Somewhere in France
15 August 1944

Grace Darling;

Still living a life of temporary ease and comparative luxury.

Last night, another Lt. + myself cooked our own supper over an open fire. We had delicious french-fried potatoes, egg + onion omelets, coffee and apple pie we procured from the company kitchen.

Sounds like pretty simple fare doesn't it? But to us it was as regal as anything you can get at the Waldorf—especially when washed down with a couple of swigs of the local bottled lightning called "Calvados."

Honestly, that is the most potent stuff I have ever encountered. Even the crude-oil they called "cognac" when I was in Spain doesn't compare with this drink for pure, unadulterated deadliness.

It's made out of apple cider. What they do, is take applejack + distill it. Result—liquid fire.

Three drinks and you're ready to take on the whole damn German Army, singlehanded and barefisted.

Don't get the idea I'm becoming a rum pot, hon. Just a snifter once in awhile.

The other Lt. I mentioned is a very nice Chinese-American boy from California.[22] He's an engineer + architect in civilian life—and probably a damn fine one, because he's smart as a whip.

---

[22] Cane is referring to Lt. John B. Wong, a fellow combat engineer who himself compiled a distinguished record in World War II, from the D-Day landings on Utah Beach to the surrender of Germany, receiving not only the Silver Star for gallantry in action, but the Bronze Star for valor, the Purple Heart, and the French Croix de Guerre with Palm. He and Cane, along with the other members of their platoon who took part in the actions supporting the lead elements of the 2nd Armored Division in Operation Cobra, also received a Distinguished Unit Citation. Lt. Wong commanded Company C of the 238th Engineer Combat Battalion during the Battle of the Bulge and was promoted to captain in early 1945. He served in the U.S. Army Reserves until 1971, retiring with the rank of lieutenant colonel. He was one of several Chinese-American veterans who were featured in the 1999 PBS documentary film "We Served With Pride: The Chinese American Experience in WW II" and who were honored at the

He's enthusiastic as hell about modern architecture for private homes. And, by God, he sure set me to dreaming about us. Maybe, maybe—Quien sabe? Why not?

But, first get this war over with—and get home O.K.

We haven't received much news the past few days. We know that the Army has swept on. We know also that we're giving the Krauts a lacing. Outside of that, <u>you</u> back home have probably got a better picture of the present front line positions.

This rest has been delicious and we'll all probably be a little reluctant and sorry when it's over. Mais, c'est la guerre.

There isn't much else to write darling, except to repeat what I'll never grow tired telling you.

I love you.

Your, Larry

238th Engr. Combat Bn.
APO 230, NY, NY
Somewhere in France
18 August 1944

Darling;

Off to the rat races again!

What tremendous events are unfolding!

We have the German 7th Army in a trap—even if half of them get out, they'll lose most of their equipment.[23] We've invaded France from the South. All railroad workers in France in the Ger-

---

White House by President Clinton on October 26, 1999. Lt. Wong's nomination of Cane for the Silver Star can be found in Appendix E.

[23] From August 1 to 26 General George Patton's (1885–1945) Third Army drove east from Avranches, then turned north along a broad front stretching to Argentan, just as the British and Canadian First and Second Armies attacked to the south as far east as Falaise. As a result, the entire German Seventh Army was enveloped in what became known as the Falaise pocket. Although about a third of the Seventh Army and the Fifth Panzers slipped through the gap and escaped, they left behind 10,000 dead and 50,000 captured, along with hundreds of tanks, nearly 1,000 pieces of artillery, and 8,000 cars and trucks. It was the worst single German defeat since Stalingrad.

man rear are on strike. Everywhere we go now we meet the Maquis, the French Forces of the Interior.[24]

On we sweep—the tanks and half-tracks, the trucks, the jeeps careening wildly, yet orderly, in clouds of choking blinking dust. Five miles, ten miles, fifteen miles, twenty miles behind the enemy lines.

To hell with the enemy!

Keep pushing. Smash through his hasty defenses, annihilate his once proud infantry, push on—nothing can stop us. Encircle him, cut his communications, sweep by his strong points—do it the Russian way.

And we keep rolling!

As inexorably as the flights of Fortresses[25] which keep droning over our heads all day long.

Nothing stops them, nothing breaks their formations. The black puffs of flak hit right inside the flight. A plane bursts into flames + it drives spectacularly to earth. But the other planes never waver. Don't even wobble their wings, just keep on going. Fate with four motors.

They drop their loads and the sound is insane—like a tornado hissing through a great forest, breaking up into shrieking whistles and then bright flame, geysers of smoke, the stink of cordite, and a crackling earth-shuddering roar.

Up goes the German dream of lebensraum and world domination. Pillboxes, fragments of men, shattered guns—up in the air.

And now push through the tanks, the infantry, the engineers, the artillery. Keep going. There must be no rest for the enemy.

That's what's going on here.

It is impossible for me to describe this push. I haven't the words.

But, it realizes the fondest dreams of the most ardent anti-Nazi.

As we sweep on, in spite of the fighting and the exhaustion there are vignettes of humor.

---

[24] The Maquis was the name given to the French guerrilla units who were part of the French Resistance. The name "maquis" comes from the French word for the thick and nearly impenetrable scrub forest in the South of France which provided shelter for the Resistance.

[25] The B-17 "Flying Fortress" was a long-range, heavy bomber used extensively by the U.S. Eighth Air Force.

At one halt on a road, there was the usual throng of French men, women, and children running up and down the column handing out flowers, cognac—shaking hands cheering, applauding.

One of our boys on a truck yells out to a French girl, "Mademoiselle. Du lait?" The young lady amusingly enough seems to have been able to speak some English.

So, she comes back with, "But m'sieur, we do not have ze time."

The G.I. looks at her dumbfounded for a minute, and then howls—"Oh my poor back. No. No. Mamselle. Lait. Lait. Comme ça." And he imitates someone milking a cow.

The mamselle sees the light. "Oui. Oui." Runs into the house and brings out a bucket of milk.

"Oh, the women in France, parley-vous."

Darling, in just about four weeks Mr. + Mrs. Cane will become Momma + Poppa Cane.

This will be a great year for our child to be born in.

It will be the year that will be known in history as the start of a great new era.

None of this milk + honey pollyanna stuff intended. But it will be a great new era.

And, darling, remember no matter what I'm doing or where I am, I'll be pacing that hospital floor.

I love you. Take care of yourself.

Your, Larry

———

238th Engr. Combat Bn.
APO 230, NY, NY
Somewhere in France
20 August 1944

Darling;

We've been traveling so fast and furiously lately that the APO hasn't been able to keep up with us. . . .

Have I ever told you what kind of boys I have in my outfit?
They're 100% G.I. Joes and they're wonderful.

About half the men in my battalion come from the South.
They're mechanics, factory hands, farmers. About 25% come
from the Pennsylvania coal mining districts. These are our demolitions men—wizards with explosives. Practically born with dyna-
mite in their hands. They can blow a pillbox, a hedgerow, a
roadblock, or work a gravel pit as pretty as you could ever want
it done. The rest come from all corners of the country, and represent all types of people. We've even got a couple of rough and
tough gangsters from Chicago—damn good soldiers, by the way.

Our mess sergeant got his experience as a cook in a reform
school for boys. From what the men say, he's still punishing people. But, he's really pretty good.

Like most of the American Army, they're not much on the spit
and polish—and they never will be, no matter how much the
West Pointers tear their hair. But they're tough, and they stay
with it no matter how hard the going.

The most wonderful thing about them is their sense of humor.
Neither the crap they have to take in our own Army, nor the
suffering + privation forced on them by the enemy will ever get
them down.

They can be staggering with exhaustion, blasted by artillery, or
be heaped with the chicken-shit that abounds in our Army—
particularly from some of these screwy West Pointers—and they'll
always come up with a wisecrack.

All I can say is what all the people back home must be saying
and thinking—"God bless 'em."

Well, we're still chasing the supermen. So far, my predictions
have been pretty good, no?

Here's hoping that all my predictions turn out to be correct. If
they do, maybe I'll be getting home to my Grace and my "Joe"
pretty soon.

That's the day I'm waiting for. . . .

Darling, one more month and the great day will arrive.

I sweat just to think about it. How I wish I could be with you
in person.

You'll take real good care of yourself, won't you darling?
Give my love and regards to everyone back home.

I love you. Larry

————

238th Engr. Combat Bn.
APO 230, NY, NY
Somewhere in France
27 August 1944

Darling;

I have seen scenes in the past few days that will remain in my
memory forever. . . .

We had to ferry some infantry outfits across a big river, near the
big town, in a night assault crossing.[26]

When we finished ferrying the infantry across, and a solid
bridgehead had been established, it was daylight—and the next
step was in order. That was the building of a pontoon bridge at
the crossing site.

So the engineer equipment which had been lined up a couple

---

[26] Cane is referring to the crossing of the Seine River at the village of Evry
Pont Bourg near Corbeil, south of Paris. Originally, General Dwight D. Eisenhower (1890–1969) had intended to bypass Paris, leaving it cut off, and to continue pursuing the hastily retreating German Army. However, General Charles
de Gaulle (1890–1970), the leader of the Free French, insisted that Paris had to
be seized and occupied by Free French troops. Eisenhower finally agreed to let
an armored division under General Jacques Philippe Leclerc (1902–1947) move
on Paris, supported on their right by Americans of the 4th Infantry Division.
When Leclerc's armored columns began their advance on August 24, 1944,
Cane's battalion was holding positions to the southwest of the city. Many of the
tank drivers in Leclerc's division were exiled Spanish Republicans who had
fought in the Civil War against Franco. When the first elements of Leclerc's
columns approached the positions of the 238th Engineer Combat Battalion,
Cane was electrified to see that the lead tanks had emblazoned on their bodies
the names of many of the great battles of the Spanish Civil War, with the very
first bearing the name TERUEL, where he himself had fought in a desperate
struggle in the depths of winter in January 1938. He leaped onto the road and
ran alongside the tanks, giving the raised fist salute of the Popular Front and
hollering at the top of his lungs (Lawrence Cane as told to David E. Cane).
General de Gaulle triumphantly entered the liberated city on August 26, 1944.

of miles away started to roll in. The bulldozers, the Quickway cranes, the $2^1/_2$ ton trucks, the jeeps, the air compressors, etc. etc.

And with the equipment came the delighted and amazed populations of the towns on both sides of the river to cheer, to exclaim in wonderment, even to pitch in proudly and hold guy lines as we put in the near-shore abutment.

We took five hours to put that bridge across, and I'll bet the people who saw it will be telling their grandchildren about it 50 years from now.

The air was filled with excited "Ooo la la's" and observations of "Quelle materiel." "Magnifique." "Vive les Americains, sauveurs du peuple Français."

The place resembled a country fair. Dozens of little boys came to swim in the river. Young girls, old women, women with babies, old men, and young men sporting the armbands of the FFI (French Forces of the Interior)[27] armed with their assorted German rifles, British Sten guns, double-barrelled shotguns, hunting rifles, pistols, knives, American carbines, Tommy guns—all lined both banks.

Even the priests and monks out of a local monastery turned out en masse to lend their praise.

The place got so crowded we had to ask the FFI boys to help us keep the people out of the way. The women with babies were especially enthusiastic. Every opportunity they could get or make, they wanted you to kiss their babies. I'll bet I kissed more babies in five hours, than any Senator ever did in a year's political campaigning.

If anyone would have told me before the crossing, that the battleground of the night before would become the picnic ground of the day after, I would have told him he was nuts.

When the bridge was finished, the chief priest asked us if he could walk across first. We told him O.K., and he proceeded to bless the bridge and then walk across looking like a kid who's just gotten a big box of candy.

When our columns stop in any of these small towns around here, the vehicles are literally mobbed. Little boys clamber all

---

[27] The FFI or French Forces of the Interior was the name of the French Resistance forces.

over, women young and old come with bottles of wine and flowers.

They want to shake our hands, kiss us, speak to us, or just even touch us. We are their heroes—no kidding.

They dance in the streets, they sing the Marseillaise, they are delirious with joy.

And Lord help the lonely jeep that visits a town alone. The cry of "Americains" is a signal for a mob scene. If the boys in that jeep can get out of town with only 1 ton of flowers, one-half their clothes, one or two broken ribs from being hugged, and just half a drunk—they can consider themselves lucky.

I saw something of what happens to those Frenchmen and Frenchwomen who were friends of the Germans.

We happened to be going through a town and the route was blocked by a shrieking, gesticulating mob—mostly women and girls.

As the jeep nosed into the crowd, it parted and we saw what the object of the commotion was.

There were four disheveled, bloody, naked women. Their heads had been shaved. Their bodies were scarred where they had been clawed or whipped, they were covered from head to foot with the spittle from these avenging women. They were being led somewhere and they were running a venomous gauntlet.

These were formerly saucy "filles du joie." But they had slept with the "Boches." And now they were receiving their retribution.

Reminded me of the terrible scene in Emil Zola's "Germinal"—where the wives and daughters of the coal miners finally take their revenge on the manager of the company store during the coal strike. Remember?

They kill him, dash his brains out, then pull off his penis and put the bloody thing on a stake and parade it around.

Zola knew his people.

Another thing I have seen is the Underground in action.

How proud I feel to know that these are the people we always said would spring up to fight side by side with us.

When the full story of the French Forces of the Interior is told, it will probably be one of the most amazing and heroic tales in the history of man's fight for freedom.

We have units of the FFI attached to all our divisions—especially the Infantry.

They go out with the advance reconnaissance elements. They know every nook and cranny, every trail, and where the guerrilla forces are behind the German lines.

When you read about our rapid advances, remember that and it will explain in part how we are able to accomplish them.

Yep, we're reaching the end of the road on this thing. Jerry is finished.

There won't be but a fraction of the German troops who were in France on D-day who will ever get back to Germany alive—and most of those will be our prisoners.

We are absolutely cutting them to pieces. . . .

Being a conquering hero is nice—but I'd trade it all just to be with you for five minutes.

Darling, even these breathtaking events don't take away the ache. I love you, love you, love you.

Your, Larry

238th Engr. Combat Bn.
APO 230, NY, NY
Somewhere in France
29 August 1944

Darling Mine;

This will have to be brief. You understand.

The radio in my jeep announces a victory parade of American troops in Paris today. Some fun. Paris is way behind us, and we race on.[28]

All fight and not much fun in these assault outfits. Didn't even ever get to see the damn place again.

I've been a front-line Joe long enough to know one thing.

The entire German Army stands on the verge of complete de-

---

[28] At this time, the 238th was building bridges across the Marne River near Meaux.

struction. Not only here, but on all other fronts. They will either have to surrender or die everywhere.

Victory for the forces of progress looms. The greatest military debacle in all history stands before the Nazis.

And it's coming faster than most people even would dare believe or hope for a little while ago.

How's your tummy darling? (Somewhat irrelevant, eh?)

Even while chasing the Boches I keep thinking of you and "Joe."

Be careful and take it easy.

I love you. Larry

―――――――

238th Engr. Combat Bn.
APO 230, NY, NY
Somewhere in France
1 September 1944

Darling;

We're stopped for a breather for a few hours, so here goes a few words.

Yesterday I had the job of reconnoitering a tremendous ammunition dump left behind by the Germans in their headlong retreat.

It was reported to be mined, and information was needed in order to determine how best to take off the materiél, and what precautions had to be taken by clearing parties that would come after us.

Well, the first thing I did was get in touch with Underground and got a scout who knew every foot of the area. The dump was in a dense forest + occupied about 20 square miles of territory.

We climbed into my jeep + took off.

When we got into the forest we came into a little valley and there in front of us lay a pretty little village.

As we approached the village, I saw people running into their houses and shutting the doors.

I asked the scout what was wrong, and he said they probably

thought we were Boches since no Americans had yet been in the area.

Well, we drove into the town square + I had the driver stop the jeep. I then instructed the FFI boy to shout that we were Americans.

He grinned, stood up in the jeep, and bellowed "Hey everybody! This is not the Boche. It's the Americans. Come on out and say hello!"

Well, you should have seen the demonstration of hysterical enthusiasm that followed.

In a minute we were swarmed with men, women, and children who kissed us, pummeled us, shook our hands, piled us with flowers, gave us plums, eggs, apples, pears, cognac, + cider.

A little girl presented me with a tri-color flag she had made from her old dresses and a handkerchief, which she had been hiding for the day the first Americans came through.

The priest came out and I had to autograph a special page in the church register.

The enclosed rose is from the pile that we were showered with.

I finally was able to beg off to get on with my mission, which we completed in a few hours.

On my way back, we were mobbed again. This time we had to eat with the Mayor. No, they would not take no for answer.

So we had a feast till the food + drink damn near came out of our eyes.

We left with their cheers ringing in our ears.

Oh, Oh—here's work.

Take care of yourself, darling.

I love you. Larry

238th Engr. Combat Bn.
APO 230, NY, NY
Somewhere in Belgium
6 September 1944

Hello Darling;

We just finished building a bridge.[29] A fine bridge, a good bridge. Now, we're watching the tanks roll over it.

We put it across the river and had traffic running across it in just under five hours. Pretty good time when you consider that we had to cross an assault party to clear the opposite bank of snipers.

Belgium is a really lovely country—but we're not getting much of a chance to see it. We've been going on through like a dose of salts.

One of the first things that hits your eye when you go through Belgium is the neatness, the modernistic architecture, the surprisingly dense population. The cities and towns are much farther advanced than England or France, and in some respects even the U.S., from a superficial view.

For instance, we saw a lot of coal mining towns without dirt, grime, and the squalor of our own Pennsylvania or Kentucky coal fields.

The houses were neat, modern, of brick construction.

The most stupendous thing to the first American spearheads here, was of course, the reception by the people of Belgium.

Yes, my outfit was with the first armored groups here.

If France of Paris and environs was delirious Belgium was stark, raving mad. The scenes of uncontained joy were absolutely indescribable.

One thing that I, as an individual, was quick to notice was the apparently very well-organized underground (which is now of course out in the open) and the abundance of Russian as well as American, British, and Belgian flags.

The boys seem to have been on the ball over here.

Fleeting side-glimpses include a man standing at a corner pis-

---

[29] The bridge was a floating steel treadway bridge built over the Meuse River at Namur, Belgium under enemy fire.

soir, doing his duty with one hand, and giving us the V-for victory with the other. A sign reading "God bless Roosevelt, God bless Churchill, and God bless Stalin." Nu, why not? An adolescent girl yelling, "I love you," at every American vehicle that passed. And a maelstrom of loving humanity that mobbed us every time we went through towns.

Enclosed are a few more trinkets. They're the shoulder tabs, insignia, and decorations of the chief of Gestapo in a large Belgian town.

By the time you receive this, I think that we as well as you shall be in the home stretch and racing towards the big event.

You, darling, will be sweating out the birth of "Joe." We, shall probably be in Germany and smashing forward to the grand finale.

To the happy culmination of both events, I look forward with the greatest eagerness.

I love you, my darling. I hope and pray that everything will be O.K. with you and the baby to come.

Your loving, Larry

———————

238th Engr. Combat Bn.
APO 230, NY, NY
Somewhere in Belgium
11 September 1944

Hello Darling;

The weather has turned cold—but fine + clear. Wonderful weather for our bombers.

Every morning they drone over by the hundreds, flying east to Germany. The preparation for the final battle—the Battle of Germany is beginning.

Personally I don't believe that it will be very long now—I give it two more months at the outside. Anyway, I fervently hope so.

How long it will be before we can get home—ça, c'est une autre chose.

I know that practically every G.I. over here is at heart a homesick pup. But, if there's anyone that longs to be home as much as I do, I'd like to meet him.

I keep thinking about the 20th of this month. I know, of course, that babies don't run on train schedules—but the 20th is a good reference date.

Very possibly you may get this letter after the event. You may even be lying in a hospital bed reading this right now. Gee, darling, I hope the baby looks like you.

And, how I would like to be with you!

This damn war is such a miserable business. . . .

Sometimes I'm so full of hate, I think the best thing to do would be to burn the whole lousy place [Germany] to the ground—with all its inhabitants.

One thing is certain, there won't be any riotous welcome for us like we experienced in France and Belgium. Even the workers of Germany failed in their historic task. Was it any easier for the Greeks, the Yugoslavs, the French, the Belgians, the Dutch, the Norwegians to organize resistance?

> Oh well, nous verrons ce que nous verrons. . . .
> Excuse the brevity darling, but we're very busy.
> I love you avec tout mon coeur.
>
> Your mari, Larry

International Brigades—Spain in 1937–1938.
Upper photo: 1937—Lawrence Cane, first row, seated at left; Lower photo: 1938—Mackenzie-Papineau Battalion parading in Barcelona; Lawrence Cane, far right.

Grace Cane in Civil Defense Volunteer Office uniform in 1942.

Above: Staff Sgt. Lawrence Cane at Geiger Field, Spokane, Washington in 1942. At right: Grace Cane and Lt. Lawrence Cane, prior to his departure for England in January 1944.

582nd Engineer Dump Truck Company, Camp Claiborne, Louisiana in September 1943. 2nd Lt. Lawrence Cane, seated 6th from left.

11 June, 1944
Somewhere in France,

Gracie Darling;

I wrote my first V-mail note to you yesterday. I'm sorry I couldn't sit down and write any sooner, because I know you've probably been worried. But I'm still alive and well and hoping that I'll remain that way.

You remember my anxiety about getting into some real action — about being up front where people like us should always be? Well, darling, I should never have worried about it. Somehow, I always get to where the fighting is hottest.

As I mentioned to you in my note, I landed in France on D-day, 6 June, 1944, with the combat engineers in the assault wave. I was in on the storming of the beach fortifications and since then have been right up in the thick of it with the parachute troops.

While we were back in England, my company was assigned as the trucking outfit for the Engineer. Combat Group that was picked to do the assault

Letter of 11 June 1944—"Somewhere in France."

THE STARS AND STRIPES

U.S. Troops Cross Seine Under Fire

Utilizing the early morning fog for cover, Army engineers ferry jeeps across the Seine at a point near Montereau as American forces crash through German defenses. The pontoon ferry was built by the engineers.

Combat engineers ferrying troops across the Seine River in August 1944 (see letter of 27 August 1944).

September 22 1964

My dearest Dad:

Do you remember the day twenty years ago, the day when I was born. Oh no, you can't because you wasn't with us then, I was alone with mother and grandma and aunt Carola, when I looked into this world the first day. You was very far away, you was in Europe, you had to fight for us, for me, for Mutti for all mankind. You had to fight to make the world to that what she is now, that we are able to enjoy a free world, a free life an understanding between the different people. You had to fight the evil, the madness who wanted to rule the world with their, you called it fashistic ideas, I can't understand what that means. But I know that you was one of the heroic men who helped us to have a happy life. I learned in history how the world looked twenty years ago and I hardly can find the understanding for it. But why do I write all of this to you. to thank you for your doing for giving us this life paid with your sweat and courage.

Yours son
David Earl

Letter to Lawrence Cane from Max Herschmann. Max Herschmann, a cousin of Grace Cane and a refugee from Nazi Germany, wrote this letter shortly after the birth of David Earl Cane. The letter was dated September 22, 1964 (see letter of 7 October 1944).

Aachen, Germany in October 1944. Upper photo: "V-13" streetcar filled with high explosives by 238th Engineer Combat Battalion and sent rolling down its tracks toward the city of Aachen during siege; Lower photo: Ruins of Aachen during clearing of streets by the 238th Engineer Combat Battalion.

— *An Editorial* —

Don't Get Chummy with Jerry

WE are fighting in Aachen in Germany. The war which the Germans began has finally completed a cycle and is back where it started. Let's look at the war for a moment —and let's look at Aachen.

This is a total war—a war of entire peoples. The men, women and children of Germany against the men, women and children of the United Nations. Who made it a total war? The Germans. Every resource in Germany is part of the Nazi war machine. Every man, woman and child. Every German factory and every German farm. That's total war—Nazi style.

The Germans practised total war another way too. They made war on the men, women and children of the nations they attacked. Remember Rotterdam? Without warning the city was bombed. Thousands of women and kids were killed. Remember the refugees on the roads of Holland, Belgium and France in 1940? They were driven there by the German Army. To ball up Allied supplies. To slow down French and British troops. Refugees were part of the master plan. They were machine-gunned a n d dive bombed by the Stukas from hell to breakfast.

That's total war à la Deutsch.

Well, the war is now in Germany. Aachen is the first big German city we've hit. Militarily the battle of Aachen is in the infantry's hands. You should see that infantry—dirty, wet, bloody, tired, miserable—but fighting and killing Germans every inch of the way. Yard by yard, street by street, Aachen is falling into the bag.

*   *   *

BUT at Aachen we may lose this war. Because here's what's going on around Aachen:

1) German civilians are giving the Yanks the V sign, the glad hand, free beer, big smiles, plenty of talk about not being Nazis at heart, and hurray for Democracy.

2) Some GIs and plenty of officers are returning the smiles, flirting with the frauleins, drinking the beer and starting to think what nice folks the Germans really are.

3) German civilians are being removed from Aachen and driven two miles in U.S. Army trucks to Lutzow barracks in Brand—a suburb of Aachen.

To move them out of the city is a matter of strict military necessity. But these Nazis are being quartered in the best buildings outside Aachen. They are being brought there in Army vehicles. There are canvas covers over them to keep off the rain.

They have already received 20 tons of Army food. Army authorities found two large cooking vats and brought them to the Nazis in U.S. Army trucks. These Germans are eating hot chow—soup, meat, vegetables, coffee, cake. They are sleeping in warm, dry rooms. They are being cared for by American and British authorities, as solicitous about these poor German civilians as a mother hen over her chicks.

General Ike spoke his piece on non-fraternization in no uncertain terms. He did so with full knowledge of the consequences of pampering the Germans, who regard kindness as weakness and who are already taking full advantage of the kindly, sentimental American sap.

This May Be Jolly...

GI JOE will obey the order not to fraternize with the Germans. It will be a tough order to obey. By nature he's friendly. He's also lonely. He's also thirsty and curious. When his arm isn't hugging an M1, it aches to hug a girl. When he's not bent on killing, he's intent on kissing. But, to repeat, GI Joe will obey it, just the same as he's obeyed every other order he's been given so far.

But the order will be tougher to obey because of what is going on around Aachen.

If an open field in the rain is OK for GI Joe, how about open fields for able bodied Nazis?

If cold chow is good enough for GI Joe, how about K-rations for Hans and Fritz?

If there are trucks enough to bring up 20 tons of food for the Germans, why are combat troops getting along on a half pack of cigarettes a day—*when they get them?*

If replacements can ride in uncovered trucks, how about a little fresh air for the Nazis?

If a slit trench in the mud with four inches of water for a mattress gives a Joe his beauty rest, why the best buildings in Aachen for the Nazis?

Yes, GI Joe will obey the non-fraternization order. He knows Joe Goebbels has told the Germans our Army is sloppy, undisciplined and over-friendly. He doesn't want to be a stooge for Nazi propaganda. So if the order is don't cuddle up with the Germans, cuddling is out.

But if Nazi-cuddling is out for GI Joe, how about putting Nazis off limits for everyone else too? How about letting the German men, women and kids know that their support of Hitler and his crowd, their racial and religous intolerance, t h e i r aggressions throughout the world, don't make us love them to the point of treating them so much better than our own boys who are being killed by Nazi guns and grenades?

How about carrying out the true spirit of General Ike's proclamation—that "we come as conquerors"—and not as *over-friendly* saps?

We're not for copying the Nazis. We're not for budging an inch from the Geneva Convention. We're not for bombing or machine-gunning civilians. We're not for concentration camps, Nazi style. We're not for kicking around babies, pregnant women, the aged and sick. We're not for being rough, aggressive, insolent or overbearing.

We are for making the Germans realize what it's like to be on the other end of a total war. We are for letting them taste the misery their kind of war has caused others. We are for starting the process of German re-education right now—in Aachen, in Cologne, in every other German city until we meet up with the Russians coming the other way.

We're for cuddling Nazis less.

We're for cuddling GI Joe more.

...But This Is Grim

Stars and Stripes editorial, October 20, 1944 (see letter of 22 October 1944).

Lt. Lawrence Cane receiving the Silver Star from
Maj. Gen. J. Lawton Collins, Commander VII
Corps, U.S. 1st Army on November 11, 1944 (see
letters of 31 July, 2 August, 12 August, and 11 November 1944).

5

The Siegfried Line and the Battle of the Bulge: Fighting in Germany and Belgium
September 15, 1944–January 26, 1945

238th Engr. Combat Bn.
APO 230, NY, NY
Somewhere in Europe
15 September 1944

Hello Darling;

Here it is the middle of September, and drawing on nigh to the big event—the birth of our baby.

Probably by the time you receive this letter we will already be mama + poppa.

I've said it many times before, but it still goes, I wish I could be with you darling. I'm so lonesome and homesick for you. Each letter I receive from you is like being home for a few minutes. When I have to burn them for security reasons, it breaks my heart.

We are in the home stretch of the war over here now. The sooner it's over, the sooner we get home—we hope.

As for the men just fighting to get home, that's not true any more. It may have been the day we entered battle, but there has been a gradual transformation. At first, when buddies were killed and the fighting became real and personal there was blind hatred. Then as we progressed through France and then Belgium, the men saw what Nazism actually meant to the people. Most of them, in my outfit anyway, are conscious anti-fascists now.

Now, with the Siegfried Line[1] and Germany ahead of us, we are for the most part, eager to finish the thing off.

---

[1] The Siegfried Line was the name for Germany's fortified western frontier.

About my Silver Star, I understand it's run into Army red tape. You see, the Silver Star, the DSC [Distinguished Service Cross], and the Congressional Medal are the three highest awards for bravery given by the Government.

Well, we engineers were attached to an armored division at the time of the big breakthrough, and any award has to come through the commanding general of that division. Of course, right now, we are attached to some other outfit, and the armored division in question is in another sector of the front.

Sooo. The general wants additional information, or maybe the t's weren't crossed properly, anyway, there's a lot of new paper work that has to be done, and the whole thing has to be re-submitted through channels.

Probably get the damn thing ten years after the war's over.

Well, take good care of yourself, darling. . . . I love you.

Larry

================

238th Engr. Combat Bn.
APO 230, NY, NY
Somewhere in GERMANY!!
19 September 1944

My Darling;

We're in the home stretch now.

This Siegfried Line is no joke, but we're busting our way through.

The last letter I wrote I had to dateline "somewhere in Europe" for security reasons.

The people here are no longer friendly. This is Naziland and they hate us.

We are no longer "Liberateurs," we are now "Invaders."

That's O.K. with us, because the feeling is mutual.

We've only seen the small border villages yet. We're still fighting for our first large town.[2]

---

[2] The town was Aachen, sometimes called Aix-la-Chapelle, located near the Germany-Belgium border. It was the first German town captured by Allied forces. Fierce fighting ensued and not until October 21, 1944 did the Germans surrender.

If the Germans decide to fight us all the way back (Something I doubt) we're prepared to make all of Germany look like Normandy in France.

I rather think, though, that organized resistance will collapse once we're on the other side of the Rhine. . . .

Today is the day before the deadline, and darling so help me, I'm a lot less worried about Jerry's artillery than I am about you.

Mentally, I'm already walking up + down that hospital corridor. Jesus, I'll sure have to sweat this one out.

Be sure to take it easy darling and don't strain yourself.

'Bye for now. Je t'adore.

Your, Larry

238th Engr. Combat Bn.
APO 230, NY, NY
25 September 1944

Hello Sweetheart;

Here it is five days after our deadline, and I still don't know whether or not I'm a poppa.

You'll never know how anxious I am about you.

What a situation! Am I or am I not? How are you? Is it a boy or a girl? Oh gosh, darling. . . .

I hope I get the dope soon.

By the way, I'm sending you a couple of Nazi flags I picked up. Maybe it would be a good idea to give one of them to my folks.

Tell them to put the Star of David on it and hang it out on Passover.

Wouldn't that be a cute one?

I've got some other stuff I can't send home in a package. Just have to hope I can get them back to you in person. . . .

Things over here are getting kind of tough as far as the weather is concerned. It's been raining like hell the past few days. Picture my enjoyment. I believe if I figured it out on paper, my feet have been dry about $9^1/_2$ days all told since I got here.

They better polish these Krauts off pretty quick, or I'll really get mad.

Oh well, there's little to write, except to repeat that I'm sweating out your confinement and I'm hoping that everything turns out O.K.

Take good [care] of yourself, darling.

I love you.

Your, Larry

—————

238th Engr. Combat Bn.
APO 230, NY, NY
29 September 1944[3]

My Darling:

Nine days after the 20th and I still don't know from nothin'. If I'm a poppa and you're a momma I probably will get a letter long before I get any cable you sent.

Among other advantages of being with you at a time like this sweetheart would be the fact that I wouldn't have to sweat it out so long. I'd just walk the hospital corridor for a few hours—but here, Jesus!

I keep hoping and praying that you came out of it O.K. and that we had a healthy squalling youngster.

Maybe I'm getting soft—but dammit I'm only human. I love you and miss you, and God a man can only know what hunger for his wife means after going through this hell.

The weather is getting raw and cold, even the sun doesn't help things when it comes out, which is infrequently. There's been a lot of rain.

Darling, I promise you if I should ever get home O.K. and someone proposes a walk in the rain, I will promptly crown him on the spot. After two wars—there'll be no singin' in the rain for this Joe. . . .

---

[3] On September 29 the 238th Engineer Combat Battalion moved into the line 1½ miles south of Aachen, relieving the 2nd Battalion of the 16th Infantry. They remained in the line, with heavy fighting, until the surrender of the German garrison on October 21.

I love you, or as the natives say, "Ich liebe dich."

Your own, Larry

=======

238th Engr. Combat Bn.
APO 230, NY, NY
Somewhere in Germany
4 October 1944

My Darling;

Gott sei dank! A seven-and-three-quarter pound David Earl has finally arrived.[4] Just imagine, Momma and Poppa Grace and Larry.

I don't have the words to describe the incoherent, giddy feeling that I have.

When I got the letter from Marge announcing the blessed event (which, incidentally, came in record time) I just let out a war whoop. Unfortunately we're not in a place where I can buy cigars and hand them out. But I sure feel like turning handsprings and yelling and singing and dancing.

Marge tells me the doctor had to perform a Caesarian section. Exactly what that is I can only guess—but it doesn't sound pleasant.

Please, please darling tell me how you are and how you feel. I am so anxious about you and hope so much that you are alright.

And darling, tell me about our son. Tell me what he looks like, and what he does, and is he a healthy baby.

Remember I told you the firstborn in my family has almost always been a boy?

Turned out that way this time, too. Didn't it?

I hope you liked the flowers, bub. I had that arranged with mother and Marge a long time ago.

---

[4] David Earl Cane was born on September 22, 1944. Grace's sister, Marjorie, sent Lawrence a telegram with the news of the birth, but the telegram was delayed. The telegram arrived three days before Grace's letter with the birth announcement.

How does our son feel to you when you hold him? Gee, I wish I could carry him around for awhile.

Gee—a son!

I'll bet the family is all excited. Mother must be running around in circles, and my Mom and Pop must be happy as all getout.

David Earl Cane—son and heir!

Whoops—PX rations just came in, including CIGARS. The Lord or somebody must be in on this deal. I'm buying a box and passing them out.

Just got news that we can officially announce that we are in Germany. I did that by mistake when we first got here, maybe it got through.

We were among the first to hit the Siegfried Line. Right now we're sitting somewhere right smack in the center of it.

We hope we don't sit too long and from the looks of things we should be moving again by the time you get this letter.

Look darling, the mailman is just about to leave, so I'm going to close now.

All my love to our son, and to you my sweet, I love you with everything that is me.

Your own, Larry

238th Engr. Combat Bn.
APO 230, NY, NY
Somewhere in Germany
7 October 1944

My Own Darling;

Received your letter with the enclosed birth announcement of our son.

Gee, its seems funny to read that "Lt. and Mrs. Lawrence Cane announce the birth of a son, David Earl."

And that little wisp of silky black hair. If the little shaver can spare that, he's way ahead of his old man already.

I received a wonderful letter from Max. I'm going to send it to you so you can read it. Save it for me darling.

I'm glad you liked the flowers. Are you still in the hospital, or have you been able to go home? Is mother staying with you for awhile, or have you made some other arrangements? And how are you feeling now, sweetheart?

Same old story, I'm consumed with anxiety.

Keep me posted, darling.

I love you, love you. Larry

September 22, 1964[5]

My dearest Dad:

Do you remember the day twenty years ago, the day when I was born. Oh no, you can't because you wasn't with us then, I was alone with mother and grandma and aunt Carola, when I looked into this world the first day. You was very far away, you was in Europe, you had to fight for us, for me, for Mutti for all mankind. You had to fight to make the world to that what she is now, that we are able to enjoy a free world, a free life an understanding between the different people. You had to fight the evil, the madmen who wanted to rule the world with their, you called it fachistic ideas. I can't understand what that means. But I know that you was one of the heroic men who helped us to have a happy life. I learned in history how the world looked twenty years ago and I hardly can find the understanding for it. But why do I write all of this to you. To thank you for your doing for giving us this life paid with your sweat and courage.

Your son, David Earl

---

[5] This letter was written in September 1944 to Lawrence Cane, following the birth of his son, David Earl, by Max Herschmann, a cousin of Grace Cane. Max, along with his wife, Carola, and daughters, Ellen and Ruth, had managed to escape from their home city of Bonn, Germany in November 1938, shortly after Kristallnacht, and emigrate to New York City.

238th Engr. Combat Bn.
APO 230, NY, NY
7 October 1944

My Dear Max;

I must sit down and answer the wonderful letter you wrote to me. I can't begin to tell you how much I was touched and moved by it.

I only hope that my son will grow up in the kind of world you describe. I hope that the future you talk about is being born now.

I'm going to save that letter, and if I'm still alive 22 Sept. 1964, I'm going to read it and see what's happened to your dreams and mine.

You must know this area pretty well, Max.[6] But, it's somewhat changed since you last saw it. We are bringing war to Germany.

It is terrible to bring death and destruction to a town that looks so pretty through my field glasses. But, no suffering and misery is too great to bring to a people who have been responsible for such horrors as the torture and burning of millions of innocent people.

I identify the German people with the war criminals because I am bitter and disappointed in them. All other people—the French, the Greeks, the Yugoslavs, the Belgians, the Dutch, the Norwegians were able to fight on in spite of the Gestapo terror. But the Germans either Heiled Hitler or stood silent. And most of them Heiled Hitler.

Today I led a patrol into that pretty town I mentioned and ordered the evacuation of some civilians.[7] You see, we can't trust them, so we have to send them behind our lines, when they're in the battle area.

There was one old lady who began to cry and tell me she wanted to find her old sister of 75 before she left. I looked at her and thought of the hundreds of thousands of Jewish mothers, sisters, wives, sweethearts that Germans have massacred, and it saved me from feeling pity. Why should I give you a break, when your dumkopf grandson is probably a Jew-killer, I thought.

---

[6] At this time the First Army was fighting near Aachen, Germany.

[7] On October 7 the dawn patrol of Company C went into a section of Aachen called Steinbruck, where it was fired on from an enemy machine gun outpost at a roadblock. The patrol returned fire, threw several hand grenades, and withdrew, bringing 10 civilians from Steinbruck with them.

Heraus!

Some day in that future you mention, perhaps we won't have to think in terms of hate.

All this will certainly not have been in vain if it turns out that way.

Give my love to Carola and Ruth and Ellen.

Yours for a speedy victory.

As ever, Larry

⸻

238th Engr. Combat Bn.
APO 230, NY, NY
Somewhere in Germany
15 October 1944

My Darling;

Another Sunday has arrived, but it's not peaceful and lazy like it used to be back home. Remember the delicious, long hours of sleep, the wonderful brunches?

They're so far away now. Like a fairyland that a child dreams about.

And the prospect doesn't look quite as rosy as it did to me on the way through northern France and Belgium. Maybe we've been in the line too long and I'm tired and bitter and dopey. But it does seem right now that we've still got a lot of war to fight.

I tell my men if we have to take this goddam Germany town by town, street by street, house by house—I'll be looking for my son to come up with the replacements before it's over.

My battalion commander congratulated me on the birth of David Earl and said, "I hear you've got a little soldier in the family now."

I answered by saying, "Soldier hell, that boy's old man has enough war in his system for all his descendants, and then some." And, I have too.

I hope to God that our boy will never have to shoulder a rifle for anything except duck-hunting.

How is our baby, darling? Your brief description of him made me long to see him and hold him and let him grab my finger. Is he a good baby or a cry baby?

I wish so hard that I could get home to the two of you. Good God, how I miss you. Gracie, Gracie I love you so much.

Maybe old Hitler thinks that because I feel this way, and maybe a couple of million Joes think the same, that it'll affect the high command, and then maybe he can negotiate a peace and save some of the pieces. You know, we get tired of the fight and say the hell with it, we'll give him terms.

But, he's wrong. We'll fight and fight. The longer it takes the more we'll hate, the more we'll destroy.

Maybe once, we were easy-going, slaphappy, naive Americans. But now we're killers. Hard and mean + we hate the Boche.

The average G.I. whose a front-line rat thinks the Krauts are a bunch of dirty bastards and only takes them prisoner because he's ordered to do so. Otherwise the list of prisoners among the Germans would be much smaller, and the list of dead would be much larger.

It's too bad that most people back home don't realize what's going on over here—And what their boys are going through. Oh hell, darling, I'm getting a little incoherent, so I'd better stop.

From the middle of the Siegfried Line, I send you my love darling. I hope that the future doesn't turn out to be so bleak, and that soon you and I and little David will be together for good.

I love you

Your, Larry

238th Engr. Combat Bn.
APO 230, NY, NY
Somewhere in Germany
22 October 1944

Hello Darling;

First chance I've had in the past few days to write to you. I was out in an isolated outpost in front of our main lines and mail was, of course, an impossibility.

We didn't fare so badly out there, especially when it came to food, drink, and smokes. There were plenty of chickens around, potatoes and vegetables in the gardens, champagne and cognac in the wine cellars, and the best cigars I've ever smoked.

We lived like kings in the midst of the wreckage and stench of battle. It rained, but we slept in the cellars with plenty of mattresses, blankets, and comforters.

Outside of having to fight like devils every once in awhile, that was the best spot we've hit yet.

The battle is over now, and it was a bloody, miserable fight.[8] You've probably read about it in the newspapers and heard about it on the radio. What you probably don't know is that the combat engineers fought as infantry here. Four weeks in the line—and no damn joke either. It was worse than Belchite in Spain. Ask any Vet how that was, and he'll tell you it was hell. . . .

I'm enclosing an editorial from the Stars and Stripes. As you can see, it's a bitch against the way Germans are being coddled by the Army officials. It expresses the sentiments of every American G.I.[9]

You see, we have orders not to be friendly with the Krauts, at the same time our Civil Affairs people are handling them as if they were victims of the Nazis instead of being the very people we are fighting.

Every man who's been at the front here is sore as hell about the setup, and the editorial puts it in words to a "T." . . .

Tell our son that daddy sends him a big hug. And you darling, all my love.

Your own, Larry

---

[8] The German garrison at Aachen surrendered on October 21, 1944.

[9] The editorial, "Don't Get Chummy with Jerry," appeared in the October 20, 1944 issue of *The Stars and Stripes*.

238th Engr. Combat Bn.
APO 230, NY, NY
Somewhere in Germany
23 October 1944

Hello Darling;

Yesterday, when I wrote you, I mentioned being in an outpost for a few days.

I'd like to tell you a little more about that, especially about something interesting that I ran across out there.

The outpost was a group of houses, all battered and smashed from shelling and thoroughly looted by retreating Germans, but excellent to fight from.

The house that I established my CP in belonged to an old, wealthy German family.

Well, naturally, when you get into a place like that, you kind of rummage around—just out of curiosity's sake.

I got into a closet that had a bunch of old papers, medals, trinkets, and picture albums.

There were relics and pictures of the War of 1870–1871 against the French. You remember, when the Paris Commune was crushed. Then there was a lot of junk from the World War of 1914–1918. But, the thing I became absorbed in was a picture life of the only son + heir of the house.

He was born in 1918, just after the end of the last war. The pictures are the ordinary thing. Proud mama + papa and little snookums.

The pictures go on through childhood, and young boyhood—shots of school, summer camps, winter sports, family groups, etc.

Then comes 1933 and the business begins.

Junior is now in the Hitler Jugend and a sturdy lad of 15. You see him with his "troop," all resplendent with his short pants and his "rucksack."

1936 rolls around, and he's now in the SA (Sturm Abteilung).

In 1937, he's in the Army.

In 1938 he's an "Unteroffizier" and is sent to Officers School in Potsdam. And, oh the pictures of the parades and goosestepping and shiny boots now!

1939 and he transfers to the Air Corps. He is now a second lieutenant.

There are pictures of airfields, and officers' quarters, and more shiny boots and more goosestepping parades.

1940 and Junior is a full-fledged pilot. Bomber pilot at that. But in 1940 the pictures stop.

Among the papers and books there were ravings of Adolf Hitler. I found a quotation that was quite appropriate from a document called "Training of German Youth for Military Service," 1935.

Translated, it goes something like this, "It is repugnant to the heroic man that death on the battlefield should give rise to sorrow and complaint. It should be regarded as the ardently longed for termination of life. . . ."

Well, maybe this time when we finish with these bastards they'll sing, "I didn't raise my boy to be a soldier," instead of "Deutschland, Deutschland, Uber Alles."

One thing, if they make us fight for every city—they're sure going to be too busy building them up again for the next fifty years, to think of building up an army.

Napoleon was the last guy to lead an army into Germany, and they had enough for about sixty years after him. . . .

Oh darling, darling. I want you so much. And if I could just get one peek at our son.

Just have to keep sweating it out, I guess, and hoping it won't be too long.

Take good care of yourself, sweetheart.

I love you. Larry

238th Engr. Combat Bn.
APO 230, NY, NY
Somewhere in Germany
27 October 1944

Darling:

We're getting a well-earned rest right now, and it sure is welcome.

I found out that my old outfit is back in Belgium not too far away, so today I took a ride back there to visit them. What a racket they've got now!

Living like kings and they never even hear a rifle shot any more. . . .

They're all O.K.—and why not?

All the guys were pretty glad to see me and flocked around when I got in.

I spent a couple of hours shooting the breeze with them, and then came back.

Somehow, I was very glad that I was just a visitor as far as they were concerned.

How's my darling and my son doing?

Can you get some pictures taken, hon? I'd love to have some of you and the baby.

Take it easy, darling.

I love you. Larry

238th Engr. Combat Bn.
APO 230, NY, NY
Somewhere in Germany
29 October 1944

Grace Darling;

. . . I received your letter of the 17th Oct. with the pictures of you and David taken in the hospital.

You ask me if I like him. Do I like him? Darling, I'm crazy about him.

I keep staring at the pictures, and showing them off. . . .

We're sorta resting now. We're living in houses outside a big city we helped to take.[10] We rotate between a day off, a couple of days of specialized training (coming events cast their shadows before), and a couple of days of work clearing mines + booby traps in the aforementioned town.

---

[10] The city was Aachen.

It's heaven compared to what we had up to now, and it's a real break now that the weather here has turned cold.

By the way, tell Max he'd never recognize the town he mentioned in his letter to me. It was an ancient + beautiful city, but now it looks like Belchite in Spain, or St. Lô in Normandy. And by God, terrible as it may sound, I enjoy seeing a <u>GERMAN</u> city destroyed.

How they've had it coming to them! . . .

Take care of yourself—for me darling.

I love you.

Your, Larry

238th Engr. Combat Bn.
APO 230, NY, NY
Somewhere in Germany
2 November 1944

Darling Mine;

. . . There's a constant roar in the sky tonight. Our bombers have been going over for an hour by the hundreds heading for the Rhineland cities. Far away you can see the red and green flares of the pathfinders over Köln, the flashes of the German flak, and the lightning of the bombs crashing. They've been doing that every night for more than a week.

To live in a German city these days must be a nightmare.

This will be a terrible winter for the people of Germany. Especially if they hold out. But it will tear the heart out of them and crush their spirit.

They will have had a bellyful of war for a long time when we are finished with them.

That's all for now, sweetheart. Take care of yourself and David for me. Give him a kiss from Daddy.

I love you. Larry

238th Engr. Combat Bn.
APO 230, NY, NY
Somewhere in Germany
11 November 1944

Grace Darling;

Well I finally got the Silver Star pinned on me.

I wish you could have seen the ceremony. You would have been so proud. All through the proceedings I kept thinking, If only my Gracie could be here, holding David in her arms, and drinking it all in.

The formation was held in the courtyard of what had formerly been a college in a small Belgian town.

We were lined up by the General's aide-de-Camp and given preliminary instructions.

Promptly at three P.M. two staff cars drove up and Major General J. Lawton Collins, commander of VII Corps, 1st U.S. Army, followed by three other Major Generals strode to the flagpole while the band played "Ruffles + Flourishes." We were brought to attention and presented arms. Then we were given order arms. The aide then read the orders of the day which consisted of the descriptions of each individual action for which the men were to be decorated.

I was in pretty brassy company. Up in front of my row stood old Major General Huebner, commander of the 1st Infantry Division, who was to receive the Bronze Star Medal. On my right there was a Brigadier-General who was to receive the Oak Leaf Cluster to the Legion of Merit.

To even things up, on my left stood a 1st Lieutenant, and ex-cowpuncher who was also to receive the Silver Star. On his left was a good old G.I. private, a medic, also up for the Silver Star.

"First Lieutenant Lawrence Cane, Corps of Engineers," I heard the aide read, "For gallantry in action during the armored break-through in Normandy, France." Then followed an account of what had happened.

"Geez," I thought, "is that me the guy's talking about?"

Finally, the orders were completed and Major General Collins got down to the business of putting on the medals.

When he got to me I was standing stiff as a ramrod, eyes front.

I saluted and he returned the salute. He grinned and said as he was putting the medal on me, "Lt., I'm very happy to be able to do this. Congratulations." I said "Thank you, sir," and he shook my hand.

After the medals were all distributed, the General put us at ease and made us a little speech. It was a good speech, a fighting speech.

After that came the National Anthem, Salute to the Colors, and it was over.

It was something I'll remember for a long time.

Maybe someday, I'll be able to take David on my knee and tell him all about it. . . .

There's a great deal of suffering and misery ahead—but there's a great day coming, honey. . . .

I love you, darling.

Your, Larry

P.S. The radio just started playing our favorite song.[11] God! how I ache for you.

238th Engr. Combat Bn.
APO 230, NY, NY
Somewhere in Germany
15 November 1944

Hello Darling;

Just received your letter of Nov. 4th.

So you participated in the election campaign for Roosevelt? I should have known you'd get in on it. Can't keep you down, eh? . . .

Talking about politics, darling, I want you to do me a great big favor. I want you to sit down and write me a long letter telling me about what we are going to do with Germany after the War? No fooling.

---

[11] Their favorite song was the Harry James' wartime hit, "You Made Me Love You."

All we get here is the Stars and Stripes, and back issues of Life, Time, Newsweek, etc.

I've read what's supposed to be the Morgenthau plan, and what some bright columnists have to say about it pro + con.[12]

But, what's the real dope, hon?

Up at the front, we're all full of hate, and our first reaction is pretty much summarized by the phrase "Kill the bastards!"

But we're not just fighting for today and tomorrow alone. I hope to God that David Earl never has to go through the things I and so many millions of others have had to experience the past few years.

Solutions that sound good on the spur of the moment, just won't work out for five or ten or twenty years.

You just can't practically destroy 43,000,000 Germans and expect it to stick. And it just doesn't seem to jibe with the picture of the democratic world of tomorrow.

Sure, destroy the Nazi State and all its organs, execute all the war criminals (hundreds of thousands, a couple of million if necessary), establish a military gov't, take away the estates of the Prussian generals, revamp the educational system, establish an international organization that will stop aggression—based on the closest collaboration between the Soviet Union, the U.S., Britain, + China.

But what about German industry, should it be destroyed? That doesn't smell so good to me. Should Germany lose her national independence permanently? I'm also suspicious of that—nothing takes root of a people so much as a war for national liberation.

And, I'll tell you another thing—much as I hate the no good Nazi sonsabitches—I still have faith in people. I believe that Germans can be like you and I, some day. I believe that they can take their place in Humanity's march to progress. And, by God, for Humanity's sake the necessary preconditions should be established.

But, what are those preconditions? That's what's bothering the

---

[12] The Morgenthau Plan was a proposal for postwar Germany presented by the Secretary of the Treasury, Henry Morgenthau (1891–1967), at the Quebec Conference in September 1944. It called for making postwar Germany an agricultural and pastoral country. The plan was ultimately rejected by Franklin D. Roosevelt and Winston S. Churchill.

hell out of me. I think I know some. But the others are not quite clear.

Help me out, will you darling?

If anything is being said about it in Church[13] these days, give me the dope—clippings, articles, etc.

Help me out, will you darling? . . .

Be good darling. I love you terribly.

Your own, Larry

―――――

238th Engr. Combat Bn.
APO 230, NY, NY
Somewhere in Germany
22 November 1944

My Darling:

Today our son is two months old. I was thinking how nice it would be if I could be home so I could buy him a present. Something crazy—like a pair of 16 oz. boxing gloves. And I could bring you an enormous bouquet of flowers. Then, after we were finished giggling over the gloves, we could look over the turkey and debate about how we'd set the table tomorrow. 'Cause tomorrow is Thanksgiving day.

But there'll be rain tomorrow, just like today and the day after tomorrow, and there'll be mud and gunfire and bitter battle, and there'll be loneliness and longing.

On the face of it, tomorrow should be just another day of war, of smashing pillboxes, of building bridges, of clearing mines, of being cold and wet and miserable and dopey with exhaustion.

But when our turkey's dished out (yes, we'll have turkey) I'm going to be thankful that I'm still alive, thankful for my wonderful wife and the baby I've never seen, thankful that I've been able to come from the maelstrom of the beach in Normandy on H-hour June 6th to the quagmire of the Siegfried Line, thankful the world stands on the verge of victory over the horror that is fascism,

---

[13] "Church" was Lawrence's code name for the Communist Party.

thankful that I have been able to contribute my two bits to the struggle, thankful for the men around me and their courage and fortitude.

Yes, darling, things will look bleak and be bleak, but there'll be a lot to be humbly thankful for.

And I can secretly hope that next year our Thanksgiving will be a much happier one.

The radio says Gen. Eisenhower believes the Nazis will fight the battle of Germany west of the Rhine.[14] In my letter to you yesterday I said just about the same thing. Me and Eisenhower, mmp!

Things are going along. The Krauts are resisting desperately and fighting us viciously, but we're crowding and pushing them back. Slow but sure. Some day, there'll be another break somewhere—when it comes we'll exploit it. Jerry can't afford many more breakthroughs, we're right inside his house now.

There isn't much else to write, darling, except to tell you that I love you and miss you like the devil. Kiss David for me and take care of yourself.

All my love, Larry

238th Engr. Combat Bn.
APO 230, NY, NY
Somewhere in Germany
26 November 1944

Darling Mine;

Well, we're up in there again.[15] You've probably guessed from the gap in the letters.

We're keeping Ike Eisenhower's promise to Germany. The heat's on and we're steamrollering ahead.

[14] General Eisenhower was the commander of the Allied Expeditionary Force in Europe.

[15] On November 24 the 238th Engineer Combat Battalion returned to the front and completed the construction of a trestle bridge over the Inde River near Munsterbusch on November 26.

The Kraut's are fighting for every foot viciously, desperately—but the American powerhouse shoves on. Their towns here are an integral part of the Siegfried Line defenses. They sit astride the main communication roads, railroads and riverways. They're highly industrialized and bristle with fortifications outside, inside, and on the other side.

So, we smash from town to town, and when we mop them up they look like Hitler's precious pillboxes—heaps of smoking, blasted rubble.

Their retreat here is still orderly, so they blow their bridges, mine their fields, booby trap their houses. Plenty of work for us engineers.

Progress is still slow and painful for us. We fight in a nightmare of mud and rain.

But, this is the approach to the industrial heart of Germany. From here comes the major portion of the Nazi war production. Soon, soon we hope to reach the Rhine. If we ever get across that in force we shall be able to tear this heart out of the living body of Nazidom—and the last great natural obstacle between us and Berlin and a juncture with the Russians will have been cleared.

A great prize which spells quick victory. So we sweat as we fight, and curse and shiver in the mud as we wait (so much of war is just waiting), and push on when we get the word.

We are going to <u>win</u>, and we <u>know</u> it.

Enclosed, hon, you'll find the official photo of me being decorated.

The guy with his back turned to the camera is General Collins. The little gink with the twisted smirk shaking his hand is, as you suspect, me. . . .

Bub, I miss you so much these days, it's impossible to explain. I find myself aching for you and feeling blue and lonely. This is a long heart-rending grind, and the worst of it for me, is my continuous hunger for you.

I love you, Grace, for all my forever.

Your, Larry

238th Engr. Combat Bn.
APO 230, NY, NY
Somewhere in Germany
28 November 1944

Hello Darling;

This will come as a surprise to you. It did to me.

I've been transferred to the staff of my battalion and am now the assistant S-2. That's assistant intelligence officer.

The funny thing is, I never even asked for it. I've been quite satisfied in my company and grew quite attached to the men and officers.

One thing about it is that I am now a staff man. And after being a line officer in command of combat troops in two wars, it's going to be kind of hard to get accustomed to working with the brass that's so frequently given me a pain.

You know me darling, fundamentally a charter member of the beefer's union.

Rumor has it that I'm eventually to become Battalion Intelligence Officer, and incidentally a captain. But, there's no sense counting the chicks before they come out of the shells.

Anyway, I'll do my best.

The job should prove to be the best and the most interesting assignment in all my military career (Which is kind of extensive by now—don't you think?).

I had a chance to go back to Belgium for 3 days, but I passed it up because I didn't want to leave the outfit right now. There's a helluva lot of working and fighting to do these days. And I wouldn't feel right lying on my fanny somewhere in the rear when I know the rest of the boys are up here taking it.

"Meshugeh," ain't I?[16]

Might not get another chance for a long time, but what the hell? The only pass I'm looking for is the one which'll be permanent—when I can toss off this uniform and hold you again tightly in my arms.

I can't tell you how much I dote on your descriptions of David Earl—his habits, his growth, his diet, and how precious he is.

---

[16] "Meshugeh" is Yiddish for crazy.

I got a letter from my folks dated Oct. 30th, and they're crazy about him. So'm I. Even way over here in the mud.

Well, that's about all I got for now. Be good, darling. I love you.

Your, Larry

————————

238th Engr. Combat Bn.
APO 230, NY, NY
Somewhere in Germany
29 November 1944

Hello Darling;

Well, assumed my new duties today. Not bad, so far.

The Colonel had a talk with me. Said he was glad to have a man of my experience in Headquarters, particularly the Intelligence section. Said my knowledge of languages should prove quite handy—etc., etc. I let him ramble and gave him the old yessir stuff. . . .

We're still pounding ahead, yard by yard, in what I believe is the bitterest fighting since we landed. It's rougher even than Normandy was, with the Krauts fighting like cornered rats, and the weather conditions absolutely appalling.

You remember how I used to hate rain? That was a heritage from Spain. But, now, I'm even worse of a bug on the subject. Jesus, sometimes I think old Noah was a piker—he only had forty days of it. And to top it all, he kept dry in his Ark.

Over here, to get in out of the rain for a few hours, to crowd a fire, to put on dry socks and clothes is a rare and heavenly luxury.

Oh, well, what's the use of bitching? Come hell or high water, we're here to win, and that's just what we're going to do.

Give David a great big hug for me. Regards to all the folks. My love to you, darling.

Your, Larry

————————

238th Engr. Combat Bn.
APO 230, NY, NY
Somewhere in Germany
13 December 1944

Hello Grace Darling;

. . . [D]on't worry about not being able to give me a pat answer on what to do with Nazi Germany after the war. I guess the best brains in the world still have to sit down and thrash that problem out.

I tell you frankly though, if it were left up to the front-line Joe, Tommy, or Ivan, I believe the German population would be slaughtered. Honestly, I have never seen such bitter hatred in the hearts of men as we have here. And to be even more honest, I feel the same way.

I'll give you an example.

Yesterday, a couple of civilians were sent to us by the Military Government. They had information about German mines and booby traps in a town a few miles back.

In my capacity as Intelligence O., it was my job to check their story. So I piled them into a jeep and went back to the town in question.

Well, they showed me the area, and it was really lousy with all kinds of mines and booby traps. They were in houses, cellars, buried in gardens, under doorsteps, in the fields—all over the place.

When I finished noting the areas on my map, one of these Krauts asked me when my men would be up to clear them.

I just looked at him for a moment, and then told him coldly that we weren't going to clear it at all, just post signs in <u>English</u>— marked "Danger Mines" so that our troops would not be endangered.

"But," he says kind of bewildered, "there are women and children who have no place to go. It's cold, winter is here. Where are they to go?"

I looked him over again—"What a spot for a Jew," I thought.

"Looka here," I said in my best broken German, "I don't give a damn where they go. Your soldiers put these mines in, you can take them out. You and your Hitler started this war. You've been responsible for the misery and death of millions of people. Now you're going to have to take a little of the stuff you've been dishing out for so many years."

I was furious but cold as I spoke.

That was all.

As I rode back, I realized I could kill every one of these bastards and never bat an eye.

But, I'm afraid that's not the solution to the German problem. . . .

There isn't much else to write. The fight is still rough, and we keep inching forward.

I love you very much

As ever, Larry

238th Engr. Combat Bn.
APO 230, NY, NY
Somewhere in Germany
18 December 1944

Hello Darling;

You're probably sweating out the newspapers and radio today—and will be for a few more days.

Jerry's "all or nothing" offensive has started.[17]

The outcome of the Battle of Germany, especially its duration, may well be decided in the next couple of weeks.

The battle is already one of the greatest fought in this war, and the initial momentum has carried Jerry several miles forward into our lines. They may continue to advance for a while in some sectors—we've got to expect that because of the size of their striking force.

But, they will be stopped, and when they are, the truth of Gen-

---

[17] This is a reference to the beginning of the major German counter-offensive, popularly referred to as the Battle of the Bulge. It represented Hitler's last effort at driving the Allied forces out of Europe. The battle began on December 16, 1944 in the Ardennes forest and ended on January 7, 1945. It was the largest battle fought on the Western Front during World War II and resulted in a decisive victory for the Allies.

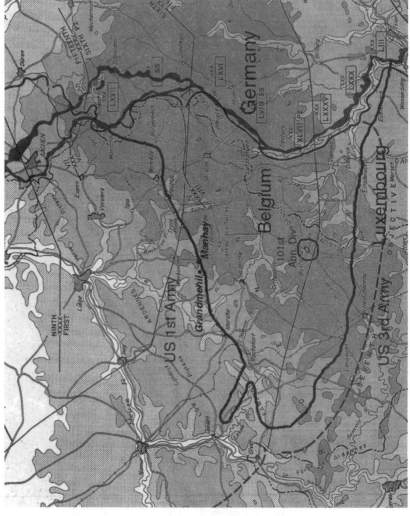

MAP 3

Battle of the Bulge, December 16–31, 1944. The dark line shows the limits of the German penetration during the Ardennes offensive. The 238th Engineer Combat Battalion supported the 82nd Airborne along the northern shoulder of the Bulge in the vicinity of Manhay and Grandmenil, Belgium, helping to repel a German armored attack the night of December 25, 1944. (Based on Map 1, The Ardennes Counteroffensive, in Hugh M. Cole, *The Ardennes: Battle of the Bulge* [Washington, D.C.: Government Printing Office, 1965].) See Appendixes F and G.

eral Eisenhower's statement that the Battle of Germany will be fought west of the Rhine, will be seen.

Don't you worry, honey, we'll take these Krauts. . . .

Do you remember last Christmas? You and mother at the Officers' Club in Claiborne? And then you and I sick in bed together the next day?

All I can do now is hope that we'll all be together safe and sound, you and I and David, before too much longer.

It's a helluva long war no matter which way you look at it.

I want you so much it hurts.

I love you. Larry

238th Engr. Combat Bn.
APO 230, NY, NY
Somewhere in Germany
20 December 1944

Hello Darling;

I know you're worried, so I'll get these few lines off. Things are hot and heavy, but the situation is in hand, never you fear.[18]

There's been no mail from you the past few days. I guess they're saving it up for me. I'll sure be glad when I get it, too.

Have you started to receive the stuff I sent you yet? Please let me know when you do.

How's David? The little fellow is almost three months old by now. They say babies really go into full bloom at about that age. If he was beautiful before, what must he be like now?

I'll bet he's really something special.

Well, there's not too much more. Don't worry too much and be a good girl.

I love you.

Your, Larry

---

[18] The Battle of the Bulge had been in progress for about four days and the Allies had only just begun to halt the German advance.

238th Engr. Combat Bn.
APO 230, NY, NY
Christmas Day 1944

My Darling;

Merry Christmas to you and David.

We've been rushed a bit these past few days, that's why I can only write you a measly V-mail.

I know you're worried, so I just want you to know that I'm still O.K. and I hope to stay that way.[19]

The situation is shaping up pretty well from where I sit, and I think Jerry is in for a big surprise.

We had a small turkey dinner today, but it sure wasn't anything like you can cook.

Darling, next Christmas I hope we'll be together again, and I'm going to sit down and eat your turkey and cranberry sauce till it runs out of my ears.

I love you as always.

Your, Larry

———————

238th Engr. Combat Bn.
APO 230, NY, NY
27 December 1944

Hello Sweetheart;

The past few days have been hectic, as you can well imagine. I'll bet you and everyone else back home has been hugging the radio and biting fingernails.

I can't say that I blame you—I've spent some anxious moments myself.

The Germans have apparently decided on a desperate gamble.

---

[19] During this period, the 238th Engineer Combat Battalion, acting in conjunction with the 82nd Airborne Division, constructed roadblocks around Manhay, Belgium on the northern flank of the Bulge and then defended them successfully against repeated enemy infantry and armored attacks by the 2nd Panzer SS Division. The purpose was to deny the attacking German army access to the main road that ran north from Manhay to Werbomont.

Faced with the inevitable loss of the war, they seem to be placing all their chips in the pile in the hope that they can either destroy a large part of our forces, or at least lengthen the war and make it more costly for us to win. Perhaps by prolonging the war they may have even hoped to get some kind of a "deal" worked out.

They hit us in a weak area with tremendous force, and it was inevitable that they should overrun our positions and make a deep penetration. But their breakthrough in no way compares with the one we achieved at St. Lô. They didn't panic us, we didn't lose our heads.

A great swirling battle is raging now—one which will go down in history as one of the great, decisive battles of all times. I say that because I believe from the way things are shaping up, that the German counter-offensive can be converted into a gigantic trap. I believe we can make even our massacre of the German 7th Army in the Falaise—Argentan pocket pale in comparison.

If things go right, this will be the last big battle on the Westfront. Because if we can trap what the Germans have here, it will become impossible for them to resist any large scale offensive successfully.

We've slowed them down now—and there's still some vicious engagements to come before the tide is completely turned. But we'll do it—never you fear.

Tell the folks back home, they can be proud of their boys. I've been in some shows the past few days that made me so proud I could have cried.

The best tribute to us that I've seen yet came from a famous Nazi paratroop leader, war idol of Nazi Germany, rescuer of Mussolini . . . , who led the airborne landings behind our lines.

He gave himself up in disgust after his units were shot to pieces and grudgingly he said, "Americans are too goddam obstinate."[20]

You bet we're obstinate. We've come a long way and buried a

---

[20] The Nazi paratrooper was Otto Skorzeny, the most renowned commando in the German Army. Among his exploits was the kidnapping of Benito Mussolini (1883–1945) on September 23, 1943. During the Battle of the Bulge, Skorzeny led a group of 500 English-speaking German soldiers, disguised as G.I.s, behind American lines where they initially caused great havoc. American forces captured many of Skorzeny's men and executed them as spies.

lot of dead—too much to have victory snatched from us when it was just within our grasp. . . .

I love you.

Your own, Larry

===

238th Engr. Combat Bn.
APO 230, NY, NY
Somewhere in Belgium
29 December 1944

Darling Mine;

Well, you can see now where I am.

Come back some, haven't we?

But, I think we've got them slowed up now, and I think also that the next few weeks may finally decide how long this damn thing is going to last over here.

If we can cut them off, and destroy what they've got in this salient, I believe the end will finally not be far off. And I'm hoping and praying that I live to see the day soon.

I hope you've been getting my mail more regularly than I have yours. It's been three weeks now that I haven't received a letter.

Be a good girl. All my love to you and David.

Your own, Larry

===

238th Engr. Combat Bn.
APO 230, NY, NY
Somewhere in Belgium
1 January 1945

My Darling;

I have just seen the new year in.

We're in a little Belgian town [Xhoris], and we had a party. There was wine and cake made by a fine old woman whose husband is a prisoner of the Germans. We sang songs—all the old loved ones that are part of the American people.

Everyone tried hard to have a good time.

But, I was sad.

My thoughts, as always, are with you.

What shall I tell you my dearest? How can I describe the terrible loneliness, the constant dull ache, the hunger for you that will never be satisfied until we have each other close again?

We have just passed through a trying period. The great German counterattack has been stopped. Whether temporarily or not remains to be seen. My faith in our ultimate victory rests unshaken. But how much longer before the beast is dead?

All through those nightmare days, I was with you and David Earl in spirit. I worried because I know with what anguish you'd read the headlines, how you'd pray for mail from me.

Grace, Grace I love you. . . .

The weather here is cold, with plenty of snow and ice on the ground. The scenery would be lovely, if we didn't have to fight a war in it.

I hope this is the year that really sees us victorious, finally. It's a grim job, with a lot of fighting ahead, but hang on and keep a stiff upper lip—they can't last forever.

Give David a hug for me.

I love you terribly, Larry

238th Engr. Combat Bn.
APO 230, NY, NY
Somewhere in Belgium
9 January 1945

Hello Darling;

I am now in one of the most beautiful sections of the Ardennes salient. Of course, it would be a lot more beautiful if viewed from the inside of a nice warm hotel room, and not from the seat of that diabolical invention called a jeep. Or, as the natives say, "a gyp."

We've been having a blinding snowstorm for the past couple of days, and in other times I might be tempted to wax eloquent describing the craggy mountains, the forests, the swiftly flowing streams, the picturesque villages covered with snow and looking like a master etching.

These days, though, as I travel the country trails inundated in snow, hunched and miserable with the cold, with a wet "derriere," my face cut by the howling wind and my ears filled with the rumble and thud of artillery—all I can think is, "Brother you can keep it. Take me back to New York."

I asked a Belgique the other day if they always had so much snow in the wintertime, and he said, "Oh, mais non, cette hiver est exceptionelle."

I had to laugh. When we fought in Normandy it rained most of the time, and the inhabitants of the bocage country said, "Exceptionelle." In France, it rained some more. Again, "Exceptionelle." In Germany rain, rain, rain—also "exceptionelle."

I asked the Belgique if he ever heard of the California Chamber of Commerce, but the crack was lost. American humor is a bewildering thing to these Europeans.

Say, darling, I never told you about my work. Here's a glimpse of a phase. It's not all that way—just the reconnaissance end of it sometimes.

The Colonel calls me in and takes me to one of those large-scale military maps that always look so impressive in the movies.

"We're scheduled to build a Class 40 bridge right here," he says pointing to a spot on the map where a main highway is shown to be crossing a river.

A class 40 bridge means it will take loads up to and including 40 British long tons.

I take a look at the map and then remark brightly, "Colonel, we haven't advanced that far yet, according to the latest reports."

"I know," he says, "but we should have passed that point by now."

"Lovely," thinks I. Aloud, "Well, sir, I'll see if I can make it."

So out I go and mount my trusty jeep, and take off for the area to be reconnoitered.

Pretty soon there are the unmistakable signs of the front— wrecked and burning vehicles, dead men in all the shattered and grotesque attitudes of violent death, littered equipment both American and German, and the marrow-chilling symphony of small-arms fire, high-velocity artillery and the roar of planes.

Better go easy now, thinks I: Better see what the hell's what. According to my map we're only a few hundred yards from the prospective bridge.

We see a couple of infantry doggies sitting at a machine-gun which is trained down the road in the direction we're traveling.

"Hey Soldier, how far down is the front?"

With a kind of snicker in his voice one answers, "You're just about at it now, Sir."

"Anything between us and that bridge that's out down there?"

"Well," says the gunner rubbing his week old stubble, "I dunno."

"Look, I've got to go down and take a look at that bridge site. How's about covering me in case anything comes up?"

"O.K. Sir."

So, I go down there feeling like a damn duck in a shooting gallery and proceed with my reconnaissance.

I look at the abutments. Measure the approaches. Look at the stream, sound it, gauge its speed. Tie a stone to a string and throw it across so I can measure the width.

"Crack." A rifle shot.

Some sonofabitch of a Krauthead is shooting at me from the woods across the river. I must look silly as hell to him, fooling around up there with a damn tape measure.

I dive for some cover. Take out my notebook and jot down my findings methodical as an Englishman and his tea. I take another peek to check on some detail. Another shot, this time it throws dirt on me. Close.

I yell back for the infantry gunners to throw a few bursts over me in the direction of the shots and tell them I'm going to run off to an angle so they can get a clear field of fire, and then come on in under cover of their gun.

The trick works, and I sprint the 200 yards in short dashes, from cover to cover, in remarkably short time.

I thank the boys for their help. One of them says, "Helluva job you got there, Sir."

"Same to you, son," says I. To my driver, "Give 'er the gun. Let's get the hell out of here."

That night a bridge goes in.[21] The next morning tanks are rolling across. . . .

Well, darling, I'm about running out of gab. Give our son an extra-special hug. And for you, all my love

Your own, Larry

══════════

238th Engr. Combat Bn.
APO 230, NY, NY
Somewhere in Belgium
16 January 1945

Darling;

. . . We're still slugging away over here. And it's still bitterly cold. Matter of fact, the place looks like pictures of the Russian front.

We've handed Jerry a solid trouncing, and I hope we'll be able to follow it up with a smashing drive.

The news from the Russian front is encouraging, and there isn't a man over here who isn't rooting for them.[22] It'll be a great day when we can meet the "Tovarische" in Berlin, and drink a couple of beers to the death of German Nazism.

And, if I can come home to you and our baby soon after that I'll be a mighty happy guy.

But, there's still a lot of fighting before that happens. . . .

Too many armchair generals had the thing in the bag. We have no illusions over here—it's costing us blood and years of our youth and happiness. But I venture to say that the ordinary Joe in

---

[21] The bridge was built near Stoumont, Belgium on the Ambleve River sometime between January 3 and 7.

[22] After stopping the German advance in Stalingrad in January 1943 and Kursk in August 1943, Soviet troops began their bloody offensive toward Berlin. During the crisis of the Battle of the Bulge, Western governments asked Josef Stalin (1879–1953) to help take pressure off of them by stepping up the Russian offensive in Eastern Europe. Stalin responded accordingly.

the foxhole has a closer picture of what it takes to win the war than most of the so-called experts.

They can sit on their big fat "rusty-dusties" and talk impressively about what's wrong with our leaders, our "intelligence," our tactics, our weapons—and then they can go to sleep in their nice warm beds and feel like intellectual giants.

But we have a calm confidence in our leaders and our ability to win. And we know that General Ike hit the nail on the head when he said, "To get peace, you've got to fight like hell." . . .

The experts can keep on moving vast armies over the table-cloths of restaurants and night clubs. We'll keep on burying our dead and doing our talking with the plane, the tank, the artillery, and the M1 rifle in the hands of the suffering, bitterly miserable and plodding dogface.

And when we win, by Christ, nobody better sell us short!

Well, darling, I hope I get a letter from you soon. I'm dying to see those pictures of David, and I hope you're in them too.

Take it easy and remember I love you. Larry

———————

238th Engr. Combat Bn.
APO 230, NY, NY
Somewhere in Belgium
22 January 1945

My Darling;

Our David Earl was four months old today. Four months old in the midst of earth-shaking events.

Some day I hope I'll be able to tell him about how his early birthdays looked to me on the battlefields of Belgium and Germany. About how we smashed and hacked away the last flowers of the German Army in the wild, snowdrifted, forest of the Ardennes. About how we stood like our forefathers at Bunker Hill, the Alamo, Gettysburg, and Chateau Thierry. And how we added among the other bloody names of this war that of Bastogne and the Ardennes.

And I'll tell him how we hoped and prayed for continued success when the stupendous Red tidal wave burst out of Poland and swept into Silesia, pointed directly for Berlin, and swirled in to the home of the warlords—East Prussia. How we listened to the communiques with unstinted admiration, and heralded each new advance of our Soviet comrades-in-arms with shouts of glee.

And I'll try to tell him how precious his heritage of liberty is, and how jealously it should be guarded—because it was won at such an appalling price. How millions of little people died on their feet rather than live on their knees—to paraphrase "La Pasionaria." . . .[23]

Give my love to our son, and tell him his daddy would like to see him.

I love you, darling.

Your own, Larry

---

[23] "La Pasionaria" is a reference to Dolores Ibarurri (1895–1989), the revolutionary political theorist, champion of women's emancipation, antifascist, and Spanish Communist Party leader. When the Spanish Civil War began on July 18, 1936 Ibarurri gave an address over Radio-Madrid in which she stated: "It is better to die on your feet than to live on you knees." Her address stirred freedom-lovers around the world and rallied the Spanish people to heroic acts of resistance. She was an international figure who symbolized the steadfastness of the Spanish Republic.

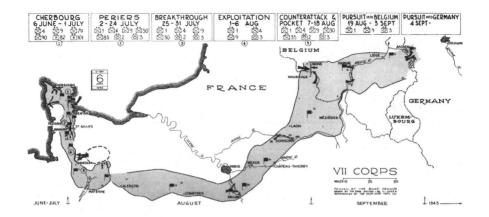

MERRY CHRISTMAS

HEADQUARTERS VII CORPS

Season's Greetings *from* Germany

With all my love,

Larry

HAPPY NEW YEAR

VII Corps Christmas card in 1944, showing the major campaigns from June to September 1944 and the route taken by the U.S. VII Corps from Utah Beach to Aachen.

Battle of the Bulge—Ardennes, from December 1944 to January 1945. Upper left photo: Lawrence Cane in camouflage uniform; Upper right photo: Lawrence Cane and driver with Nazi Mark V "Tiger" tank knocked out by minefields laid by Company C of 238th Engineer Combat Battalion near Manhay, Belgium, December 25, 1944; Lower photo: Lawrence Cane, reconnaissance, Liernieux, Belgium (see letters of 18 December and 25 December 1944 and 16 March 1945).

A. Bridges built by the 238th Engineer Combat Battalion. Upper photo: Seine River, Evry Pont Bourg, just north of Corbeil, France, August 27, 1944, floating steel treadway bridge (see letter of 27 August 1944). "JEAN" was the code word used to designate the 238th Engineer Combat Battalion; Lower photo: Meuse River, Namur, Belgium, September 6, 1944, 564-foot steel treadway bridge (see letter of 6 September 1944).

B. Bridges built by the 238th Engineer Combat Battalion. Upper photo: Roer River, near Birkesdorf in Düren, Germany, February 23 to 24, 1945, floating steel treadway bridge built by Company C under direct enemy fire (see letter of 28 February 1945); Lower photo: Rhine River near Bonn, Germany, March 21, 1945, 1,320-foot steel treadway bridge built by Company C of the 238th in collaboration with its sister battalion, 237th Engineer Combat Battalion, in record time of 10 hours, 17 minutes. Sign reads "The Beer Bridge. Shortest Route to CBI" (China, Burma, India). VII Corps Commander, General J. Lawton Collins, promised each man a beer if the bridge were completed in less than 10 hours (see letter of 19 March 1945).

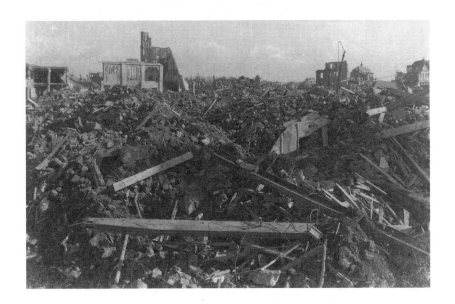

Germany in ruins. Upper photo: Kirkenhausen, Germany, March 1945; Lower photo: Cologne, Germany, March 1945. Sign placed by 238th Engineer Combat Battalion reads: "Gebt Mir Fünf Jahre Und Ihr Werdet Deutschland Nicht Wiederkennen" Adolf Hitler; "Give me five years and you will not recognize Germany" JEAN S. (see letter of 6 March 1945).

Liberation of the Dora-Mittelbau extermination camp, April 1945. Able-bodied men from nearby Nordhausen, Germany were brought to the camp at gunpoint by the U.S. Army and forced to bury the dead (see letter of 15 April 1945).

WHEN YOU MEET THE RUSSIANS

THE first Russian soldier you meet will come from one of the 16 countries in the USSR and he may be tall and blonde or short and dark. He will be a great guy for discipline, and you'll find he will salute on the slightest provocation. He received elementary military training in school between the ages of 12 and 15. If he went to a technical or high school, he got three more years of part-time training in the Red's equivalent of our ROTC.

Russian women serve in some branches of the army and most reports describe them as pleasant but strictly business. Unlike our Wacs they participate in combat, and Soviet girls have gained fame as pilots and guerrilla fighters.

Russian equipment, supplemented by our lease-lend material, is regarded as good by our military authorities. Most doughboys will prefer their M-1 to the Russian rifles, but Soviet heavy artillery and tanks are said by some to be tops. Their heavily armed, low-flying fighter planes have had spectacular successes against tanks.

The advance of the Axis stopped first at Moscow, and Gen. Douglas MacArthur called the Red defense "the greatest military achievement in all history." Soviet soldiers are as cocky about their accomplishments as Americans and are equally gusty about drinking, singing and dancing. They call each other "Tovaritch," and their old man is known as "Tovaritch Stalin."

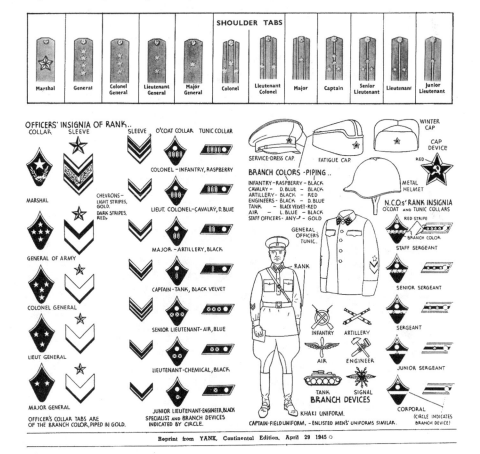

Reprint from YANK, Continental Edition, April 29 1945

Leaflet distributed to U.S. troops, April 1945 (see letter of 25 April 1945).

Liberated Russian prisoners of war, May Day celebration, 1945. Beneath the portraits of Stalin and Marshal Zhukov, the banner reads "Happy 1st of May! Hail the Red Army and the United English–American Forces. Death to the German Occupants!" (see letter of 1 May 1945).

238th Engineer Combat Battalion Headquarters Staff, Eisleben, Germany, May 1945. First row: Capt. William S. Sweitzer, S-4 (Supply); Maj. Martin F. Massoglia, Exec.; Lt. Col. Jay P. Dawley, Commanding; Maj. William N. Poe, S-3 (Operations); Capt. Arvo J. Ryoti, S-2 (Intelligence); Second row: Capt. George W. Cline, Asst. Div. Engineer; Capt. Raymond D. Zimont, Battalion Surgeon; 1st Lt. William F. Rule, Adjutant; Capt. Sydney M. Allinson, Battalion Dentist; 1st Lt. Lawrence Cane, Asst. S-2; 3rd row: Warrant Officer; 1st Lt. Stanley Bass, Asst. S-3.

Counter Intelligence Corps assignment, Lawrence Cane, occupation duty in Eisleben, Germany, May 1945 (see letter of 4 May 1945).

Back home. Capt. Lawrence Cane with his son, David, age 16 months.

Anti-Vietnam War march on Washington. Lawrence Cane (right) with David Cane, November 15, 1969. Button reads, "Volunteers [of the International Brigades] for Peace."

6

The End of the Third Reich:
Belgium, Germany, and France
January 27–May 8, 1945

238th Engr. Combat Bn.
APO 230, NY, NY
Somewhere in Belgium
27 January 1945

Hello Darling;

For a long time now I've been promising myself to sit down and have another long range discussion with you about Germany.

With the Eastern front cut to ribbons by the great Red Army, and with us getting set for the K.O.—anything can happen. . . .

And as we storm on towards the destruction of our enemies, I think that we're also beginning to realize that Peace, as well as war, must be <u>organized and waged</u>.

Without an alert and wise organization, without a constant sensitivity and reaction to threats whatsoever the source, Peace will remain a mere subject for babbling at cocktail parties, or brave but ineffectual struggle by small groups of people. It will remain what it has always been—a desperate and futile wish in the hearts of men. . . .

The first thing I want to get across, is despite the fact that I've fought Nazis and Nazi ideas all along the terrible road from Madrid to these last battles that face us, I am not one of those who offer the seemingly easy but impossible solution of, "Kill the bastards—physically and materially."

I want to see Germany handled so that some day—not tomorrow or maybe even ten years but, certainly a generation—Germany will be able to take her place in the family of nations. Her position not one of sword-rattler, but a country in which a man's fundamental dignity is recognized, and which has passed from the category of criminal to reformed member of society.

How?

First, the repressive measures.

The surrender, in toto or piecemeal, or the destruction of the German Wehrmacht in the field does not automatically end the war. It ends the largest phase of it, which most of us have been concerned with these past few years. From there, it takes a new turn.

The Nazi State, and all its organs must be destroyed.

That not only entails decrees, but must be backed up with the force at our disposal.

Since a State, any State, is an organization of people and is run by men, the destruction of that State—to be complete—will necessarily entail the destruction of its leaders, or a good percentage of them.

All war criminals, and there must be a list long enough to fill the Encyclopedia Britannica, must be apprehended—be they dumbkopf babykillers or shrewd industrialists. They must be brought to trial, their crimes made public, and then executed or imprisoned for long terms.

I prefer shooting—but perhaps that's because I've done my arguing with Nazis at the point of a gun for so long.

All attempts at guerrilla warfare, sabotage—whether of the mind or of the more evident variety—must be ruthlessly suppressed.

Some people might be squeamish about more blood-letting. But, the surgeon spills blood when he cuts out a cancer. And Nazism is a malignant, tumescent growth which has damn near destroyed civilization.

What else?

Well, I think we'll have to break up the political conglomeration known as the Third Reich. . . .

Broadly speaking, I think that the division should take this form.

Austria becomes Austria again—and not Germany. Occupied by a military commission for a transition period to be determined by history and their own development, and eventually made independent.

That's not a hard one to take because Austria was a political entity for a long time before Hitler took over, and I dare say most Austrians would want their independence once more.

The next split I believe should take place is East Prussia to Poland.

I know that historically East Prussia is German, even before the emergence of Germany as a modern unified state. I know also that such a move is fraught with possibilities for future discontent.

But I think the times require it.

First, because a strong, independent Poland that is shaping up for the future must be economically stable.

While there are no really large industries in East Prussia—there are ports, vital to the well-being of any nation's economic existence.

Second, because continuing Polish unity requires compensation for land that will be part of Soviet Russia.

The Polish Committee in London can be very easily told to blow it out their barracks bags, and the Polish people will be behind it.

And thirdly, the vital interests of the Soviet Union, our future friendly next-door neighbor require it.

What about the people of East Prussia?

We can give those that want the honor, transportation to postwar Germany.

I know that we are creating a new minority when we do this. But that doesn't necessarily result in a revolt for national liberation.

The French in Canada have been calling themselves Canadians for a long time. The Flemish of Belgium call themselves Belgians.

With proper handling, some day East Prussians may call themselves Polish.

The Sudeten lands back to Czechoslovakia—of course. With the same opportunity to those who ask for it, to go back to Germany.

What have we got left?

Roughly, a Germany that encompasses old Prussia, Bavaria, and Baden.

Have we destroyed the German nation? Not at all. The Nazis might think so, but I don't.

The next thing to consider is German economy.

Germany is the industrial heart of continental Europe.

Now, should we destroy this industry, and make of the Germans a nation of "potato-pickers" as Goebbels puts it?[1]

I say no.

But I do say there should be some great changes, commensurate with the kind of country Germany must emerge.

With a reduction in size, with the urge for empire no longer the dominant idea—German economy will become agrarian as well as industrial, maybe 50–50.

This natural trend must be channelized and given impetus and direction in the postwar plan.

How do we do that? One way is this.

It stands to reason that there's going to be a lot of machines lying around unused in Germany after the war. Instead of letting them gather rust, they can be used to pay part of the inevitable reparations to the Soviet Union, France, and other countries. There, they can be used to rebuild what has been destroyed.

Enough should be left to Germany to furnish the fundamental commodities necessary to her own population, and rebuild her own shattered utilities and cities. But absolutely no production for war, and very little luxuries for a long time.

And now, what about democracy. How do we transform the minds of a people traditionally warlike. How can we change the animal philosophy of a whole younger generation.

Much of the answer lies in the revamping of the whole educational system. That doesn't mean only the schools but the press, radio, movies and all organs of propaganda. They must be given a "democratic" direction.

But, that is not enough. The Germans will have to learn the democratic way of life by <u>practicising</u> it.

The fact that I believe that there must be a complete military occupation, negates any repetition of the Weimar republic. We just can't say to the Germans, "O.K. have yourselves an election and vote in a government, and you'll have democracy."

---

[1] Joseph Goebbels (1897–1945) was chief of propaganda for the Nazi Party. In this reported comment about making Germany a nation of "potato-pickers," Goebbels was parodying Morgenthau's proposed plan for a postwar pastoral, agricultural Germany.

No, the practice must begin in the fundamental economic and social organizations of the people.

It can start with such things as voting by secret ballot for administration in the countless small towns and villages, and then the cities. By the organization of democratic trade unions once more. . . .

Other organizations to satisfy economic, cultural, and regional needs can spring up. Other rudimentary democratic processes can be nurtured.

As the years go by the chances are good that the Germans will get the <u>feel</u> of democracy.

This process can be closely observed, and military measures can decrease in severity in direct proportion to the growth of democratic consciousness of the people—until the day arrives when the last soldiers can leave Germany.

There are a great many other things that will inevitably enter into the postwar arrangements for Germany. There are details of all kinds which are for history to write.

But these are my opinions about the biggest problems which will have to be solved. They may not be the correct solutions. It's pretty hard to think clearly about the future when you spend your time staying alive at the front. And when you have very little opportunity to exchange ideas, either by reading or discussion.

And don't think that I believe that the world will live happily ever after, merely as a result of the correct solution of the German problem.

That's only part of the job.

The living standard of the steel worker in Youngstown, Ohio, the well-being of a Chinese peasant standing barefoot in his flooded rice-paddies, the liberty enjoyed by the Untouchable Indian, the educational facilities at the disposal of a Negro share-cropper, are part and parcel of the problem of maintaining the Peace.

And remember, all these things must be handled by a world predominantly capitalist, a system which contains within itself the seeds of war.

Great objectives can be achieved, yes. But, it'll be a fight every foot of the way, with dangers on all sides.

There you have it, darling. The longest letter I have ever written you.

Tell me what you think about it.

The time is rapidly approaching when our dreams of being together again may be realized soon.

I am hoping and praying that I live to see the day.

I love you as always. A big hug to our son.

Your own, Larry

238th Engr. Combat Bn.
APO 230, NY, NY
Somewhere in Belgium
31 January 1945

Darling;

. . . The admiration of G.I. Joe for G.I. Ivan is boundless. It's something that's going to have great implications after the war. Because this feeling of Joe's is going to tide America over some rough spots that certain people will be bound to create.

We heard Hitler last night. What a pitiful speech for the would-be ruler of the world!

I think the Russians will take Berlin, but barring an internal crackup, the war will continue for awhile more. We'll probably have to bust through across the Rhine on a wide front and link up with the Red Army before she'll be over.

Of course, with panic spreading in Germany, demoralization and disorganization will inevitably follow. Anything can happen—but we can't count on it. All we can depend on is the force of our arms. We must not under-estimate the monster that is Nazism.

However long it takes, the Red offensive has brought the day of our homecoming closer.

No matter how short it is, though, it'll be too long for me. . . .

They don't have Valentine cards over here, Bub.

But, remember the first one I ever sent you? I said: "I'm all yours—hook, line, and sinker."

Still goes, darling.

I love you. Larry

238th Engr. Combat Bn.
APO 230, NY, NY
Somewhere in Germany—Again
4 February 1945

My Darling;

We've come back [to Eschweiler, Germany]. This time we're going to make it stick. If the war in Europe isn't over by Spring, it won't be because we didn't try.

Believe you me, I'll be damn glad when it is.

I miss you darling, miss you so terribly much. It's been such a long time, and without you I'm just half of me.

You know, when most writers try to describe war, they attempt to capture the horror and terror of battle. Yet, somehow, that's not always the worst thing.

The physical hardships, the suffering, the nervous strain is something you can get away from when you get away from the front.

You get to a place where there are people—no matter how wretched and miserable the war has made them—the sound of artillery is faint and far off, or not heard at all, there is no mad spitting of small arms fire, you get a roof over your head—even if it is a ruined house or a stinking barn—you get some hot chow, a shower, a shave, a change of clothes, and physically you're comfortable. Death is a little farther away.

But yearning for the one you love, the deep all-pervading ache—that stays. It even becomes more intense during rest periods.

I miss you. Miss the smell of your hair, your head on my shoulder, the feel of your body at night. I miss the sound of your laugh, the perfume behind your ears, your warm lips under mine. I miss your biscuits, the way you walk in to a room, the desk crammed full of your junk. I miss our constant exchange of thoughts and ideas, our growing up together, our dreaming of the future. And I wish I could see and hold our son—part of both of us. . . .

I love you as always.

Your own, Larry

238th Engr. Combat Bn.
APO 230, NY, NY
Somewhere in Germany
15 February 1945

Hello My Darling;

The last few days have been wonderful for me as far as mail is concerned. I've received a whole slew from you, and one from Mark, my Pop, Alan Wolfson who's in Paris the lucky stiff, and Jim Greene.

All of the letters rave about you and the baby. Mark and my Pop say you're wonderful. Alan and Jim say you're more beautiful than ever. And all of them say the baby is the most gorgeous, wonderful, etc. etc. they've ever seen.

Mark says he'd like to have a son like him. And Alan, who reminds me that he's a proud Papa himself, says he's never seen a kid like our David.

From the pictures you sent, I got a pretty good idea what he looks like—in a blackout, anyway. Darling, I love you, but you can't take pictures indoors worth a damn.

I was saddened to hear about Bottcher[2] and Saully Wellman.[3] I hope Saully pulls through O.K.

Funny thing about Saully. I was with his outfit during the Bulge fight and I had a hunch he was around somewhere. Never did have a chance to look good for him—we were kinda busy.

---

[2] Herman Bottcher (1909–1944) emigrated to the United States from Germany in 1931 and applied for American citizenship. He quit his college studies in California to fight with the Abraham Lincoln Battalion in Spain. When he returned to the U.S., he learned that his application for citizenship had been revoked because of his participation in the Spanish Civil War. Following Pearl Harbor, Bottcher attempted to enlist in the Army, but he first had to convince Army officials that he was an acceptable candidate even though his application for American citizenship had been revoked. He was sent to the South Pacific where he was known as the "one-man Army of Buna." While fighting in the South Pacific, he finally received his citizenship papers. He led a guerrilla unit for 57 days behind Japanese lines. He died in combat on Leyte on December 30, 1944, after a mortar shell blew off his leg. He was twice awarded the Distinguished Service Cross.

[3] Saul Wellman (1912–) was the political commissar of the Mackenzie-Papineau Battalion.

Been reading about the Big Three conference in Yalta. Needless to say, I'm enthusiastic about the results.[4]

I'm feeling a little smug secretly about my own opinions which I wrote you about just before the conference. I hit the nail on the head pretty much, didn't I? (Cane you goddam boaster).

We're still waiting—but hold your breath honey. There's a big ratrace acoming, and I'm saving a bottle of Scotch (Yes, we get a ration of scotch each month) to swap for a bottle of vodka with the first Russians I see.

Oh, my back, what a day that'll be!

The way the Russians are going these days, by the time we get across the Rhine there'll be nothing in the German rear but the Reds.

You should hear the Kraut radio broadcasts these days. They call us the Anglo-American Bolshevik gangsters. And they're screaming about the results of the Big Three meeting like mad dogs. When we break loose, they'll be milling around like the inmates of a nuthouse on a rampage.

Well, Bub, be a good girl and don't worry too much about me. I love you. A kiss for David Earl.

Your own, Larry

238th Engr. Combat Bn.
APO 230, NY, NY
Somewhere in Germany
28 February 1945

Hello Darling;

We're on the move again, and I'm just grabbing a few minutes to let you know that I'm still O.K.

Was in on the Roer crossing, and while the papers may write

---

[4] Churchill, Roosevelt, and Stalin met in Yalta in the Crimea from February 4 to 11, 1945 to plan for the postwar world. Although Cane expressed enthusiasm for the Yalta Conference, the decisions that were reached, especially concerning Poland, Yugoslavia, and Greece, served as the basis for the rigid political divisions between Eastern and Western Europe that occurred over the next half century.

about the doughs and the tanks, it was strictly an engineer show. We ferried the assault waves, cleared the mines, and then put the bridges in that crossed the armor.[5]

It wasn't exactly a picnic.

We're making good progress now and I sure hope we can keep it up.

It feels good to be moving again, because every mile forward is a mile nearer home.

The Roer's behind us, the Rhine's in front of us, and the end is in sight.

I love you.

Yours, Larry

———

238th Engr. Combat Bn.
APO 230, NY, NY
Somewhere in Germany
2 March 1945

My Darling;

. . . I guess you've been following the news pretty avidly these days. We've been making some nice headway, and it's only the beginning.[6]

One of the interesting things about the past few days is the fact that we've been overrunning towns that civilians are still in. We evacuate them as fast as we can root them out and as their legs will carry them (we waste no transport at the front). But the thing I find interesting is their reactions.

At first, of course, they're terrified because the Nazi propaganda has painted us as "Bolshevik gangsters." But when we go right

---

[5] The 238th Engineer Combat Battalion supported the crossing of the Roer River by the U.S. First and Ninth Armies, operating against fortification systems on the far shore and the industrial section of Duren known as Birkesdorf. Bridges were built under intense machine gun and artillery fire as well as enemy bombing. American armor began crossing the bridges on the morning of February 24.

[6] The battalion supported the 104th Infantry in the assault crossing of the Erft Canal. Just ahead lay the last major obstacle to the invasion of the German heartland, the Rhine River.

on about our business fighting the war, and just simply ignore them and any overtures that any of them might make, they just look as if they can't figure it out.

We herd 'em up and send them to the rear, and pay them no mind as they string along the roads—a wretched, bewildered motley representation of the Herrenvolk.

They are puzzled and don't know what to expect. I believe some of them would be relieved if we just did something, either kicked them in the pants or said hello or something.

As it is, the cold shoulder treatment must be giving them the Willies.

Another thing, when they see our endless columns of tanks, guns, trucks, and motorized or marching infantry, our planes roaring overhead, they seem as is if they are simply overwhelmed. They seem as if they can't believe it, that it's a dream, that it just can't be true.

But, it's true allright. They're getting some of the stuff they dished out—with interest.

Certainly going to be a ruined nation when this war is over.

Well, hon, better catch up on my shuteye (haven't had any for 48 hours).

All my love to you and David.

Your own, Larry

———————

238th Engr. Combat Bn.
APO 230, NY, NY
Somewhere in Germany
6 March 1945

My Darling;

Today was a rather notable day. I went into a very historic city which you've probably read about by the time you get this letter.[7] We're still fighting for it, but it will soon be ours.

———————

[7] The city was Cologne on the Rhine River.

The place is a shambles.

There were a surprising number of civilians around, and while they didn't cheer and give us the V–sign, some of them gave us hesitant smiles and tried waving—all of which was ignored.

My first impression of these people tells me they're beaten. For them there is no "Mit Hitler zum Sieg." And their slogan, "Trotz terror, Ungebrochen," like most other Nazi garbage is a lie. For they <u>are</u> broken.

While their soldiers were off looting and plundering the rest of Europe, the war was a wonderful thing to them. Now when they themselves are homeless, or forced to live like pigs, and their country shattered, they think it's outrageous + they're quitting.

Too damn bad about them.

Another thing I've been seeing is the liberation of the slaves.

Thousands of Poles, Russians, Ukrainians, Czechs, Frenchmen, Belgians, Dutchmen, Byelo-Russians, White Russians, Norwegians, etc. Women, children, men old and young—all trekking towards the Displaced Persons Centers which have been established to handle them.

They seem happy in a stunned sort of way. Unbelievable but true. The hated German is no longer over them. They are going home. Can you imagine? Free and going home.

The tales they have are absolutely fantastic. The women especially tell stories of German depravity which are so shocking they are hard to believe, until you see the truth in their eyes.

Talk about oppression and misery. Christ! We Americans are lucky that we hardly know the meaning of the words.

Since my last letter to you, hon, I've become the acting S-2 [intelligence officer] of the battalion. If everything goes O.K., there'll probably be a promotion for me in a couple of months. Here's hoping I do allright in my new job.

I've been getting a big kick out of showing off David's pictures. Everyone agrees that he's a beautiful baby. They all ask me how come I got a kid like that, and I tell them his looks are a present from his mother.

Gosh, darling, I'm sure anxious to get home—and that's putting it mildly. It'll be a great day when I can hold you in my arms again, and kiss you, and tell you over and over how much I love you.

Your own, Larry

======

238th Engr. Combat Bn.
APO 230, NY, NY
Somewhere in Germany
9 March 1945

Hello Darling;

. . . Well, the big news for us is that we've got people across the Rhine. As usual, the 1st Army was first again.[8] It wasn't in the cards, and I believe we were about as surprised to get across as the Krauts were to hear about it. . . .

The war, darling, is in its final stages over here. It shouldn't be long now—really not.

These Krauts are beat—the people are beat—they've had enough. They're a dead nation, and what's going on now is post-mortem convulsions.

You should see how miserable these Herrenvolk look as they pick their way through the ruins, like alley-cats over a garbage heap.

It can't be too soon for this Joe.

I love you so terribly, and want so much to be with you and the baby.

Good night for now, sweetheart.

All my love.

Your, Larry

======

[8] Units of Combat Command B of the 9th Armored Division, assigned to occupy the west bank of the Rhine at Remagen, southeast of Bonn and Co-logne, arrived in the city on March 7 to find one of the railroad bridges across the river still intact. They rushed across under enemy fire before German engineers could detonate the charges which had been set on the bridge. The bridge-head was rapidly exploited by the First Army.

238th Engr. Combat Bn.
APO 230, NY, NY
Somewhere in Germany
12 March 1945

Bub Darling;

. . . We're on the Rhine right now from north of Coblenz to Holland, and across it at one spot.

This one crossing has probably changed all our plans for the conduct of the offensive in the West.

As for the fear that some people had about guerrilla warfare in Germany—that was wishful thinking on the part of the Nazi leaders. Germans are not Russians or Frenchmen or Yugoslavs or Greeks. They have no fierce pride in freedom because they never have really been free. And their Volksturm, romantic as the name may sound, now is busy cleaning streets for us and falling over themselves in their eagerness to show us that they're really "good" people and never did like those nasty Nazis anyway. . . .

I love you.

Yours, Larry

———————

238th Engr. Combat Bn
APO 230, NY, NY
Somewhere in Germany
16 March 1945

Darling Mine;

. . . Say, hon, . . . did you see the Feb. 5th issue of Life? It has a pictorial story entitled "Last Days of the Ardennes Battle." There's one picture that shows five tanks knocked out near a road junction, and explains that they were spotted by planes and knocked out by artillery.

Well, the story is all wrong. Those tanks were knocked out at 1100 PM Christmas eve, when it was so dark you couldn't see your hand in front of your face, much less observe from a plane— and our battalion got those tanks.

The road you see in the picture runs between the towns of Manhay and Grandmenil, Belgium—Manhay being at the top and Grandmenil just off the horizon.

We laid a minefield in those fields to the right of the road, and just to the entrance of Grandmenil we had placed a roadblock, manned by a platoon from my old "C" company.

When the tank column came down the road to attack Grandmenil, the men on the block opened fire. The Krauts, seeking to deploy around them, ran off the road and one after another were disabled by our mines—A neat little job which went off exactly as planned.

I felt impelled to tell you about that because it's one of the many things you never hear about. Combat Engineers, and my outfit in particular, have been in on so many big events in this war, and have received such little credit.

Not that it matters too much, but when you do a good job and lose people doing it, you like to get at least a pat on the back.

The best tribute to combat engineers I've ever seen was a Sad Sack cartoon in Yank. It was labeled "Armored Drive," and it depicts a road choked with tanks and armored vehicles all following Sad Sack who's plodding along wearily with a mine-detector. . . . [9]

This is such a long, damn war, and we've missed so much of the best years of our lives together. But, if the sacrifice will guarantee our son, and his brothers and sisters (am I too ambitious?) the opportunity to grow up without fear of the same old insane story, I guess it's worth it.

Take care of yourself, Darling.

I love you with all my soul.

Your, Larry

---

[9] Sergeant George Baker (1915–) created the Sad Sack cartoon during World War II to depict what Army life was like for the bewildered civilian trying to be a soldier.

238th Engr. Combat Bn.
APO 230, NY, NY
Somewhere in Germany
19 March 1945

Hello Darling;

The last time I wrote to you I was still on the west bank of the Rhine. Now, I'm somewhere in the bridgehead on the east bank—the pay-dirt side.[10]

As you can well imagine, there's a lot of engineer work in this operation. The Rhine is a real river, even by American standards.

It's pretty noisy here just now, with our big guns on the other side of the river firing just over our heads and making an infernal racket.

We've put our headquarters in what was formerly the District Nazi Party Center. It's a beautiful setup—big rooms, beds, easy chairs, and we've even picked up a generator and have electric lights.[11]

We sure fight this war in style whenever we get the chance. . . .

Enclosed you'll find a clipping from the Stars and Stripes. I think you'll find it highly interesting. Especially since I can verify it as having seen it with my own eyes.[12]

As in everything else in this Theater of Operations, the good old First Army is first in this too. It's an outfit that will occupy a proud niche in American military history, and in the world's fight against Nazism.

I've had the rare privilege to fight in the International Brigade and the First U.S. Army (the crack Seventh Corps, no less). Not

---

[10] On March 17, 1945 the 238th Engineer Combat Battalion crossed the Rhine, arriving at Konigswinter, a few kilometers to the northwest of Remagen. Shortly thereafter, Company C participated in the construction of a 1320-foot steel treadway bridge in the record time of ten hours and seventeen minutes.

[11] This turned out to be the home of Dr. Robert Ley, leader of the Deutsche Arbeits Front, which had been responsible for the destruction of trade unions in Nazi Germany.

[12] The article in *The Stars and Stripes*, dated March 18, 1945, was headlined, "Negroes Join Front Units As Infantry." The article emphasized that "White and Negro infantrymen are fighting shoulder to shoulder against the Germans." It went on to state that "this break with traditional Army policy of separation of units according to race became a reality with the assignment of Negro platoons to rifle companies of infantry divisions of the First and Seventh Armies."

too many men have been fortunate enough to have such an opportunity.

I hope to live to see the day when I can tell our David a little bit about how dearly his liberties were purchased, and maybe make him sit open-mouthed at some tall tales of "derring-do."

Be a good girl darling. Take good care of yourself. Never mind about the gefüllte fish—I'll settle for some real sardines if you can get them.

And remember I love you always.

Your, Larry

====

238th Engr. Combat Bn.
APO 230, NY, NY
Somewhere in Germany
24 March 1945

Hello Darling;

I'll bet you're holding your breath these days, listening to the radio and following the headlines which announce our spectacular successes on the Westfront.

For us too there is an electric feeling in the air—a feeling that Victory is within our grasp now.

There are unmistakable signs of disintegration beginning to appear in the West.

I'm moved to take out my crystal ball and predict that the collapse of the German Armies in the West will come in the next few weeks.

Our meeting with the Russians somewhere in the center of Germany is not too far away.

I wish I could tell you some of the things I know. In my job now, I get a lot of information that will probably never even appear in the history books, let alone the papers. That's why some of the things I've predicted have turned out to be true.

Believe me, short of some kind of evil miracle, the Krauts are finished. . . .

Gee, darling, I'm a lonely guy. I'm in the midst of tremendous events, the things I've believed in and fought for so long are near achievement. I should be excited and happy, I suppose. But, the deepest emotion I feel is intense longing for you.

As long as we are not together, I shall never be happy.

I love you, my wife, my comrade, my sweetheart.

Your, Larry

238th Engr. Combat Bn.
APO 230, NY, NY
Somewhere in Germany
5 April 1945

Darling;

Tonight I'm feeling kinda blue—and peeved too. The mail came in and everyone in the outfit got an armful of letters. But, me, I didn't get a stinking one.

Not only that, I haven't received anything from you in over a week. And what I did receive up to then was some dehydrated V-mails. . . .

One of the things I used to wonder about was where the hell did the Germans get all their soldiers? I know now. I've seen thousands upon thousands of released prisoners of war and "slave-laborers"—Russians, French, Poles, Belgians—trekking down the roads.

These are the people who worked the farms and produced in the factories while the German men went off to war.

The strange thing to me is that none of these enormous groups of people have done anything to help us in the line of our advance. No strikes, no violences, no last minute sabotage or guerrilla activity, not even any passive resistance.

Just goes to show that nothing can be done with large masses of people without organization. . . .

I say again—using radio parlance—I want mail: Over.

I love you. Larry

238th Engr. Combat Bn.
APO 230, NY, NY
Somewhere in Germany
8 April 1945

Hello Darling;

No sooner do I finish writing you a petulant letter, caterwauling about not receiving enough mail from you when I get three luscious ones in rapid succession—and a beautiful package. . . .

Hon, the ratrace continues, and I don't think I'm overly optimistic in saying that the German Army will not be able to establish a continuous front before us, or prevent our meeting the Russians soon.

The process of the piecemeal disintegration of the German Wehrmacht has already begun—and will be accelerated as we advance.

Right now, as you know, we have many thousands trapped in the Ruhr pocket, with two alternatives—Surrender or Die! More pockets are coming, and quickly.

Not only that. The morale of the Nazi soldier is crumbling. Every day we pick up soldiers who have thrown away their uniforms, their weapons, even in their panic have destroyed their identity papers. They hope, naively, they can fool us this way and get home. There are tens of thousands (without exaggeration) doing this.

Their attitude can be summed up in the statement one of them made to me today.

The war is lost. Further resistance is madness. Why should I be killed in the last days of the war? . . .

Say, I've got a little sidelight you'll probably get a kick out of.

We've got a former Red Army cavalryman who's attached himself to us. He wants to stay with us until we tie-up with the Russians, then he'll go over to them. We just liberated him a few days ago.

We put him to work in our headquarters kitchen, where he puts in more work than the rest of our permanent KP's combined.

The Colonel thought he ought to be investigated before we attached him on the Q.T. so I called him in.

He came into Headquarters and gave me a smart russki high-ball.

I put him at ease (He speaks broken German).

"What's your name?"

"Bagramian. Ivan Bagramian, sir!"

"Isn't that the name of a famous Russian general?"[13]

"Yes," with pride.

"Tell me Ivan, where do you come from?"

"Baku, sir."

"What did you do in civilian life?"

"I am an oil-worker."

"How old are you?" "Twenty-three."

"Ivan," I look at him casually, "Sind Sie Komsomol?"

"Yes sir," again with pride.

"I'll tell you what Ivan. If you agree to question Russian and Polish workers in the towns we stop in, and find out who are the new faces, the leading party members, the soldiers in hiding you can come along with us."

"Oh, Lieutenant, that will be a pleasure."

To date I credit Ivan with information leading to the capture of 22 Nazi soldiers, including 4 SS sabotage agents.

Good, eh?

Darling, it's getting late and I'm sleepy. I had promised to write a letter to David, the first from his daddy. But, I'm too tired right now. . . .

I love you always.

Your, Larry

---

[13] Soviet Armenian General Ivan Bagramian (1897–1982) was the hero of the Baltic Front during World War II.

238th Engr. Combat Bn.
APO 230, NY, NY
Somewhere in Germany
15 April 1945

Darling;

Last night we heard the broadcast of the funeral services for Pres. Roosevelt.[14] We were all saddened to hear the news of his sudden death.

There isn't a soldier overseas, no matter what his political beliefs, who didn't feel a sense of personal loss.

We need no historians to prove to us that he was one of the great leaders of modern times, and a president who will be enshrined forever in the story of our United States.

Such a pity for him to go when the greatest victory of mankind is just around the corner. . . .

You say when I get home you'll make me talk and talk. That'll be O.K., hon. But there're some things that I have seen on this drive into the center of Germany that I will refuse to talk about.

In my rather extensive career as a soldier I have seen much death and a great deal of suffering. But since this final push has been under way we have been overrunning some of the indescribable murder mills that have been running full blast since the Nazis came to power twelve years ago.

Here were scenes so monstrous, so grisly that the imagination palls. Never, so long as I live, will I forget the horrible sights, the tales of the pitiful survivors whom we liberated.

The worst one of all that I have seen was a concentration camp for politicals.[15] Nothing in all the written history of man can

---

[14] President Franklin D. Roosevelt died of a massive cerebral hemorrhage at his cottage in Warm Springs, Georgia on April 12, 1945.

[15] This is a reference to the Dora-Mittelbau concentration camp at Nordhausen. Dora-Mittelbau was originally a satellite camp of the larger Buchenwald concentration camp for politicals. It became a separate camp in October 1944 with more than 30 of its own subcamps. Inmates, many of whom came from Buchenwald, were used as slave laborers in large underground factories manufacturing V-1 and V-2 rockets. The Nordhausen camp, a subcamp of Dora-Mittelbau, was created by the SS for prisoners too weak or ill to work in the tunnels of Dora and was termed a "Vernichtungslager," or extermination camp. Unlike the factory-like extermination camps of Auschwitz, Sobibor, or Chelmno, most of the prisoners of Nordhausen were allowed to die of starvation or

equal, or even approach, the infamy and the degradation, the sadistic depravity, the barbarism of Germany under Hitler.

By all previous standards it would be just for the entire population of Germany to be condemned to death for these crimes. It's too bad that it cannot be done.

Despite everything that my reason tells me, I shall always hate Germany and Germans. There are no good ones. Those that were decent have long ago perished in these concentration camps or gotten out.

The rest, down to the children are polluted to their roots.

It will take a generation, at least, to begin to remove the taint.

There is no Germany of Goethe, Heine, of Beethoven. They belong to us, to civilization.

There is only a Germany of Hitler. A nation of criminals.

So, remember, darling. Don't ever get me to talk to you about the concentration camps. You will only be shocked and sickened.

Our tanks plunge onwards these days, we go forward unchecked. We shall meet the Russians soon. When we shake hands on the battlefield we will cement a bond which will last a long, long time.

We're about to load up to move again. So, 'bye for now darling.

I love you. Here's a kiss for David E. and a great big one for you.

Your own, Larry

---

total lack of medical care. Nordhausen was liberated on April 12, 1945 by the U.S. 104th Infantry Division. Upon entering the camp, the American troops found only a handful of survivors among more than 3,000 corpses. Units of the 238th Engineer Combat Battalion operating in support of the 104th Infantry were brought in with bulldozers to prepare the mass graves. Able-bodied, mostly older, German men from the nearby city of Nordhausen were brought at gunpoint by the U.S. Army to the Nordhausen camp and forced to view the thousands of corpses and to bury the dead.

238th Engr. Combat Bn.
APO 230, NY, NY
Somewhere in Germany
1 May 1945

Darling;

May Day greetings from the ruined citadel of Nazism!

Today was cold and crisp and clear. A day of mixed happenings and emotions for me.

In the first place, things didn't start out so good. In the morning after breakfast, the Colonel called me in and told me that orders had been received making another Joe from one of the other battalions in the Group the new S-2.

This new fellow is a West Pointer who's been out of the Point two years now and still a first looie.

Nothing wrong with my work, of course. Matter of fact it's been more than good. But, the old school tie takes precedence. And to give a captaincy to an ordinary mug like me when there's a West Pointer drooling around is unheard of.

So, he gets the captaincy and the title—I'll probably still do the work as his assistant.

Naturally, I'm a bit disappointed and resentful. Particularly since I would have liked for you to get that raise each month.

Well, after that I had to go out and do something I didn't like to do.

As you know, we're on temporary military government duty—as are many other First Army combat units. (Combat in this theater is over for First Army).[16]

The way it works, we more or less supplement the regular military government setup.

We got the guns, so we're more or less the cops. Not actually openly, but that's about the size of it.

Well, there's this Burgomeister in a little town we control who wants to publish a notice commemorating May Day. He wants to tell his people that for the first time in thirteen years May Day has come to their town freed from fascism. He wants them to

---

[16] Battalion headquarters was situated in the Chateau of Baron von Krosygk at Helmsdorf. The baron, suspected of complicity with high Nazi officials, was kept in house arrest in his servant's quarters.

commemorate this day in quiet remembrance of the millions of lives lost and the ruined country brought on by the Nazis. He wants them to pray today, that someday May Day will be celebrated joyously in a free and democratic Germany.

Not a bad little notice. The first time I've heard a German say these things. You'd think it would be O.K., wouldn't you?

But no, this phoney (M.G. [military government] officer) in charge of the Kreis (District) says he suspects the Burgomeister of communistic intent. He says we've got to stick to the middle of the road and be especially certain that no extremists right or left gain the upper hand.

So, I gotta go and tell this Burgomeister he can't post his notice.

How do you think I felt doing it? Yeah, that's right.

Some day I'll tell you what I think about our AMG [American military government].

Coming back in my jeep I passed one of the camps we're running for Russian PW's. There, my heart jumped about 15 feet for joy.

The Russkis were celebrating May Day the old-fashioned way. They'd cut down some trees and constructed an archway over the entrance to their camp. The arch was painted red. On the top center was a huge red star flanked by charcoal drawings of Stalin and Zhukov.[17] Red flags were streaming in the brisk wind. An altogether stirring sight.

I stopped the jeep and got out to snap a picture, and as if by magic the Russians started to flock around. They saluted me and smiled and laughed when I pointed to the decorations and said "Prima." And then when I motioned for them to get in the picture they about knocked each other down in their eagerness.

I said "Das vadanyah" to them and took off for our area, and do you know something? I passed through three towns, and each one of them had at least one red flag flying somewhere!

All I could say was, "I'll be go to goddam." . . .

I'm hoping I'll be lucky enough to be with you soon. This show is just about on the verge of being over. Surrender is in the air. But, even if they don't quit, complete occupation isn't far off.

---

[17] Georgi Zhukov (1896–1974) was the most capable Soviet field commander of World War II. For his great leadership and strategic abilities, he was awarded the rank of Marshal of the Soviet Union.

I love you, bubby. A hug for David.

Your, Larry

238th Engr. Combat Bn.
APO 230, NY, NY
Somewhere in Germany
4 May 1945

Hello My Dearest;

There's certainly been a lot of big news the past few days—Hitler + Mussolini dead, surrender in Italy, brilliant progress wherever the Nazi lunatics insist on fighting.[18] Perhaps by the time you receive this letter there will be even greater news. . . .

Right now, I'm about forty miles from my own outfit on a special little job of ferreting out Gestapo and SS leaders.[19] I'm unfortunate enough to be able to speak this damn lingo after a fashion, and someone seems to think I know something about Nazis and how to contact people who can tell me something about them. I wonder why?

Incidentally, former church-goers are quite helpful these days. . . .

The most terrible part of this war for me has been the separation from you. Maybe I've said it before, but a man can become inured to all kinds of hardships and dangers, but I can never become used to being away from you.

My loneliness and longing has become intensified daily. And now that we've just about completed this job here, it's well-nigh unbearable.

---

[18] Mussolini was hanged by Italian partisans on April 28, 1945. Hitler committed suicide two days later at the Fuhrerbunker in Berlin. On September 3, 1943 General Dwight D. Eisenhower announced the formal surrender of Italy. However, fighting in Italy, mostly against German troops, continued until May 1945 when in the last days of the war in Europe, the German Army in northern Italy surrendered.

[19] Cane was put in command of a Counter Intelligence Corps (CIC) detachment of four German-speaking enlisted men, working in and around Eisleben, Germany.

I just want one thing—to be home with my Grace.
I love you terribly.

Your, Larry

238th Engr. Combat Bn.
APO 230, NY, NY
Somewhere in Germany
6 May 1945

My Darling;

V–E day is just around the corner. . . .
We have already started on that damnable period of marking time, of performing odd jobs, of training, of gossip, speculation, and rumor-mongering, of being consumed with anxiety over our future.

All of it is, and will be, a big pain in the behind. The all-important question is do we get to go home? . . .

All these small fry Nazi big-shots, these Kreisleiters, these Gestapo and Sicherheitsdienst agents, these Allgemeine and Waffen S.S. leaders, these bastards who murdered Jews and enslaved and terrorized millions, who strutted around in gaudy uniforms and had the gall to believe they were Herrenvolk all turn my stomach.[20]

I have them arrested and brought to me for questioning, and they are so servile, so fawning. They roll their eyes to heaven and proclaim their innocence. When the absolute evidence is placed before them they sweat and lie for their lives, they beg for consideration, for mercy. Dammit, they disgust me!

I haven't met one with courage.

If the veteran commander still says the Germans will wage guerrilla warfare, I still say he's off his trolley. There may be attempts and some small-scale successes here and there, but widespread sabotage will be a miserable failure.

---

[20] Cane is referring to Nazi elite organizations that included the secret police, labor, and intelligence.

Like the National Redoubt, it's all a feverish Nazi pipe-dream.[21]

I'm enclosing a copy of a leaflet that most front-line troops received just before we linked up with the Russians. The little blurb on top is the tipoff on how far we've come since the war started.

We like the Russians. . . .

Just about running out of news for now.

Good night, sweetheart. My love to our son.

> I love you as always. Larry

> 238th Engr. Combat Bn.
> APO 230, NY, NY
> Somewhere in Germany
> 8 May 1945

Darling;

V-E today!

What can I say? How can I describe my feelings? Shall I tell you how I longed to be with you, to kiss you, to put your head on my shoulder and say quietly—"We made it."

Such a long, hard, bitter road had been the painful trek from Madrid to Berlin. So much suffering, so much heartbreaking loneliness and longing for you, so many comrades lost.

The German church-bells tolled the end of the war in Europe, the people walked through the streets as usual. Here there was no wild-rejoicing. Nor were there tears of happiness.

I thought back, back to the long ago of 1937.

I wondered that day, as I stood on the top deck of the Acquitania and watched the Statue of Liberty, if I would ever see her again.

---

[21] The National Redoubt represented what was thought to be Nazi strongholds in the Bavarian Alps. Created by Nazi propaganda, the National Redoubt did not exist, but Allied intelligence believed in its existence and planned for ways to destroy what turned out to be a phantom.

Then came France and the romantic and exciting secret moves via the underground railroad.

The hike over the Pyrenees and finally the thrill of being stopped by Spanish sentries.

The first three days in Spain at that old fort. The filth, the human faesces, the rotten wine, my first introduction to baccalaue and garbanzas.

Enlistment at Albacete. The training period under the hot Spanish sun at Tarazona de la Mancha.

Then, the bloody street-fighting at Quinto and Belchite, the suicidal charge at Fuentes del Ebro, where I got myself hit.

The stay in the hospital. Typhus—and the raging delirium.

Then, the silly running away from the hospital to the Battle of Teruel. The incredible suffering and hardships of that campaign.

The attack at Mont Atalaya and Seguros de los Baños, which they called the most brilliant tactical maneuver of the Spanish Civil War.

The terrible retreat in Aragon. The weeks spent behind enemy lines, and final escape to our own forces.

The assault crossing of the Ebro and the Battle of Gandesa.

Then battles at Sierra de Caballs, the fantastic and grewsome Sierra de Pandols, and the Sierra de Laval de la Torre.

Then, our retirement and the stay near Puigcerda in the Pyrenees. The trip home.

And you darling, I thought about you and our marriage and the indescribable love that I have for you, and how I cry inside for you all the time.

And then Pearl Harbor, and the Army and war again for me.

I thought of H-hour, D-day and how I with several hundred others in assault teams stormed ashore on Utah beach in the Cotentin peninsula. The bloody mess on the shore that day, the exhaustion which dulled any enthusiasm that might have been aroused at seeing the rest come in and the realization that I had helped to make it stick.

Then, the sweep to Cherbourg.

After that St. Lô and the breakthrough. The Falaise-Argentan gap. The swirling battle through France. The violent short-lived battle of Mons.

Then, the bitter, rain-soaked battle for the Siegfried Line. The

Battle of the Ardennes. The crossing of the Roer, the Erft, the Rhine. And the final smash that ended with the linkup with the Russians, and the final surrender of the Germans.

A helluva lot of combat. And, now even though Japan has yet to be defeated, I want to go home.

I can't help feeling—Jesus, haven't I been in enough?

Who, even among those who are left from Spain have lived through so many battles? I'm the only man in America who fought in Spain and landed with the assault wave on D-day.

Perhaps it's wrong to feel this way. Perhaps I'm selfish.

But, sometimes I feel I can't bear my separation from you much longer.

I want to be with you and love you again.

I want to lie locked in each others arms at night. To kiss you and kiss you and tell you how much I love you. To whisper the secrets of my heart. To be so close that we are one, lip on lip, heart pounding against heart.

I want to play with the son I've never seen. To help make his formula. Even to change his diapers. To wheel his carriage of a Sunday morning, with you on my arm.

Oh, my God, how I want to be with you my darling.

If you've ever wished hard for anything, wish that I'm one of the lucky ones who comes home soon.

I love you, love you, love you. Larry

7

Waiting to Come Home
May 9–October 29, 1945

Hqtrs. 238th Engr. Combat Bn.
APO 230, NY, NY
Somewhere in Germany
11 May 1945

Darling Bub;

Back with my outfit again.

Didn't exactly enjoy the job I was on, but had my first real opportunity to talk to all kinds of Germans. I met a wide variety of people—bankers, industrialists, peasants, workers, big-shot and little-shot Nazis, Gestapo agents, spies, rank and file soldiers, officers, SS men and women, Hitler Jugend, housewives, children, young girls of the Deutsche Bund Mädel, former inmates of concentration camps, Communists, former social democrats, members of the German Nationalists, Centrum of Catholic party, priests, doctors, lawyers, teachers, and others.

I think I've got a pretty good idea of the German people now.

It can best be put in the words of an old German, who had spent three years as a "political" in Buchenwald.

He said, "Germany, <u>particularly its youth</u>, is rotten to the core. Fascism has perverted and degenerated my people. The world will make a tragic blunder if it trusts us for at least 25 years."

I know we can't exterminate or destroy them, which is the wild urge you have in combat, but I think that this must be borne in mind in all our future dealings with this nation. This is the human material we have to work with—to live with.

About our life right now. We're pretty comfortably situated. Live in the best houses in town. Good chow, and for us an officers' mess. A good athletics program. An educational program being organized. Movies every night. Not much work. A good deal of the old Army chicken shit. . . .

I didn't tell you about my meeting the Russians.

I tried to get to Berlin the other day. But when I got to the Russian lines, I was stopped by a couple of smiling Ivans. I asked them to take me to their company commander, which one of them did.

We shook hands and I pulled out my bottle of Scotch and presented it to him, and then I asked him for a bottle of vodka which he delightedly gave me.

We sat around shooting the breeze in German, which he spoke excellently.

He was a Moscow man and a University graduate. As a couple of big-city slickers we compared notes on our home towns.

I asked him about General Rodimstev,[1] who fought as a captain in Spain, and when he learned I had been with the IB [International Brigades] he gave me a special grab on the shoulder and an enthusiastic "Tovarich."

When I told him I wanted to go to Berlin just for the special personal satisfaction of walking up the Unter den Linden and standing in front of what was left of the Reichstag.

I was sure disappointed when he told me, "My dear Tovarich, I am so sorry, but it is verboten."

So, we polished off the vodka. Shook hands. Saluted all around, and I took off with his "God be with you" (Surprising?)

Anyway, I met the Reds.

That'll be another tale for Davie some day. Got a lot of them, haven't I?

Well, hon, I'll say goodnight to you now.

I love you.

Your, Larry

---

[1] General Alexsandr Rodimtsev (1905–1977) fought in the Spanish Civil War, under the name of "Pavlito." He also fought at the defense of Stalingrad during World War II. He wrote several books, including the two-volume work, *Under Spanish Skies,* published in 1974.

Hqtrs. 238th Engr. Combat Bn.
APO 230, NY, NY
Eisleben, Germany
16 May 1945

My Darling;

Today I had a rare treat.

I met and talked to two former functionaries of the KPD (Communist Party of Germany).

They have spent twelve years in the infamous concentration camp for politicals at Buchenwald.

Twelve years!

And they were still sane, in fair physical condition, and most important of all—the fire still burned bright within them.

Theirs was a tale of personal tragedy and suffering, of steadfastness, loyalty and heroism so inspiring that I was thrilled and entranced.

They told me about the first terrible days in 1933, when the Party organization was smashed and its leaders executed or jailed.

Then the long terrible months and years in the camp. How they organized themselves under the noses of the guards and the Gestapo.

They told me how Ernst Thaelmann died—murdered in August 1944 by the SS in Buchenwald.[2]

They described how they began to arm themselves with revolvers, rifles, machine-guns. How they made bombs and Molotov cocktails, waiting for the day when we would come near.

Yes, right in Buchenwald!

They told me how they performed the amazing and hazardous feat of constructing a radio transmitter and receiver. And how they used it to establish contact with our bombers which flew over nearby Weimar! How in the last days, when it looked as if all thirty thousand inmates would be executed, they begged our planes for instructions and were told—"Wait, we are coming."

---

[2] Ernst Thaelmann (1866–1944) was a leading figure in the German Communist Party. He organized and led the fights in the streets against the Nazis in 1933. He was imprisoned by the Nazis and murdered by the SS in Buchenwald in 1944. The German brigade with the international volunteers in Spain was named for him.

How they arose and killed all the guards when the first American tanks broke into Weimar.

I asked them how it felt to be free again.

They said it was strange and unreal.

One, with coal black hair, streaked with white at the temples, said he used to be married. After being in jail for five years, his wife wrote that she was jobless, starving, and felt that she could not remain faithful to him any longer. So, he said, since his future put him in no position to ask a woman to wait for him, it was not fair, and since he was not the kind of man who could stand being married to a woman who was not true to him, he asked her to divorce him—which she did.

Now, he said, although he was once quite normal—he felt no sexual desire upon seeing women again. And he was only 40.

The other, the one with the steely grey eyes, the broken nose, and the close cropped blond hair said his wife, also a functionary, was beaten and tortured to death in 1935. He too, was not able to feel any sexual passion.

But, aside from that they said they were both O.K. And that there was lots of work to do in Germany.

It's high time for a change, they said. And they were going to pitch right in to help.

What a pair of battlers!

I wanted to yell right out loud and tell them how much I was pleased to meet them.

How brave and noble our people are.

Things here are pretty much the same as they've been for the past few days. The C.O. is driving everybody crazy thinking up new nonsense every day. But, I tell the other officers on the staff if they could live through what we've been through, why it oughtn't to faze them.

Hell, it's the old Army game.

Tell my Davie his daddy aches so much for his Mommy it's driving him goofy.

I love you forever. Larry

Hqtrs. 238th Engr. Combat Bn.
Assembly Area Command
APO 752, NY, NY
Eisleben, Germany
22 May 1945

Hello Darling;

Got a physical exam today—the whole Army's getting them over here. After going through the whole rigamarole, I was pronounced disgustingly healthy, emotionally and physically.

Still 1-A in the Army. . . .

Say, hon, I had a funny one happen today.

A wizened, dark-haired character was ushered into my office. He had been picked up by a guard at one of the road-control points.

I looked him over, and I had a strange feeling of pushcarts on Hester St., clothing stores on Canal St., an automat in the garment district during lunch hour.

I spotted him in a minute, but I had to work him over. There's been some strange things happening in Europe in the last few years.

"Well, what are you here for?"

He gave me one of those shrugs—one of those unmistakable, intangible motions which only one people in the world can give.

"I don't know."

"You don't know, eh? Where's your papers?"

"I haven't got any."

"No papers. Hmm. Where are you coming from?"

"Poland."

"Poland! For Chrissakes! Where do you think you're going?"

"Portugal, Lisbon."

"Portugal! Oh, my aching back! Wait a minute. What's your name?"

"Wolf Scheinaug."

"Now look, Wolf Scheinaug, you say you're coming from Poland and you're trying to get to Portugal. How did you get through the Russian area?"

"Oh, I came with French soldiers who were on their way home to France."

"Well how did you work that? Can you speak French?"

"No." Another one of these gestures. "All guards ever said was, 'Parlez-vous francais,' and all I ever said was 'Oui, Oui,' and they used to wave me on."

I couldn't keep from laughing any longer. So, I burst out in Yiddish "Goyische Kopfer."[3] And you should have seen the expression of joyous wonderment on my landsman face.

I told him he didn't have to be afraid and hold back any more. That he was dealing with an American and a fellow-Jew. I told him to let his hair down and tell me everything straight.

Then, he told me his story—which I interrupted from time to time for clarification (My Yiddish is rusty).

He had left Poland and gone to Portugal with his family in 1936. In 1939 he had returned to Warsaw to marry a second cousin of his.

That, incidentally, is an old-world Jewish custom. It's something that's decided even before kids are born. Ask my Pop, he'll tell you.

Well, he got married and then came the German invasion. He was stuck—couldn't get out.

In 1940 his wife and infant baby were sent to the murder camp at Maidenek.[4] There, they met the fate of millions of Jews—murder and burning.

He himself was sent to another camp.

From then, until his liberation by the Russians, he went through a fantastic life of suffering and torture.

Now he was trying to beat his way back to his family.

I asked him why he didn't stay in Poland, especially since the Russians were there now. But, he said Poland is a place of too many horrible memories. He wants to be with his parents and his family in Portugal.

Well, I had to tell him he couldn't do that right now.

I sent him to the Burgomeister and got him some identification papers.

I also gave the Burgomeister orders that he was to be provided

---

[3] The literal translation of "Goyische Kopfer" is "Gentile brains." It is a not very complimentary way of saying, "What would Gentiles know about a Jew?"

[4] Maidanek, located close to the Polish city of Lublin, was the second largest Nazi concentration camp. Originally built as a prisoner of war and slave labor camp and run by the Waffen-SS, it became an extermination camp where be-

with food, clothing, and shelter in a private German home until travel restrictions were lifted, at which time steps were to be taken to send him home.

And I also told Wolf Scheinaug that he was to take crap from nobody. That if anyone wanted to know who and what he was, he was to hold his head up proudly and say he was a Jew, and what about it.

When he left me he was crying he was so happy. . . .

I love you, Larry

Hqtrs. 238th Engr. Combat Bn.
Assembly Area Command
APO 752, NY, NY
Reims–Chalons-sur-Marne, France
6 June 1945

My Darling;

Back in France a year to the day after we surged up on the Normandie beaches.

Our return was a helluva lot less spectacular than our arrival.

This time they set us down in a Godforsaken sprawling tent area which has been erected for the purpose of re-deploying the American Army in the ETO [European Theatre of Operations].

The area is divided into numerous camps and our job is going to be to scatter our people through them, and supervise all engineer and utility work in the assembly area. . . .[5]

We're supposed to be entitled for handling under the point system as well as anyone else. But, the way it looks to me, we're going to get screwed on the deal until this thing gets going properly.[6] And that should be at least a couple of months. . . .

---

tween 200,000 and 350,000 Jews, Poles, and Soviet POWs perished by mass shootings or gassing.

[5] Seventeen redeployment camps were established in an area 50 × 100 miles near Reims; later five more "temporary" staging areas were created in Le Havre. Boredom and low morale were widespread in these centers.

[6] In order to determine who would go home first, a point system, whereby service personnel received points for time in service, overseas duty, combat,

In 10 days, we will have been married five years.

I want to wish you a happy anniversary darling. As happy as you can make it under the circumstances. . . .

The war has kept us apart for a long time—a heartbreaking time. We'll never be able to get it back but, darling, I'll sure try hard when I get back to you.

I love you terribly—and miss you, now more than ever.

Your own, Larry

Hqtrs. 238th Engr. Bn.
Assembly Area Command
APO 752, NY, NY
Camp Oklahoma City
Sissonne, France
16 June 1945

My Darling;

Five years ago today—The most important day of my life

Five years we've been married, and we've spent almost as much time apart as we have together.

It's pretty hard for me to put down on paper just how I feel right now. Impossible for me to describe the depth of my loneliness and longing and love for you.

All that I can say is that I'm praying to be with you again as hard as I ever prayed for a chance at the future while sweating out a bombing without cover.

I love you my Gracie. . . .

Love to my son, and to you, darling, all my love for all my forever.

Larry

and parenthood was instituted. Service personnel regularly groused about the unfairness of the point system. In actuality, the frustrations expressed by the troops came mostly from their unhappiness at not getting home sooner. Eventually, the point system was modified to include considerations such as special skills needed by the military, availability of transport, and location of unit.

Camp Oklahoma City
Sissonne, France
3 July 1945

Darling;

Yesterday I visited Al Tanz, the first vet I've seen since coming overseas.[7]

He's a 1st Lt., also in the Corps of Engineers, but hasn't seen any combat in this war.

He's been in an Engineer Depot outfit—which is the kind of bunch that handles an Engineer supply depot.

Right now he's stationed about 10 kilometers from me, near the town of Laon, + I think we'll be able to get together quite frequently.

Maybe you know him. He's a lawyer and used to work for the same firm that Jerry Lurie clerked for.

We chewed the rag for a couple of hours, exchanging news. We also talked about church.

He's in the same boat I'm in with regard to knowing what's happening—and he's also waiting for news from home. . . .

It's mighty hard to arrive at an independent opinion over here. We get so little news of that type—and what we do get is distorted.

While military operations were going on, I used to be able to see what was coming weeks, and sometimes months, in advance.

That was because as Bn. [battalion] Intelligence O[fficer], I had access to information which even the most prominent and trusted correspondents couldn't even dream of obtaining.

But this thing is something else. I don't know what the devil is happening.

By the way, if you can get me a copy of Duclos' statement, I wish you'd send it to me.[8]

---

[7] Al Tanz was a Spanish Civil War veteran. In December 1936 he was one of the ninety-five original American volunteers to form the Lincoln Battalion. He served two tours of duty in Spain and was wounded twice. After joining the U.S. Army in World War II, he served in the Office of Strategic Service, parachuting in France prior to D-Day, in preparation for the Allied invasion. He then served with the Army Engineers for the remainder of the war. He died in November 2000 at the age of 94.

[8] This is a reference to Jacques Duclos (1896–1975), French Communist party leader who helped organize French resistance during the German occupation.

Tanz also told me that Doc Hene was one of the Americans murdered at Malmedy during Von Rundstedt's breakthrough last winter.[9]

It was the 1st SS Panzer Division, "Leibstandart Adolf Hitler" that pulled that job.

They're the babies we helped to destroy on our sector of the Bulge.

It doesn't bring Doc back, but at least there was one vet that helped to get revenge for his death.

We got a shipment of high-point men today. Looks as if they're beginning to fill the outfit up with guys to be discharged.

You just keep wishing hard darling, and I'll be coming down that gangplank in New York yet.

Give Davie a big hug for me.

All my love all my life, Larry

═══════════

Camp Oklahoma City
Sissonne, France
13 July 1945

Darling Mine;

This redeployment is running way ahead of schedule. If it keeps up this way they'll have practically everything out of here by the end of the year. And we should certainly get home this fall some time.

You're not the only one waiting impatiently for the summer to end. . . .

He was a principal architect of the Paris uprising of 1944. In April 1945 Duclos sent a letter to the American Communist Party condemning Earl Browder, the leader of the American Communist Party, for abandoning the class struggle and for preaching a doctrine of peaceful coexistence between the United States and the Soviet Union.

[9] Dr. Julius Hene was an American who was chief medical officer with the Mackenzie-Papineau Battalion during the Spanish Civil War. He was killed at the Malmedy Massacre on December 17, 1944 when German S.S. troops herded about 100 U.S. soldiers into a field at a road junction near the Belgium town of Malmedy and murdered them with machine gun fire.

Going to visit Al Tanz tonight. We're going to have a good old bull session. He tells me another vet, a doc by the name of Bill Pike and who's a major, is in one of the camps and waiting to be redeployed to the Pacific.[10]

We're going to try to get together with him before he pulls out.

I met another guy who was in Spain, but who was a phoney and deserted during the retreats.

He's the provost marshall of the camp I'm in and, of all things, also a major.

He was one of those soldiers of fortune guys who found out that there was no romance and fortune to be found in the Spanish Civil War.

When I walked up and said hello to him, he almost keeled over he was so embarrassed.

Last time he saw me, I was in kind of a hot spot. So the first thing he blurted out was, "How the hell come you're still alive?"

I just grinned and looked right through him and said, "I guess I've been kind of lucky."

He left me with an uneasy "Come up and see me some time" remark.

Davie sounds like he's getting hard for you to handle. Just you hold the fort, sweetheart, I'll be there soon to help.

Honest, I'll do all the floorwalking at night and I won't mind it a bit. Anyway, not much.

I love you, darling.

Your, Larry

—————

Camp Oklahoma City
Sissonne, France
16 July 1945

Hello Darling;

. . . The other night, Al Tanz and I got together and we had a real old-fashioned bull-session. We beat the Spanish War to death.

---

[10] Spanish Civil War veteran Bill (Doc) Pike died in April 2000.

He says I've got enough war stories between that one and this, to keep David fascinated from the time he starts to talk till he's a grown man.

We got to talking about the vets, and we suddenly realized I had a darn good chance of being able to go to the Christmas eve dance this year in New York.

Oh, darling, wouldn't that be wonderful?

I'm hoping it turns out that way.

I love you terribly

Your own, Larry

Camp Oklahoma City
Sissonne, France
27 July 1945

My Darling;

They've thought up something to keep me busy again. I'm now a traveling lecturer.

What I do is visit our platoons which are scattered through these camps in the Assembly Area, and talk to them on various timely topics. Such things as Bill of Rights (G.I.),[11] the Potsdam Conference, Japan and the War in the Pacific, etc.[12]

I don't mind—matter of fact, I rather enjoy it.

I've been going buggy with nothing to do, and this gives me a reason for beginning to read and study again.

Besides, it's a good thing—if you know what I mean. . . .

Can't you feel me yearning?

---

[11] In order to ease the transition from military to civilian life, Congress passed the GI Bill of Rights in June 1944. This landmark legislation provided veterans with funds for education and training, low-interest loans, unemployment insurance, and job guarantees.

[12] The Potsdam Conference, held from July 17 to August 2, 1945 in a suburb of devastated Berlin, determined key decisions about postwar Germany. Germany was divided into four occupation zones (U.S., British, French, and Soviet); Berlin, located in the Soviet occupation zone, was also divided into four zones. While at Potsdam, President Harry S. Truman learned of the successful testing of the atomic bomb in New Mexico.

This waiting is so damned hard.

Darling, how I miss you. Comme je t'aime!

One of these days, though, I'll come back to you. When I do—darling, there'll be lots of loving.

I adore you. Larry

=====

Camp Oklahoma City
Sissonne, France
29 July 1945

Darling;

. . . I got the Volunteer from the Vets, and read about a lot of the boys being back home already. How I envy them.

I also received your copy of Political Affairs.[13] You know, of course, that Saully already sent me a copy.

The setup is pretty straight in my mind now.

I read today that the Church has been reorganized. That's good, because there's lots of work to be done in the world. And it's a damn good thing that the day-dreaming has come to an end.

The papers are also full of the story about the bomber crashing into the Empire State building. That must have been quite a mess.[14]

Just multiply that a couple of thousand times, and think of it happening day after day and night after night, and you'll have some idea of what we did to the cities of Germany and what's going on in Japan right now.

Give David a kiss + a hug for me.

I love you always. Larry

=====

---

[13] *Political Affairs* is the theoretical journal of the Communist Party, USA.

[14] In 1945, at the end of World War II, an Army Air Forces B-25 twin-engine bomber plane crashed into the 79th floor of the Empire State Building during a dense fog.

Camp Oklahoma City
Sissonne, France
31 July 1945

Hello My Darling;

The end of another month.

Another month nearer home and you and Davy.

How time crawls these days!

This time last year we had just finished the first phase of the stupendous breakthrough. We were sitting on our first objectives—filthy, bone-weary, unshaven and triumphant.

Already it seems so long ago—like something remembered from a dream.

My thoughts were full of you then, as they are now, as they have been and will be so long as I live.

How many times have I told you, darling? I love you. Each time is as new and full of wonder as if I'd never said it before.

I'm so proud and lucky to have you for my wife. To have such a wonderful son.

And I'm so damn lonesome for you.

God, I wish homecoming time would hurry up.

I read today where Bill Z. took over the reins.[15] He's a solid sender from way back. We ought to get some real work in, provided too much time isn't wasted in bickering. . . .

We confine ourselves to our own entertainment facilities on the post—movies, USO shows, some athletics, and chewing the fat over some cognac at the Officers' Club. A helluva existence, but qu'est-ce qu'on peut faire? . . .

It just boils down to one of the most realistic soldier songs I ever heard—which I learned in Spain. "Waiting, waiting, waiting always—waiting."

And my waiting is for the day I'll hold you in my arms again and kiss you and love you and tell you how beautiful you are.

---

[15] Bill Z. is a reference to William Zebulon Foster (1881–1961), radical labor organizer and leader of the Communist Party, USA. In 1924, 1928, and 1932 Foster ran for the presidency on the Communist Party ticket. In 1932 he suffered a serious heart attack and stepped down as leader of the party. In 1945 he again became chairman of the American Communist Party.

I love you, darling.

Your own, Larry

================

Camp Oklahoma City
Sissonne, France
2 August 1945

Hello Darling;

. . . I wonder why there's been so much confusion about this business of discharging men. I'm almost ready to believe the war with Germany ended sooner than the arm-chair generals in the Pentagon building expected.

There must be something else too—something besides inefficiency and shortsightedness.

And so far as the confused policy with regard to officers is concerned. I don't get it all.

All this insistence on "military necessity" is the bunk as far as I can see.

We're expendable as hell in combat—especially junior officers. We get knocked off up there with the rest of the men, and get replaced just as fast. Now, we're suddenly essential.

That's a crock of manure. There isn't a platoon sergeant or first-sergeant in the Army who can't replace his officer, and who hasn't done it when his officer has bumped off—especially the ones with combat experience.

How about a more liberal policy of direct commissions for the hundreds of thousands of capable NCOs? There's your reservoir of replacements for officers.

Or is that too democratic?

Ah, me, I'm still a member of the Beefer's Union. The best thing to do, I guess, is just sweat it out, and hope for the best.

But, I'll tell you this, darling, when the day comes that I've got my honorable discharge in hand, I'm going to be pretty damn glad.

And if it was tomorrow, it couldn't be too soon.

I'm living for the day I come home to you again.

I love you terribly.

Your, Larry

==========

Camp Oklahoma City
Sissonne, France
12 August 1945

My Own Darling;

What an incredible five days, have been the ones that just flew by.

First, the Atomic Bomb.[16]

I was leery of accepting the first accounts at face value. We had heard so much about German secret weapons, and when they were introduced we saw they couldn't possibly alter the course of the war. And anyway, revolutionary as they were, they were just another kind of bomb. V-1, V-2, etc.

But this fantastic thing! A small bomb, whose actual explosive charge weighs no more than five pounds—and it wipes out 250,000 souls, a whole city, in one gigantic clap of doom!

Jesus!

Here is a source of power, which if harnessed, makes practically anything you can dream of possible—running through the air like Superman, taking a trip to the moon, anything.

That old joke about the drunk who bet he could dive out the fifth floor window, fly around the block, and come back in again won't be funny in a hundred years. I'll bet they'll be doing just that.

Then, the Russians came in with us.

I had been hoping so much that they would. Not only because it would shorten the war and save American lives, but also because of what it will mean for the Far East and for the future friendship of the Russians and ourselves.

We're going to be friends for a long time. Not that there won't

---

[16] The United States dropped two atomic bombs on Hiroshima and Nagasaki on August 6 and August 9, 1945. On August 14 Japan unconditionally surrendered.

be plenty of bastards who'll try their damnedest to split us. But, the economic, political and moral factors that make for getting along together are going to be so strong now, that the watchdogs of the friendship will have a better time of it. Our kind of people being the watchdogs, of course. . . .

And, now, we are sitting and waiting eagerly for the Japanese reply to the last United Nations surrender offer.

Imagine, in a few hours, it may be over. It doesn't seem real or possible. But we're waiting and hugging the radios all over camp.

Our prayers, dreams, and hopes are on the verge of being answered. . . .

I love you, sweetheart.

A bientôt.

Your, Larry

Camp Oklahoma City
Sissonne, France
15 August 1945

My Own Darling;

It's over! Really over!

We got the news at 1 A.M. this morning.

I can't describe how I feel.

This should speed up my coming home. The whole redeployment plan is knocked into a cocked hat. Category IV units and high-pointers will probably have priority on shipment now.

Hold tight, bub, I'll be there soon. . . .

(The radio is broadcasting celebrations in New York, Washington, Philadelphia, Chicago, San Francisco. The din is terrific. I can't even hear myself think. Wonderful.). . .

Oh hell, I can't write. These guys are making too much noise. I love you.

Tell Davy his pop will be there to give him a piggy-back soon.

I adore you. Larry

Camp Washington
Sissonne, France
19 August 1945

My Darling;

The customary dreary French weather for this time of year is beginning to set in. It's been raining the last couple of days. . . .

This job I'm on doesn't require too much effort although I've got a machine shop, a plumbing shop, a carpentry shop, a paint shop, a blacksmith's shop, an electrical shop, a rock-crushing, concrete-mixing, and tarmaking plant, a tools' warehouse, and I'm in charge of such enterprises as road-building and surfacing, the camp water supply, and landscaping—to mention a few.

The reason I'm not pressed is because we've got about a thousand Krauts doing all the work. About all I have to do is ride around and supervise, and try hard to stay away from the camp engineer. . . .

I love you.

Your, Larry

Camp Washington
Sissonne, France
24 August 1945

Darling;

. . . I see so much crap going on.

All this brass over here, trying desperately to keep their jobs as long as they can, so they can exercise their petty tyrannies a little longer, and live like kings, and take their little side excursions to the Riviera, or England, or Switzerland.

They want their tight little empires to continue. What have they got but demotions or return to unromantic civilian status staring them in the face?

This whole Assembly Area Command isn't worth a tinker's damn now. There are 17 camps, capable of accommodating more than 250,000 men at one time, and they've been empty for a month now. The only people in them are poor jerks like ourselves whose job it is to run and maintain them.

And we aren't doing a goddam thing.

Just piddling, stupid jobs like landscaping, or building a desk for the Commanding O., or installing a shower for officers.

A criminal waste of money, and a callous, rotten treatment of thousands of men who have been through hell and are pining for home and families.

My God! I hate this Army now. It's a vast jail.

When the war was on it worked, it clicked. In spite of all the misery, the hardships, I was proud to be in it, to be destroying fascism. But now, the Saints preserve us. . . .

But, even though I feel low most of the time, just as you do— we've just got to keep our chins up. I'll be with you darling. Interminable as it will seem, it won't be long. . . .

I love you and miss you.

Your, Larry

———————

Camp Oklahoma City
Sissonne, France
29 August 1945

Hello Darling;

Spent the afternoon reading Bill Mauldin's "Up Front With Mauldin."[17]

If you can get hold of it, don't hesitate to do so. It's really excellent.

The cartoons are biting and the script, which is more or less a running commentary on the drawings, is as honest and true as anything ever written by Ernie Pyle.[18]

---

[17] Army Sergeant Bill Mauldin (1921–) depicted the GI view of the war in cartoons that he drew for the Army newspaper, *The Stars and Stripes*. These cartoons were published in a book, *Up Front*, in 1945.

[18] Ernie Pyle (1900–1945) was America's best-known war correspondent. He received the Pulitzer Prize in 1943 for his writings. His columns were collected in a book, *Brave Men*, published in 1944. He was killed on April 18, 1945 during the assault on Ie Shima, a small island just south of Okinawa, where the battle against the Japanese was raging.

Looks like we're getting set for the big shipments of men home this September and October. And the way things are shaping up, I should be on one of those boats in either of the two months— probably October though.

Who knows? I may yet walk in on you with the house in a mess, your hair in curlers, your face covered with cold cream, and Davy in a demanding mood.

Wouldn't that be wonderful? . . .

Well, be good, darling.

I love you.

Tell Davy, Pop sends him a kiss.

Your own, Larry

238th Engr. Combat Bn.
Assembly Area Command
APO 752, NY, NY
15 September 1945

Hello Darling;

Leaving tonight for one-week tour of Switzerland.

Been going nutty hanging around camp and sweating out return home. So, this morning when they asked me if I wanted to go, I said yes after figuring it would be a good way of taking up the slack time.

I should be homeward bound shortly after getting back next week.

The trip through Switzerland is the regular prewar Cook's tour, and I'm told it's pretty interesting.

Should be nice to see one country that hasn't been scarred by the war anyway.

I love you.

Your, Larry

238th Engr. Combat Bn.
Assembly Area Command
APO 752, NY, NY
Schaffhausen, Switzerland
19 September 1945

Hello Darling;

Have been traveling around all over the place the last few days.

I must say that it's really beautiful here. The only thing wrong is that I'm not with you.

Am leaving for Andermatt tomorrow morning, and after that Lausanne, Berne, and a short hop to Geneva.

Visited the biggest steel works in the country today and had a fine time sticking my nose everywhere and talking production with the plant managers, and wages, hours and unions with the workers.

I hope like hell that when I get back to camp I'll know definitely what date I'm leaving for home.

The sooner the better.

I love you always.

Your, Larry

———

Camp Oklahoma City
Sissonne, France
26 September 1945

Hello My Darling;

Well back to Alcatraz after being in civilization for awhile.

God, I never realized how poverty-stricken and beat up, physically and spiritually, France is. You can only really see it when you get a chance to compare it with what a well-ordered, prosperous country is.

The trip was very nice, but as usual, nothing holds my interest any more—nothing but getting back home to you.

One of the things I did, besides looking at scenery, was to talk to people—all kinds of people. Kind of like a traveling reporter.

Incidentally, you'd be amazed to hear me talk French and German these days. I've become pretty fluent—and in Switzerland it came in handy because those are two of the three official languages spoken there.

Most people in Switzerland are worried about their future. They collaborated with the Nazis, you know—at least their government did to a certain extent. And the people feel guilty and are anxious to know what we Americans are thinking—not only of them but of the Russians. . . .

I was told today to be prepared to leave within two weeks, three weeks at the most.

As if I have to be told.

They could wake me up in the middle of the night and tell me I had to make a boat in Le Havre in five hours, and I bet I could catch it running on foot.

You just keep saving your love for me. I'll use it all.

I'm crazy about you.

Your loving, Larry

Camp Oklahoma City
Sissonne, France
28 September 1945

Darling:

Gee, time drags when you're on the verge of great happiness—doesn't it? . . .

Say, Bub, I forgot to mention it before, but I was really amused by your account of how you and Davy went on the picket line.

How did he like it?

I wonder what he'll say when we tell him some day that he was picketing before he could walk.

If you only knew how much I want to see that little rascal and hold him in my arms.

I'm afraid you'll have to check me constantly to keep from spoiling him.

One of the officers in the battalion is getting married in Paris tomorrow.

It's a real old-fashioned, story-book romance. She's an American nurse whom he met in the hospital when he was wounded.

We're going down to attend the ceremony and give them a sendoff. . . .

Je t'aime, je t'adore, je t'embrace mille fois, et je t'attendrai.

Your, Larry

Camp Oklahoma City
Sissonne, France
1 October 1945

Hello Sweetheart;

Got your letter describing Davy's birthday. I'm glad he had such a wonderful time. Tell him his daddy was thinking of him on that day and wishing he could be there to play with his toys.

I'm really on tenterhooks right now because I'm expecting orders at any time shipping me home. I couldn't be more impatient if I were a prisoner of war awaiting liberation.

God, this waiting is awful.

To make things really ironic, I'm supposed to be the battalion's recruiting officer right now.

You know, of course, that the Army is embarking on a campaign for voluntary re-enlistments. And they've picked me to handle it in our outfit. Me of all people!

Why, I think anyone below the rank of full colonel who wants to stay in this blankety-blank organization has got stones in his head.

I told the CO, he could appoint me, but I'd be damned if he could get me to drum up trade. He said that was O.K. with him as long as we could show a recruiting officer on the books.

It's silly as hell, because I'll be gone soon and they'll just have to get someone else. But, that's the lunatic asylum they call the Army. . . .

Gee, darling, I want you so much. I'm so lonely for you, so lovesick. Que j'ai le cafard!

Give my son my love.

And you too, bub.

I love you.

Your own, Larry

―――――

Camp Oklahoma City
Sissonne, France
10 October 1945

My Darling;

Stop the mails! Poppa's coming home!

I take it back about miracles, they still happen.

Tomorrow morning I leave for a reinforcement Depot in the vicinity of Paris (Fontainebleau to be exact).

There I'll be processed and made ready for shipment.

You can look for me around the end of the month.

Á bientôt, <u>really</u>.

My own dear heart, I love you.

Tell Davy he'll see his old man soon.

Je t'adore

Your, Larry

―――――

Camp Twenty Grand
Rouen, France
22 October 1945

Hello Darling;

Arrived here 5:00 A.M.

This is the last stop before the boat. From here, when we finally move again it will be, Gott sei dank, to a tub.

Now, exactly when that will take place I don't know. But, it should be within 10 days at the latest.

Boy, if they had taken so long getting us over here and moving around in combat, I believe we'd be PWs for the Krauts right now, instead of the other way around.

The only thing that keeps me from blowing my top is the knowledge that I'm actually traveling home, and that in a few weeks I'll be finished with all this chicken and stupidity.

You should be getting a phone call from me not too much after you receive this letter.

Take it easy, sweetheart.

I love you.

Your, Larry

[TELEGRAM]

1945 OCT 29 AM 5 07

HRCD8 HAVRE 19 29
VLT MRS GRACE S CANE
233 WEST 77TH ST NEW YORK=
SAILING LEHAVRE 48 HOURS HOME SOON
HALLELUJAH LOVE=

LARRY

APPENDIX A

History of *The Ticker*

THE TICKER *was founded in 1932 at City College School of Business (Baruch College of City University New York). Following a tumultuous two-year history marked by disputes over journalistic freedom, Lawrence Cane (then Cohen) was elected editor in 1934. What follows is an excerpt on the history of* The Ticker *that appeared in the 1935 edition of the college yearbook,* The Lexicon.

At the end of the [Spring 1934] term, The Ticker Association met to select a new editor. Neither Dorothy Wein '35, nor Lawrence Cohen '35, former sports editor, could receive a sufficient number of votes to be elected to the position during the meeting. After the meeting was adjourned, one of the members of the association suddenly decided to swing his vote to Cohen, and wrote a letter to Professor Maximilian Philip, chairman of the association, stating his intention. Since such a vote was not in accord with correct parliamentary procedure, the recipient of the editorship still remained undetermined. Cohen was later officially appointed editor of the newspaper.

Cohen was even more militant than [his predecessor] Charles Reichman and constantly got into trouble with his vehement editorials. Leonard J. Hankin '36 was his managing editor. Together, the two had worked on *The Ticker* for years, storing up a knowledge of the fundamentals of college journalism, and the ways of college administrators. Hard-boiled and thoroughly disillusioned, they were both imbued with a social consciousness which they were determined to impart to the student body. To them, college was not a place to bury one's self in outworn theories. They were alive to the outside world and its inconsistencies. They felt that it was the vital concern of all students to become aware of the problems of war, fascism, labor disputes, ignorance, poverty, and misery.

Cohen began a campaign for a charter, knowing that without

such a guarantee, free expression would be curtailed as soon as anything deemed to be in "poor taste" was published. After a few weeks, the faculty met his insistent demands, and gave *The Ticker* a charter which allowed almost complete freedom, and took most of the regulatory powers out of the hands of the Dean.

About this time, the notorious anti-fascist riot took place in the Great Hall uptown. Cohen had previously written an editorial criticizing the administration for extending an invitation to some visiting Italian students. When the expulsions and suspensions took place, he wrote several blunt editorials attacking the administration's policies in this matter. Realizing, however, that his course would eventually lead to disaster and the complete loss of the bitterly won freedom that *The Ticker* had acquired, Larry changed his tactics entirely. By publishing sarcastic editorials, he managed successfully to continue his original editorial purpose unhindered.

Reappointed editor for the spring, 1935 semester, Larry Cohen immediately began an anti-Hearst campaign. Furthermore, in the hope of giving the student body a Student Council which would concern itself with something more than petty politics, *The Ticker* introduced another innovation into the extra-curricular affairs of the College by endorsing certain candidates for office.

The newspaper then actively engaged in a state-wide drive to defeat a loyalty oath for students proposed by Senator Nunan in the State legislature. Cohen was appointed to an executive committee composed of college editors and student council presidents of the leading colleges of New York State. A *Ticker* delegation visited Albany to take part in the concerted lobbying which defeated the Nunan Bill. After this campaign, *The Ticker* continued its active existence by plunging into the anti-war strike movement to complete an enviable record for 1934–1935.

APPENDIX B

Lawrence Cane's Request for Reassignment to Combat or Airborne Engineer Battalion[1]

FIVE HUNDRED EIGHTY SECOND
ENGINEER DUMP TRUCK COMPANY

Camp Claiborne, La.
August, 1943

SUBJECT: Reassignment
TO: Chief of Engineers, U.S. Army, Washington, D.C.
(Through Commanding General, EUTC, Camp Claiborne, La.)

1. The undersigned officer of the 582nd Engineer Dump Truck Company, Camp Claiborne, La., feels that he has been misassigned and requests reassignment to any combat or airborne engineer battalion.
2. The officer has had almost two years of combat experience, having been a lieutenant in the infantry of the Spanish Republican Army during the recent Spanish Civil War.
   He is also a graduate of the following service schools:
   a. Engineer OCS, Fort Belvoir, Va., Mar. 3, 1943
   b. Military Intelligence Training Center, Camp Ritchie, Md., May 11, 1943
   c. Cadre Officers' Course, Fort Belvoir, Va., July 31, 1943
3. The officer feels that this background of practical and theoretical experience together with his enthusiasm for combat work qualify him to contribute much more to the Service in a Combat or Airborne battalion than he is capable of doing in his present assignment.

---

[1] Letter in possession of David E. Cane.

4. He has no experience with motors or motor vehicles, and knows nothing about their repair or maintenance, which is the main problem for a truck unit in any theater of operations. This being the case, he cannot feel any enthusiasm about his present job.
5. Since a man's performance as a leader of soldiers depends chiefly on his enthusiasm for his work and "knowing his stuff" the officer, despite a conscientious attitude, feels that he is handicapped. He will be able to function at only a fraction of his capacity in his present assignment.
6. On the other hand, assignment to a combat or airborne battalion will place him in a position where he can use his experience and training to the best interest of his troops and his Nation.

LAWRENCE CANE
2nd Lt. CE.
582nd Eng'r Co. (DT)

APPENDIX C

Diary of Lt. George A. Worth[1]

The Briefing

The moment we trained months for was at last at hand. Our Commanding Officer, Captain Edward J. Blumenstein, of New Jersey, stood before Company B, 238th Engineer Combat Regiment in the briefing tent, somewhere in England, and said: "Well men, this is the real thing!"

The slight tightening around my heart was reflected in the many expressions seen on the faces of the men around me. The easy going farmer from Georgia, the ex-coal miner from Pennsylvania, the tall, lanky Texan, the hill billy from Tennessee, the snappy Brooklyn boy, all were taking it in without more than a murmur, but relief, apprehension, worry, gladness shown from their faces.

Honest sweat lay like raindrops on their foreheads. A few sat with eyes gazing unseeing at their shoes, hands held between their knees. All listened intently to the few remarks pertaining to the job ahead for our particular unit. Company "B," our company, was to build the TX, a new Army bridge for crossing swampy ground. Company "C" was to clear the Assembly area of mines. Company "A" was to assist in demolition work on whatever was ordered by the Battalion Commander, Lt. Col. David G. MacMillan, of Alabama. Each of us felt that our Company was carrying the load of the Campaign.

Meeting of Craft Commanders

Those four words were to become nightmarish for the Junior Officers of the Battalion. All platoon commanders were assigned a craft load, 60 to 70 men and 6–11 vehicles. He was responsible

---

[1] Lt. Worth's diary is reprinted in Major Ernest C. James, U.S. Army (ret.), "238th Engineer Combat Battalion in Action in World War II" (privately printed, 1990). Reprinted by permission of Major (ret.) George A. Worth, Moncks Corner, South Carolina.

for supervising the mess, administration and security regulations from the day of the briefing until the craft was fully loaded in England and emptied on the shores of France.

Nothing seemed sacred to the Group Commander, Lt. Col. Rogers, as he called the meeting of craft commanders two, three, four times a day. Relaxation, a movie, meals were shattered by runners bringing new times for these meetings. Seemingly, every possible detail was covered, some needless, some essential.

My craft, an LCT, was to be loaded with 58 men from our battalion, 8 men from a colored trucking company, and four men from a heavy steel treadway bridge company. 1st Lt. Lawrence Cane, of Connecticut [sic], was the only other officer aboard my craft. A small statured, bespectacled, quick-witted Yankee, Lt. Cane had fought two years in Spain on the Loyalist side and knew the Nazi from what he was really cooked up to be. We immediately became cronies and the bull flew thick and fast between us. He told me that he wanted to be with his wife, and expectant mother once more, and that he loved her. He would spend his fourth wedding anniversary, June 16, in France.

Loading

We departed from the marshalling area at 1005 on 1 June 1944, and convoyed in trucks to the embarking yards at Torquay, England. My throat was sore from yelling at my men, when finally the craft was fully loaded and the ramp door pulled up in place. Each man now had a life preserver, two vomit bags, and assault gas mask, his M-1 Garand or M-1 Carbine, a steel helmet and combat pack, all worn over gas resistant impregnated clothing, which he wore 24 hours a day. In the belt around his waist he had 80 rounds of ammunition, 80 rounds of death for the Germans was his wish. Eleven combat loaded vehicles were lashed to the deck of our Landing Craft Tank/Truck (LCT) #2331, and American made boat launched 12 October 1943. Her all British crew was commanded by Sub. Lt. J. F. Oakley, RNVR, a genial Cockney from London. His second in command, Midshipman George Boulton, was a 19 year old, who was sweating out his first ring. He tended to orienting the personnel aboard.

Today we suffered our first casualty. The craft had to be beached for repair of a hole in one of her tanks. It was dried out.

I unloaded the men on the beach for calisthenics. While playing tackle football with a steel helmet, Pvt. Louis L. Powell dislocated his right shoulder in a fall. The intense pain was not relieved when I gave him a shot of morphine, so I summoned a doctor from a nearby field hospital, Capt. F. V. Edwards, who recommended he be removed from the ship. Powell certainly hated to leave the gang. Missing the big show hurt him as much as the injury. My last words to him as the ambulance pulled away were: "I'll get an extra Jerry for you Powell." Powell answered in his slow drawling voice: "Thank you suh, I'll shore appreciate it."

Life Aboard LCT 2331

At the moment, I am standing on the small 6' by 10' uncovered bridge of the craft. Below and before me are the men and material at my command. There is a mixed feeling of hope, dread, sorrow and pride inside me as I look at my men. T/4 Jesse R. Winkles, from Carrol County, Georgia, my carpenter and proud father of a new born boy he has never seen, is sitting on top of one of the overloaded trucks, looking through field glasses at the shore line of the Brixham Harbor, where we are anchored waiting for other ships to join us. A good God fearing man he will do more than his share in the coming fight. Pvt. William C. Agnew, Jr., a little man from Mississippi with the driest sense of humor I've ever encountered, is busy cleaning and oiling his rifle. Pvt. Richard E. Hoefert, Alton, Illinois, the newest member of my platoon, is sitting on the pontoon bridge material talking with Agnew. Hoefert is the platoon radio operator, and I believe him to be excellent non-com material. T/5 James E. Thompson, a huge, tough, well-liked and respected Texan, who is in charge of the truck drivers, is busy pasting a 12″ letter "N" on the windshields of all our vehicles. The "N" will assist the beach M.P.'s in guiding our vehicles to the initial battalion assembly area. Pvt. Michael M. Esler, my Joliet, Illinois assistant Jeep driver, is practicing semaphore with Sgt. Donald W. Ray of Mineo, Oklahoma, my quiet dependable 2nd squad leader. Pvt. John E. Tyminiski, Queensbury, N.Y., a quick-tempered, competent Polish lad with 6 years of service under his belt, is my demolition expert in the platoon. I've often wished that the quirk which possesses Tyminiski, and causes him to remain a private would make itself known, so that I could help him fight it off.

Also on board are the eight colored men from the dump truck company. I'm now watching the glowing white eyeballs of Cpl. Leon W. Davis, from Erie, Pa., as he lays on his back covered with blankets, looking at the barrage balloons hovering protectively over the harbor. PFC George S. Berkner, Eleanor, Pa., a deeply religious man whom I've never heard utter one swear word in nine months, is standing on the deck, a Life magazine under one arm and his canteen cup under the other. The letters from Berkner to his family and many friends which I censor are an inspiration to me in his pride of being a man of God. Private Kireakos A. McRoyal, of Sarasota, Florida, better known as "the Greek" is adjusting the blasted life preserver, which is continually falling around his hips, contrary to safety regulations.

The men who built the LCT never had to make a voyage on one, I'll bet. Every square foot of the deck space is covered by vehicles. The men are swarming under, on, and over the trucks like mighty ants. They will sleep where they are swarming. I pray that no rain will fall tonight or during the voyage. Our ration is the new Army 10-in-1, a delicious, well planned, balanced diet that is contained in a box $8'' \times 15'' \times 24''$, enough for 10 men for 3 meals for 1 day in each box. They will be eaten cold except for a few staples, beans, cereal, bacon, and coffee, which will be served hot by S/Sgt. Norman R. Roberts of Florida, the mess Sgt. for the voyage. Give my men something to eat and clothes to wear, and they will get along.

The Harbor

Around our anchored boat are dozens of similar boats, huge Landing Ship Tanks (LSTs), and many small surface boats. Just a small drop in the bucket full that will assault the Madman's Lair on "D" Day. In sight are 49 of the huge, white balloons which prohibit sneak strafing attacks by night fighter planes. The most protecting and glorious sight of all is the American Flag flying from the mast of every craft in the harbor. One of the men is now whistling the Star Spangled Banner. Oh, Merciful God, make us worthy of our heritage as we go one day nearer the day of destiny, "D" Day.

Waiting

Three hours ago, the skipper received notice to leave the harbor at 1730. At the time, I was talking to the men assembled in the tiny, cramped bow of the LCT. I was handed a piece of paper by the skipper, and immediately told the men by saying: "We will be on our way to France at 1730." Never will I forget the look of happiness that greeted my words. The men are actually wanting to get into the scrap!

At the moment, I can see all types of small craft pulling out of the harbor. Men are clustered along the rails, on top of trucks, peering at the activity around them with naked eyes and field glasses. My men are unusually calm. The majority are eating their evening ration. S/Sgt. John. J. Kochan, my efficient, well liked and respected Platoon Sgt., is reclining bareheaded atop a truck reading a book with Cpl. Thompson and PFC Marian E. King, also of Texas, and the pals are jabbing away at each other.

Under Way

With the words: "Stand by, mid-ships" from the skipper, Lt. Oakley, down the voice pipe at exactly 1807, we are underway to our great test. Only 5 powerful motor torpedo boats are left in the harbor. I just waved "so-long" to Lt. Edgar G. Wilson of North Carolina, the Commander of the 2nd Platoon, as his craft passed by. "Good luck, Ed."

Lt. Oakley, with four ratings, is standing at attention on the port bow as we leave the harbor entrance. The examination vessel is being passed, the crew stands at ease, the skipper is giving commands, and we are just another boat loaded with yanks bound for battle. The waters are filled with ships of war. As I look astern at the little English village, I see perhaps for the last time the rows of neat stone houses, green hedge-rowed fields, circling sea gulls feasting on the refuse of departing ships. God Save The King.

On the Open Sea

An unforgettable sight of countless ships, strung along for miles, evenly spaced, is now before me. The foamy wake of the American manned LCT 525 ahead of us reminds me of the sudsy top of a mug of beer from Izzy's Log Cabin, down at Valdosta, Georgia, my hometown. A teetotaler, I've nevertheless seen many a glass of suds go down the hatch. We are now approaching a priceless marker to the Navy, a swept channel marker denoting a mine free path through the troubled waters of the English Channel from Lands End to Dover. S/Sgt. Herman S. Crawley, Washington, D.C., is having his curly hair cut by T/5 Clarence O. Johnson, of Dallas, Texas. These colored boys are good soldiers and do a good job with their trucks.

Every mothers heart would be gladdened if they could stand beside me on the bridge of this craft, observing the casual, care-free, happy manner my men have assumed. I thank God I am not their enemy. Pvt. Albert L. Rael, New Mexico, is rechecking his life preserver. A quiet, easy going lad, Rael will probably never rise higher than PFC, but he will still be a soldier that any state could be proud to claim as her own son.

The sea is getting rougher and the flat bottomed LCT is starting to pitch and jounce with the waves. The sea sick preventative pills, passed out on sailing by Pvt. Frank Quatramani, New York City, my Italian First Aid man, may yet come in handy. Mountains behind the shore line bring back memories of the torturous cold of McComb Reservation in Plattsburg, New York and Elkins, West Virginia, where we spent many hard days of training in preparation for the job ahead.

Wireman Jack Robertson of Scotland, a signalman off duty, is clad in a thin white shirt, trousers, and a jaunty hat, and has his pre-chewed gum stuck behind his right ear for future use. He is looking ahead at history being made. These English lads amaze me with their acceptance of every pittance granted them with a calm, unsmiling face. As I look forward and aft of this English flagged vessel, I see Old Glory snapping in the breeze, shouting the spirit of America to me.

Our Skipper, binoculars hanging from his wind-tanned neck, keeps a piercing crow-footed eye cast on the ships about us. LCT 2074, commanded by a red bearded, hard eyed and handsome Australian is leading our craft at present. Every confidence is felt that the Skipper will beach us on the coast of France in a manner satisfactory to all. On the horizon are hundreds of ships, wearing flags of the world's most powerful navies. Our craft is wearing a new ensign, which the Skipper hoisted with exclamation "I'd reserved this for peace, but this is too blooming good a chance to miss."

The wind is getting colder. I'm afraid the boys won't sleep very warm tonight. Lt. Cane, four Staff Sergeants and myself are taking turns about standing watch with the Naval Watch on duty, just in case something might happen before beaching.

In the last few hours, I have watched a miracle of navigation as scores of LCTs have come out of harbors along the southeast coast England, joined our convoy which now stretches far beyond eye-sight, and become part of our big family. How welcome is that beautiful flotilla of destroyers that hover protectively about the convoys!! Gone are the balloons of yesterday. The English coast is still in sight. The sun is setting radiantly behind the hills. Land will be gone in the morning. Next stop: France.

While writing this, I am in the Captain's cabin, a tiny cubicle 10′ × 10′, set directly over the pounding diesel engines. The skipper is catching a few minutes needed relaxation on the bunk behind me before his all night stay on the cold bridge. The hammering of the anchor chained in its bed behind the craft sounds like an angry bull kicking in the side of his pen. Lt. Cane is on watch now, so, I can relax for awhile, if relaxation is possible with thoughts running in my mind. The automatic blackout switch which throws the entire cabin and mess deck into darkness when the door to the main deck is opened causes a little irritation trying to write. War!!

I've often wondered about the thoughts of a man bound for his first battle. Now I know. Surprisingly few thoughts of home, loved ones, old times or friends have entered my mind thus far. The preparation, briefing, study of maps and aerial photographs, feeding the men, thinking of their individual problems and possible reactions, and gazing wide-eyed at the night around us has occupied my mind. Of course, a memory or two of my personal life slips in occasionally. I wonder what the kids of Valdosta, Georgia are doing tonight. Most of all, I worry about my mother. God, give her the strength to carry on when she hears the invasion news. Pvt. Daniel T. Ardis, Atmore, Alabama, who never learned to read or write is thinking of his mom too, for he asked me this evening to write her for him if any harm came. I was honored by his request and confidence.

The skipper has gone to the bridge for the night and I am alone, pad on my knee, pencil in hand, trying to write an article that will probably never be published. A cup of coffee was just brought to me by the ship's mess man. Darn nice of these English men. Their cup of tea, or coffee must be had, regardless of the situation. I wonder what I can write that would be of interest. My untrained mind can't make up subjects. A New Testament and prayer book is at my elbow. Tomorrow, God permitting, we shall have a religious service aboard on deck led by Pvt. Berkner. When I suggested that he arrange a short program, his kind eyes seemed to fill with tears of gratitude and renewed confidence in that God did exist, even in the heart of his cursing, hell raising platoon leader. Yes, Berkner, we need Him more than ever before.

The First Officer has entered, red faced from the wind, with a cup of cocoa and a butter sandwich, hoping to get some rest before the skipper calls for him to return to the bridge. I read this diary to him for comment. He stated "It's jolly good, hope you get it back, for it will make good reading after the war." I feel flattered and very glad that I started this "on the scene" story. Mr. T. C. Merchant of Madison, Florida, the man who used to pay me by the inch for articles for his paper, would get a big kick out of watching me scribble away.

I have just returned to the noisy cabin from the deck where a beautiful bright moon is shining. Oh the memory of moonlight and courtships in Florida and Georgia. The skipper is cursing the Australian ahead of us for weaving aimlessly back and forth across the bow of our craft. His polite remarks about the man ahead are quite different from the sound cussing out I would hand a fellow for such doings.

The ghostly silhouettes of surrounding boats means a tiresome night for the skipper and watch. The men are asleep under their blankets, trusting their lives and future to the competent mind and hands and the minor role the two American Officers are playing. Twelve o'clock, midnight now, so I shall try to get a little sleepy-eye, as called by Pvt. Joe S. Harrell, Mitchel County, Georgia, in his letters to his wife, nicknamed "breadburner." My prayer for Divine protection.

Sunday Together
Sleep was fitful and unrestful last night. The hammering anchor often startled me. Seasickness has affected half the men. I am too

ill to leave the small cabin. The hour of history has been set for 0630 tomorrow, June 5th. All men are eating their rations and preparing to leave their home of 4 days for the first venture on enemy shores.

Monday Afloat

The patrol craft just announced that D-Day has been postponed until Tuesday morning. Mixed emotions greeted the announcement. Our craft has started a long circling movement to delay approaching the beach. Planes overhead gives us assurance of reaching "home in France."

Tuesday, D-Day

The thunderous roar of naval gun fire from the mighty battle ships supporting the invasion awakened us. The most inspiring sight greeted my eyes on mounting the bridge. Ships of all description covered the ocean like a blanket.

[Lt. Worth's diary ends here. Shortly thereafter, Lt. Oakley gave the order to prepare to go ashore; he was taking them in to the beach.][2]

---

[2] For the D-Day landing at Utah Beach, H-hour was scheduled for 6:30 a.m. LCT 2331 landed at Utah Beach approximately twenty minutes later.

APPENDIX D

Lawrence Cane's Silver Star Citation[1]

HEADQUARTERS 2D ARMORED DIVISION
Office of the Division Commander
APO 252

200.6 Cane, Lawrence
SUBJECT: Award of the Silver Star
TO: First Lieutenant Lawrence Cane, 0-1110976
Corps of Engineers, United States Army

Under the provisions of Army Regulations 600-45, as amended, you are awarded the Silver Star for gallantry in action by Section I, General Order Number 43, this Headquarters, dated 25 September 1944, as set forth in the following:

CITATION

First Lieutenant Lawrence Cane, 0-1110976 Corps of Engineers, 238th Engineer Combat Battalion, United States Army. For gallantry in action on 30 July 1944 in France. During the night of 30 July 1944, the advance guard of Combat Command "B," 2d Armored Division, consisting of some thirty medium tanks and forty other motor vehicles, was in danger of encirclement and annihilation by superior enemy forces attempting to break out of a trap. Lieutenant Cane, despite intense enemy small arms and mortar fire volunteered to personally reconnoiter a route for these vehicles and tanks in order to contact friendly forces. The reconnaissance was made in complete darkness at a time when the enemy situation was unknown, and resulted in encountering strong enemy patrols which infiltrated into the area and cut the roads. The enemy halted Lieutenant Cane's repeated attempts to find a route with intense machine gun and small arms fire. Despite

---

[1] Silver Star Citation in possession of David E. Cane.

these factors and with complete disregard for his personal safety, Lieutenant Cane voluntarily and determinedly continued his reconnaissance and found a safe route of withdrawal. By means of the route discovered by this reconnaissance, the tanks and vehicles were safely evacuated to the 2d Armored Division Reserve and saved from possible encirclement and destruction. Entered Military Service from New York.

> S/E.N. Harmon
> T/E.N. HARMON
> Major General, U.S. Army
> Commanding

OFFICIAL SEAL
2d Armored Division
"I certify that the above is a True Copy"

> WILLIAM F. RULE
> 1st Lt. 238th Engr C Bn
> Adjutant

APPENDIX E

Silver Star Affidavit[1]

HEADQUARTERS
238TH ENGINEER COMBAT BATTALION
APO 230, U.S. ARMY
7 August 1944

A-F-F-I-D-A-V-I-T

Personally appeared before me, the undersigned, authorized by law to administer oath, in this and like cases, on John B. Wong, 01109765, 1st Lt., 238 Engrs

Who Deposes and Sayeth:

"On 30 July 1944, I was a witness to Lt. Cane's Gallantry in action against the enemy. I personally saw Lt. Cane, under intense enemy machine gun, small arms, and mortar fire, voluntarily evacuate some seventy vehicles, including 30 tanks, that were the advance guard of one of our columns and which was in danger of being cut off. Lt. Cane, without regard for his personal safety and in complete darkness proceeded the column and drew fire, which was the only way of determining which roads were cut, thereby finding an escape route for the column."

Further Deponent Sayeth not:

John B. Wong
1st LT CE

Subscribed and Sworn to before me this 7th of August 1944

William F. Rule
1st Lt., 238th Engr. C. Bn.
Adjutant

A-F-F-I-D-A-V-I-T

---

[1] Silver Star Affidavit in possession of David E. Cane.

APPENDIX F

History of the 238th Engineer Combat Battalion

(U.S. Army Document)[1]

The 238th Engineer Combat Battalion was activated at Camp Bowie, Texas on 13 June 1942 as the Second Battalion of the 51st Engineer Combat Regiment. The unit moved to Plattsburg Barracks in October 1942 and received filler replacements in January 1943. Basic training was completed in April and unit training in July 1943. After participating in the West Virginia Maneuvers at Elkins, West Virginia the battalion prepared for overseas movement, embarking from Hampton Roads on 13 October 1943. Arriving in Oran, Algeria on 2 November the battalion was moved into a staging area while awaiting further movement orders. On 5 January 1944 the battalion left North Africa arriving in the United Kingdom on 20 January.

Upon arrival in the United Kingdom the battalion began an extensive training program in preparation for its part in the assault of fortress Europe. During this period the unit participated in Exercise "Tiger," a full scale rehearsal of the actual landing on Utah Beach.

Landing on Utah Beach on D Day as part of the assault waves, the battalion supported the landing of the Fourth Infantry Division. The original mission assigned the battalion was the opening and maintenance of the exit roads on Tare Green Beach. However, due to the commitment of other units in the 1106th Engineer Combat Group the 238th Engineer Combat Battalion opened and maintained the roads in the entire Utah Beach Area. From D Day to D plus three the battalion continued on this work. Upon being relieved of this road assignment the unit con-

---

[1] Copy in possession of David E. Cane.

structed a treadway bridge across the Douve River. This bridge was a vital part in the link between the Omaha and Utah beachheads, and is believed to be the first military bridge constructed in France during the invasion. Upon the completion of this task the battalion was attached to the 101st Airborne Division, to whom was assigned the mission of providing security for the VII Corps South flank during its drive to Cherbourg. The battalion laid approximately 13,000 anti-tank mines in the area doing a great part of this work in areas under direct enemy artillery fire. Subsequent to this attachment the 238th Engineer Combat Battalion was employed in the improvement and maintenance of roads in the Cotentin Peninsula. These roads played an important role in moving men, equipment and supplies for the breakthrough from this peninsula.★ (★Under the command of Lieutenant Col. Jay P. Dawley, 0–21750 at this point (13 July 1944) onward.)

During the Marigny-St. Gilles break-through the battalion was placed in direct support of the Second Armored Division, and by such support assisted the Armored Division in performing its assigned mission. Elements of the battalion moved the Second Armored Division's organic and attached artillery across country when it would have been impossible to move this artillery along the roads. A platoon of the battalion, part of the advanced guard of an armored column, spearheaded the entire breakthrough and assisted in repulsing an enemy counterattack. Upon being relieved of this support mission the battalion moved into a rest area.

After being in a rest area for a short time the battalion was again placed in support of the Second Armored Division during the closing of the Falaise-Argentan gap. During this phase the battalion installed and manned a band of obstacles eight miles long protecting the exposed flank of the Armored Division. The battalion sector was later taken over by the Fourth Infantry Division.

Closely following the advance of VII Corps towards Paris the battalion did extensive road work. On 27 August 1944 a 540-foot steel treadway bridge was constructed across the Seine River near Corbeil. This bridge crossed the combat elements of three infantry divisions. At Meaux, France, one bridge was erected and three strengthened across the Marne River. A 110-foot triple-single Bailey bridge was put up across the Oise River at Etreaupont.

The battalion entered Belgium on 5 September in support of the Third Armored Division, and in response to General Collins' personal wishes as VII Corps Commander, commenced bridging operations across the Sambre and Meuse Rivers at Namur. A 564-foot treadway and a 150-foot triple-double Bailey bridge, later reinforced to Cl 70 by the installation of a bailey pier, were erected across the Meuse River while the enemy was still shelling the area. During the same operation a 150-foot single-single Bailey was constructed across the locks on the Sambre. All three of these bridges were constructed simultaneously. In addition an existing class 40 bridge over the Sambre was reinforced to class 70. Upon relief from support of the Third Armored Division the battalion worked on the Corps MSR improving and strengthening existing bridges to carry class 70 loads.

On 20 September the battalion entered Germany in the Aachen area and was assigned the mission of rendering useless the part of the Siegfried line in the area held by our forces. On 29 September the battalion was attached to the First Infantry Division and committed to a portion of the sector as infantry. The battalion manned this position until the capture of Aachen on 21 October. Two members of the battalion were taken prisoner during this operation. When the situation was finally considered hopeless by the enemy commander, these two soldiers were instrumental in arranging for the surrender of the city and its 1600-man German garrison.

The battalion was next assigned the responsibility for the maintenance of lines of Communication in the VII Corps area. During this phase the battalion cleared a route through Aachen. During the period 23 Nov. to 13 Dec. the battalion constructed 13 bridges of combined length of 1330 ft., six of these along the Autobahn and the remainder across the Inde River. The bridges across the Autobahn and the Inde at Weisweiler were constructed at night as the enemy had direct observation of the work sites. When the German counterattack in the Ardennes was launched the battalion was soon ordered to that area, promptly moved there and was attached to XVIII Corps (Airborne). Its first mission was the construction and manning of a barrier line in the vicinity of Manhay. Working against time in the face of an imminent enemy attack the battalion established and manned a barrier line about six miles long. On Christmas eve elements of the battalion assisted in stopping and breaking up an enemy attack of considerable force which was apparently the final German effort in this sector. Five Mark V tanks were knocked out in one of the minefields in this barrier line. When the German forces had been contained and our offensive started the battalion performed normal engineer duties in support of this operation. In direct support of the 82nd Airborne Division the battalion constructed under enemy fire three treadway bridges across the Ran De Baleur. At Trois Pont, in spite of direct enemy artillery fire falling on the immediate site, a bailey bridge was constructed across the Salme River. Upon reduction of the Ardennes salient the battalion returned to Germany and began preparation for the crossing of the Roer River.

The 238th Engineer Combat Battalion was placed in direct support of the 104th Division during the Roer River crossings. It was assigned the mission of constructing two treadway bridges and one bailey bridge in the vicinity of Birksdorf and Duren. Working under intense enemy fire and most hazardous conditions the battalion accomplished its mission. All three bridges which required the efforts of the entire battalion were completed in record time. Over these bridges were crossed the necessary armor, tank destroyers and artillery to support the advance of VII Corps. The forces that completed the capture of the City of Duren were crossed over one of the bridges constructed by the battalion. Closely following the advance of the 104th Division, the battalion supported the division's crossing of the next river barrier, the Erft River. Within a twenty four hour period one company of the battalion constructed four bridges in support of the crossing. After the Erft crossing the battalion was engaged in construction and maintenance of the roads in the 104th Division area. Plans were made for the Rhine crossing and a training program started. When the Remagen bridge was seized intact and a bridgehead established the battalion was ordered across the Rhine and performed normal engineer duties in the lively initial bridgehead.

During subsequent bridging operations of the VII Corps, the 238th Engineer Combat Battalion provided the far shore security for the working part. When the 1106th Engineer Combat Group was assigned the mission of constructing a treadway bridge across the Rhine in the vicinity of Bonn, one company was attached to the constructing battalion. During the construction of the bridge the efforts of this company were highly instrumental in the rapid completion of the 1320-foot steel treadway bridge in the record time of ten hours and seventeen minutes.

After the Rhine crossing had been secured and the exploitation and advance into Central Germany started the battalion was placed in direct support of the First Infantry Division. During this phase the battalion opened and maintained lines of communications in support of the division's advance. During the assault crossing of the Weser River the battalion was assigned and completed the task of constructing a 320-foot infantry support bridge in the First Division zone. During this period one company was attached to the 4th Cavalry Group and supported its advance.

After the crossing of the Weser River on 9 April the battalion less the company attached to the 4th Cavalry Group, continued to operate in direct support of the First Infantry Division until the Harz Mountain pocket had been eliminated. During this period the battalion constructed three timber trestle bridges and three bailey bridges and cleared many abatis. During the entire operation east of the Rhine the fighting value of the battalion was of considerable benefit in providing its own security and that of adjacent units against by-passed enemy troops. In addition to performing its normal engineer work the battalion captured approximately 300 prisoners. Upon closing of the Harz pocket the company attached to the 4th Cavalry Group reverted to battalion control.

V-E day found the battalion engaged in Military Government duties. The unit continued performing these duties until 1 June when it was transferred to the Assembly Area Command, where it is at present performing duties as utilities engineers in nine camps.

APPENDIX G

Selected After/After Action Reports[1]

238TH ENGINEER COMBAT BATTALION
APO 230, U.S. ARMY

AFTER/AFTER ACTION REPORT

1 July 1944: Total strength of the Battalion at the beginning of the period was 33 Officers, 3 Warrant Officers, and 674 Enlisted Men. Companies B & C ran an infantry attack problem. Co. A on group security. No Engineer casualties suffered.

2 July 1944: Reconnaissance party made a reconnaissance for gravel pit; water point set up at (396846). Company "B" assigned job of maintaining and repairing road by-passing Carentan. One squad of Company C assigned demolition job for AA unit Penrod.

3 July 1944: Company A assigned mission of lifting our minefield in Blackstone area. Company C will assist Company A in lifting minefield.

4–6 July 1944: Co's A & C engaged in removing minefield in Blackstone area. Work delayed by enemy artillery and small arms fire, but no casualties suffered. Company B maintained MSR in Blackstone area.

7–12 July 1944: Battalion engaged in maintaining roads in Blackstone area. One company C jeep ran over an enemy mine killing Gravette, Donald C., T/5 34502070 and wounding Rowe, Arris M. T/5, 34598030.

---

[1] National Archives at College Park, Maryland, World War II Operation Reports, Record Group 407, Box 18763.

13 July 1944: Company A constructed bailey bridge across Tribe-hou causeway. Major Dawley assumed Command of Battalion at 1000 hrs.

14 July 1944: Company C built the second bailey bridge across Tribehou Causeway making it two-way traffic.

15 July 1944: Company B removed TX bridge by-passing the bailey bridge on Tribehou Causeway. Other companies maintaining roads.

16 July 1944: Removed 3 minefields for 552 Field Artillery.

17 July 1944: Road maintenance in Blackstone Area.

18 July 1944: Maintaining roads in group area; one cow set off a booby trap in "A" Co. bivouac area but no casualties suffered.

19–20 July 1944: Road repair and maintenance in VII Corps area. Co. C moved out to join Co. B in bivouac area.

21–22 July 1944: Light road maintenance, care, maintaining and reloading equipment. Gas alarm sounded from Adjacent Unit about 2400, 22 July, but no gas was detected.

23–26 July 1944: Road repair and maintenance in group area. Co. B lost one truck which was bombed, while maintaining road net. Champion, James L., Pvt. 34762829 was slightly wounded.

27–30 July 1944: On 27 July Cobra operations began by order of the CG VII Corps. This Battalion less one company was put in direct support of the 41st Armored Infantry which was the 2nd Armored Division reserve. Co. C this unit was in direct support of CCB of the 2nd Armored Division, one Platoon being with the point. The purpose of this campaign was to cut off the enemy facing the VIII Corps and to assist the VIII Corps in the destruction of the enemy. During this campaign this Unit was engaged in repairing, and clearing of roads in 2nd Armored area. Also the construction of road blocks, and landing strips for powerhouse artillery. On the night of the 29th July the enemy counterattacked in vicinity of St. Dennis Le Gant with approximately 5 tanks and 300 infantrymen. Two captured enemy trucks, loaded with American Engineer Equipment, [were] knocked out by a German tank while being delivered to Princess C.P. by Co. B, however no casualties suffered from this. On 29 July, P.F.C. Tony A. Scenna, 33567186, Co. C, was killed in action by enemy fire when his platoon was pinned down by fire with the point of CCB. On the 30th July, T/5 Lonnie A. Hood, 34536547 Co. C was killed in action. T/5 James F. Clifton, 34538869, Co. C, was slightly wounded in action. Sgt. Anthony P. Filipiak, 33405926, Co. C was seriously injured in action. Sgt. Donald J. Smith, 33876459, Co. C was seriously wounded in action and Pvt. Paul V. Trembley, 31323512, Co. C was slightly wounded in action. Co. A captured one German officer, Captain, and Co. B captured 20 prisoners, including 5 officers. This campaign ended temporarily for this Bn. 30 July when we were relieved from support of the 2nd Armored Division.

31 July 1944: Co. C relieved from CCB and returned to Battalion. Total strength of organization at end of period: 36 Officers, 3 Warrant Officers and 658 Enlisted Men. 3 Officers gained and 16 Enlisted Men lost.

══════════

S-E-C-R-E-T

S-E-C-R-E-T
Auth: CG VII Corps
INIT: [WM]
DATE: 5 Jan. 1945

HEADQUARTERS
238TH ENGINEER COMBAT
BATTALION
APO 230, U.S. ARMY

AFTER/AFTER ACTION REPORT
FOR DECEMBER 1944

1 Dec 44 to 2 Dec 44
The battalion continued its work on roads in the vicinity of Eschweiler.

"A" Company reported an extensive Teller minefield at CR 867454. Mines were buried and excellently camouflaged.

"B" Company located and marked a Holz minefield at K 891443, and also found a large ammunition dump.

Enemy reconnaissance planes were fairly active during these two days, and shells of 170 MM Cal. fell in the immediate vicinity of the battalion C.P.

3 Dec 44 to 7 Dec 44

This period was marked by heavy enemy air activity, with battalion anti-aircraft machine guns participating in the shooting down of one enemy aircraft.

"C" Company completed the construction of a two-way Class 70 timer Trestle bridge in place of the Bailey Bridge at Weisweiler. The work was completed without interruption to traffic in spite of sporadic enemy shell fire.

"B" Company completed a Class 40 Bailey Bridge on the Autobahn over the Inde River at Coordinate F 013493. This work was also done under shell fire at night.

Lt. Worth of "B" Company received light wounds as the result of an air-burst in darkness while supervising an angledozer making a ramp off the Autobahn 1/4 mile east of Inde River Bridge.

Eschweiler was also heavily shelled during this period. At one time 3 shells scored direct hits on the buildings in the vicinity of the battalion C.P. S-2 and S-3 equipment were damaged and the S-# trailer was destroyed.

On the night of 3 Dec., the entire battalion was alerted for a possible counterattack by the 10th SS Panzer Div. The attack did not materialize.

Several new minefields of all kinds, Riegel, Teller, Topf, Holz, and Schu mines were reported by the companies and by Battalion recon parties.

8 Dec 44 to 12 Dec 44

Heavily mined areas were encountered during this period. All the standard types of German mines were included, and anti-personnel mines and booby traps were found to be liberally sprinkled through the fields. All areas were marked off and fenced in.

The companies worked on maintenance of assigned road nets.

Sporadic shelling in the vicinity of forward bridges on Autobahn continued.

On the 12th Dec, Major Hutson, S-2 of 1106 Engr C. Group, Capt. Reichmann, CO of Company "A," were badly wounded, and 2nd Lt. McLure of "A" Company was killed by mines while checking a Holz minefield at K-951490.

13 Dec 44 to 16 Dec 44

Companies continued maintaining and guarding bridges and working on assigned roadnets.

More minefields were located and squads from each company fenced and posted them.

17 Dec 44 to 21 Dec 44

Heavy enemy air activity during this period, with enemy parachute troops dropped throughout the area. Were part of group that were scheduled to drop in the Malmedy-Monschau area as part of the big German counterattack launched at right flank of 1st U.S. Army.

Companies guarded bridges and fenced in enemy minefields.

Layed [sic] an extensive friendly minefield which was part of defensive plan of 104th Infantry Division. 5,000 mines were laid in Lucherberg-Inden area.

22 Dec 44

Battalion left Eschweiler, Germany, and moved to Xhoris, Belgium. M/R 1:250,000, to engage in battle to stop German counterattack.

23 Dec 44 to 25 Dec 44

The battalion, less company kitchens, and administrative echelons of H/S Company moved out of Xhoris, Belgium at 2230 hours 23 December 1944 and proceeded to the crossroads at Werbomont. It was here that the Battalion Commander who had gone on ahead to XVIII Corps Headquarters met the battalion and explained the battalion's task. Barrier Lines were to be prepared along the roads Manhay to Bra, Manhay to La Fourche, and Manhay-Grandmenil-La Forge. These lines were designed to prevent enemy entrance into the area, and deny him access to the main road Manhay-Werbomont.

"A" Company was assigned the road to Manhay to Bra; "B" Company the road Manhay to La Fourche; and "C" Company the road Manhay to La Forge. Battalion and Company CP's were established at Chene-al-Pierre. After preliminary reconnaissance "A" Company began work at 0330 hours, 24 December 44, "B" Company began at 0400 hours and "C" Company at 0445 hours.

All companies prepared their assigned roads with road blocks of daisy chains, prepared trees for felling as abatis, prepared roads and culverts for demolition, and layed mine-fields. See attached overlay for a more detailed picture of the work. The work was completed by 1600 hours 24 December. All road blocks and minefields were covered by machine gun and bazooka posts.

During this period, all companies received light shelling along their road areas, but no casualties occurred, and the work was not delayed. After 1600 hours, the companies began improving the barriers that had been established. They buried their minefields, doubled the strength of their road blocks and dug in their outposts.

At around 2300 hours, 24 December the enemy attacked up the road to Manhay, overrunning two road blocks which had been constructed by "B" Company but which were being manned by another unit that had started to relieve "B" Company.

Other "B" Company men remained in position north of Manhay. Some friendly infantry elements withdrew past them. At 2355 a German tank column began an attack at Grandmenil. An estimated ten or twelve tanks, supported by infantry came into "C" Company's area. Here too, men manning the blocks at the town remained in position, although ordered to fall back by friendly officers from nearby units.

"C" Company immediately began construction of additional road blocks and mine belts and reinforced their existing road blocks. During this period they received light shelling.

Back at Chene-al-Pierre, on the road between Manhay Werbomont, some of our friendly armor and half-tracks and some infantry were moving back to the rear past our battalion CP. Wild rumors of a big German push were received. The battalion commander began investigation of this rumor and determined that the battalion would stay where it was, until either relieved or driven out.

All company commanders were contacted to determine the extent of enemy activity in their areas. Existing road blocks, able to be reached, were checked to see if our men were properly manning them. It was found that all men contacted were still holding their ground. The battalion dump of mines and demolitions which had been established at Chene-al-Pierre was evacuated to battalion rear echelon to prevent the possibility of their falling into enemy hands.

The battalion commander then organized a straggler line, and picked up several truckloads of friendly infantry and sent them back to a defense line that was being organized just north of Manhay. Manhay and Grandmenil fell into enemy hands but all battalion road blocks and outposts stayed in position just outside these towns. At about 0330 hours 25 December "C" Company had one truck demolished and six enlisted men wounded by an enemy shell. They also reported as missing four men from a roadblock at Grandmenil. When last seen they were engaging enemy tanks that had entered town. Later it was discovered that they had managed to get out by hopping on the last scout car to leave town.

The enemy made no concerted attempt after this to proceed further in the defensive barrier. Contact was reestablished all along the line, and the situation was stabilized in our battalion area. By 1200 hours 25 Dec. all companies had been relieved and returned to bivouac area at Xhoris.

SUPPLIES USED DURING OPERATION

Mines, AT M1	9,960
TNT, 1/2 Lb. blocks	1,800
Barbed Wire	60 rolls
Pickets, medium	110
Caps, blasting non-elec	220
Fuse, blasting time	200 Ft.
Fuse, blasting prima cord	900 Ft.
Rocket, AT, 2.36	20
Casualties	6 EM wounded

26 Dec 44 to 31 Dec 44

Battalion in direct support of the 82nd Airborne Division.

Constructed barrier lines consisting of preparing trees for abatis, bridges for demolitions, prepared road blocks, and put in mine-fields throughout the Divisional Area which roughly was bounded by the Lienne and L'Ambleuve Rivers. Company "A" moved to Paradis (k-548037) and the entire company (93 men effective) was in position manning and guarding the barrier line La Fourche—Targnon.

At the same time the companies improved existing bridges and repaired and improved the road network within the divisional area.

APPENDIX H

1972 WBAI Radio Interview with Lawrence Cane[1]

February 12, 1972

Tony Elature: . . . My name is Tony Elature and I'm here with three members of the Lincoln Battalion who this Saturday February 12, . . . on Lincoln's birthday will be celebrating their 35th anniversary, anniversary of their baptism by fire in Spain. Why don't you introduce yourselves?

Steve Nelson: My name's Steve Nelson.

Larry Cane: My name is Larry Cane.

Sam Gonshak: My name is Sam Gonshak.

TE: Larry, you were going to read a poem by . . . .

LC: Yes, this is a poem that was dedicated to the Veterans of the Abraham Lincoln Brigade. It was written by Genevieve Taggard[2] who was a well-known American poetess and it goes like this:

> [To the Veterans of the Abraham Lincoln Brigade]
> Say of them
> They knew no Spanish,
> At first, and nothing of the arts of war
> At first,
>   how to shoot, how to attack, how to retreat
> How to kill, how to meet killing
> At first.
> Say they kept the air blue

---

[1] WBAI interview of February 12, 1972 is reproduced with permission of Valerie van Isler, general manager, WBAI, 99.5 FM, New York, New York.

[2] American poet Genevieve Taggard (1894–1948) was a lifelong supporter of radical causes. Her social poetry dealt with the issues of war, race and class prejudice, and the problems of the working class.

Grousing and griping.
Arid words and harsh faces. Say
They were young;
The haggard in a trench, the dead on the olive slope
All young. And the thin, the ill, and the shattered,
Sightless, in hospitals, all young.

Say of them they were young, there was much they did not
    know,
They were human. Say it all; it is true. Now say
When the eminent, the great, the easy, the old,
And the men on the make
Were busy bickering and selling,
Betraying, conniving, transacting, splitting hairs,
Writing bad articles, signing bad papers,
Passing bad bills,
Bribing, blackmailing,
Whimpering, meeching, garroting,—they
Knew and acted
                understood and died.
Or if they did not die, came home to peace
That is not peace.
                Say of them
They are no longer young, they never learned
The arts, the stealth of peace, this peace, the tricks of fear;
And what they knew, they know.
And what they dared, they dare.

TE: Why don't you talk about what it was like in this country
before you went to Spain and what it was that prompted you to
go to Spain in relation to this country and the situation in Spain.

SN: Yes, I'd like to comment on that. It's hard for the present
generation to realize how ominous the picture seemed to us at
the time, being that Hitler had just come to power in Europe and
he was threatening the nations around him. He went and instituted the notorious raids against organizations and people who
didn't agree with him and he began to brand people because of
their nationality and began to build the gas chambers.

However, many Americans at that time did not believe that he was really a concern of ours. There were people in this country who thought that we could do business with Hitler. That was the general attitude. There were organizations who favored him, who thought that he was a good model for America. They even called upon a General of the United States Marines—fellow by the name of Smedley Butler—called on him to do the same thing as Hitler did in Germany as a way to meet the depression that we faced at the time in the Thirties when unemployed people were clamoring for bread and support and the Nazi solution was to put them in the army or compel them to do the things that the State wants them to do.[3] And there were those who wanted to do the same thing in this country.

Then came a day when Hitler began to move against other countries, move into Austria, move into the Rhineland, threaten France, and Mussolini moved into Ethiopia, and we saw this as not only as a menace to Europe, but a menace to us.

It was just about at that time that the Spanish people held an election and they elected a . . . legitimate government which was overwhelmingly democratic, 487 deputies for what was known as the Popular Front to 300 for the opposition. And it was against that government that the fascist generals in Spain in connivance with Mussolini and Hitler attacked the Republic and tried to overthrow it. And it was at that moment that people called upon assistance, the Spanish people called for assistance. They wanted to buy things from the democratic countries but France, and England, and the United States refused to sell legitimate things to a legally elected government.

And this was our answer. We responded in a sense saying that if Hitler wins, the second war will be on us. We better go there and help the Spaniards; maybe we can stop him. And this was essentially the reason why we responded, those of us who were conscious of the menace of fascism here.

Of course, we were active here. When the Nazi ship came into

---

[3] U.S. Marine Corps Major General Smedley Butler (1881–1940) was twice awarded the Congressional Medal of Honor. In 1933 bond trader Gerald MacGuire, with significant financial backing from wealthy businessmen, approached Butler about leading a coup d'etat intended to remove President Franklin D. Roosevelt from office. Butler flatly refused and went public with the information in 1934.

the New York Harbor, our men climbed the mast and tore the Nazi swastika down. Of course the Hearst press at the time, and the Ku Klux Klan, the Nazi Bund and the Black Legion and Father Coughlin and the whole crowd that's now forgotten, they were on the scene saying, "These people are creating trouble by messing around with Hitler's business. We want to do business with him. He's not harming us." But we thought otherwise, and it appears to me that in retrospect now, even the blind can see, so to say, that had we won in Spain, we would have probably delayed a second World War for much longer. But in view of the fact that we lost the war because we couldn't get enough assistance from democratic countries, even at that, we delayed the war for three years. And we think that was a gain by democratic powers.

So those of us who saw the picture, many of us saw it from a different angle. Some trade union fellows saw it as a menace to unions: if Hitlerism comes you'll have no unions. Others who were of a particular national group felt that it had no chance to survive if Nazism ruled here. The black people certainly felt that, many of them. The Jewish people, the national minority groups in this country, and so forth. And then decent Americans who cherished democracy felt the same thing. And though there was a lot of support for us amongst the people, the government acted as if we didn't exist. And there was only one congressman who dared to take a stand to support our position.

TE: Was there any direct opposition, or was it all indirect opposition, to your going to Spain?

SN: Well, it was an opposition that was done in this manner: our passports, for example, were marked *NOT VALID FOR SPAIN.* It was illegal to go to Spain. That was one thing. And the Spanish government couldn't buy anything that they wanted here, that was another way. Hitler had no trouble buying stuff here through his concerns, and so that 50% of the oil that Franco used in Spain came from the United States and 55% of trucks that they used came from Detroit. Franco didn't have to buy it here. Hitler bought it through his concerns and shipped it in his boats, protected it with his U-boats . . . while the Loyalist government had no chance to do that. They bought a few shiploads and they were sunk on the way.

TE: How much of what was happening in Europe and especially in Spain was known here? I being young and of a younger generation . . . have been led to believe that we didn't know. Say, for example, the bombing raids on Guernica and what was happening in Germany. People said, "Well, we didn't know what was happening." Was that true, or was it known here what was going on?

LC: No, that's not true. I would say that the headlines of *The [New York] Times*, the daily headlines in *The Times* carried news about Spain and the fighting in Spain for all of the time that fighting took place.

One of the interesting things about the press in this country in spite of the fact that our government officially was supposed to be observing what they called neutrality but it was neutrality really in favor of the fascists on Franco's side because they were getting materiel through Germany and Italy, even from the United States, as Steve has just mentioned. The interesting thing about the press in this country was that the most important newspaper people, the greatest names of the time, Hemingway, Vincent Sheehan, Martha Gellhorn and many many many others, were all reporting from the Loyalist side in Spain. In spite of the fact that our numbers as a unit was comparatively small, just remember, only about, what was it, 3,300?

SN: Yeah.

LC: 3,200 of us went there, and perhaps another 35 to 40 thousand from all the other countries of the world sent volunteers, or volunteers came from those countries.

The activity of the International Brigades captured the imagination of literally millions and millions of people all over the world and the events that transpired in Spain were reported, well reported, brilliantly reported. If you ever take the trouble to take a look at the morgues of the various newspapers dealing with the events of the times you will see that they were very well reported.

So I don't think that it's possible to say that we did not know what was going on. Literally not only did millions of people know, but millions of people in this country, millions of people in France, millions of people in England, and millions of people in other countries of the world supported the cause of Loyalist Spain. So that there was no misunderstanding, there wasn't the excuse that they didn't know what was going on.

In spite of the fact that so many millions of people did know and tremendous movements were established in all countries of the world in order to assist the Loyalists, the movements were not strong enough to create the kind of unity between the so-called democracies of the West that finally eventually unfortunately had to be established in the middle of World War II to defeat the common enemy. The very fact that we went to Spain, one of the main reasons that we went, was to eliminate the possibility of such a war taking place, because we could see that it had to come, that the fascist powers led by Hitler and Mussolini were bound on world conquest and that the only way really to stop them, this was the first time to stop them militarily. But it was not to be because of the tremendous divisions that existed both here and in Great Britain and in France.

SN: I had a point that Larry just made about the public attitude here. There was a Gallup Poll taken during 1937 and of all the people that were asked which side they were on, 73% said they were on the Loyalists' side, that is, on the side that we fought for. And concerning writers, out of 300 writers who were asked where they stood on the matter, 299 said they were on the side of the Republic and one fellow said he was on the other side and I can't remember his name now to tell you, but it's a known fact. People that are interested should look that up.

SG: The main reason was that the war was lost in the capitals of the major democratic countries, in Washington, in Paris, and in London. Unfortunately although the people of these countries, the average person on the street, he was in favor of the Republican government in Spain. But unlike the situation of today, none of the people that were actually dying there touched us here, and the democratic sentiments and feelings of the people at that time was not expressed in real massive demonstrative actions so that pressure could be exerted on the officials of the countries to take a different position, these countries. And this I think was the key to the main reason for the loss of the war by the Loyalist government.

And I want to mention that all of the time that I was in Spain, from the time I was in the Lincoln Battalion to the . . . complete withdrawal of Internationals from the scene, I had occasion in the latter part of my stay there to be connected with the brigade transports and I . . . was able to travel to many towns and cities and in all of my experience in Spain I never had a feeling . . . that the Spanish people did not welcome us there. I don't remember . . . one instance whereby local reaction that the Spanish people that I met, all of the individuals, didn't by this type of expression show a fondness for us, and a friendliness to us.

And in this connection, I want to mention one thing which struck me very forcefully. When we were approaching Quinto, before we took Quinto, there was a line of fortifications, trenches, in front of the town, and we had to storm these trenches in order to proceed into the town. And one of the Spaniards of the Franco troops there, during a lull in the fighting, shouted, which was heard by us, shouted, "We're going to defend, fight to the last, but please be good to our women and children." I was stunned by this. I was stunned at the time because I realized what lies the fascists must have told the people under their control, what lies they must have told them in order to get them to fight against the Republic of Spain.

SN: Yeah. They gave the impression that there was going to be rape and murder and so forth.

SG: That's right. And I was stunned by that. And I realized that if they weren't given this type of indoctrination that . . . many of them were very very good people. Very good people. And I was stunned by this statement, to what extent they lied in order to get these people to fight against their own interests.

LC: I wonder if I can't tell you a little story about the attitude of the Spanish people, not so much what it was then, because I think Sam's experience was an experience that every one of us had.

But I want to bring it to today. I recently had the opportunity to talk to a young Spaniard who was studying and working in this country. He was a friend, well he *is* a friend, of my eldest son, and when he heard that I was a member of the Lincoln Brigade he wanted very much to meet me. During the course of a very interesting evening, I asked him, "What do the Spanish people think of us? I mean, do they know anything about us? Are we part of their existence? Do they know anything about the International Brigades?" And he said to me, with a smile, and it was a very gentle smile, he said, "Mr. Cane, they don't teach us anything about you in our schools. But we Spaniards, we Spaniards, we know all about you."

Now this is a young man who was born after the civil war was over, and there are many many stories like this that can be told. Many of our people have gone to Spain and had some fascinating experiences.

Another one, for just a minute. One of our vets went to Spain a couple of years ago, and as a result of his experiences there, he is currently making a documentary film about Spain. But one of the experiences that he relates goes this way: He was in the city of Valencia two years ago, and he has a beard. His beard became very straggly, and he decided he wanted it trimmed. So he looked around and he found a barber, went into the barber shop, and began to talk to the man.

Now apparently, Spaniards don't wear beards usually, even today. And the barber was having a little difficulty trimming the beard. And so he began to talk. Now, this friend of ours, like most of us, can talk Spanish passably well. I mean, not grammatically, but well enough to be understood and to understand what's being said to him. And so they had this conversation.

He was in this barbershop, sitting in the chair, and the barber said to him, "You know, you don't look like a hippie. What do you do for a living?"

Well, this friend of ours, for convenience sake, had been masquerading as a professor of history, and he said, "Well, I'm a professor of history in the United States. I teach history in college."

All that was understandable to the barber. He said, "Oh, well, that . . . That makes sense. Now we know why you've got a beard, you know. That's understandable, you know. Intellectuals like you, it's not out of the ordinary to wear a beard." He said,

"Tell me, what branch of history, is there a special branch that you're interested in, that you're a specialist in?"

"Yes," he said, "yes, there is," he says, "as a matter of fact, my particular interest in history is the Spanish Civil War."

And the barber looked at him and he said. "Oh, really?" He said, "Well,"—now he's fishing you see—"well, what do you know about the Spanish Civil War?"

So this friend of ours, this vet, said, "Well, I can tell you for example that the city of Valencia was for a period of time the seat of the Republican government. It was a major port of entry for materiel that was coming in, and for that reason, for political ramifications, it was not very frequently bombed. The other cities were bombed. Madrid was bombed, Barcelona was bombed. Valencia wasn't bombed too much." He said, "Militarily, probably the most exciting thing that happened was that you were shelled by the battleship *Deutschland* and a number of people were killed."

The barber says to him, "You know, that's right!" He said, "That's right." He says to him, "Tell me, did you ever hear of a general by the name of Campesino?"

Now Campesino was a nickname of a general by the name of Valentín Gonzalez, and he was a very famous general on the Republican side during the Spanish Civil War. And of course my friend said, "Oh, yeah, I know all about Campesino." And he began to rattle off the numerical designation of his division and so on and so forth, and the barber then with his buttons bursting, stands up stiff and he says, "I was a soldado, I was a soldier in Campesino's division, and after the war I spent six years in jail because I fought against Franco."

And then my friend, knowing where this guy stands, says to him, "Oh, really?" He said, "You know, it may have been, it may have happened that on one cold winter night we passed ourselves on a dark road either going into a position or going out of a position."

Whereupon the barber rears up, and he says, pointing to him, "Tu, Lincoln! You, Lincoln!" And my friend grinned, you know.

He ran, he closed the shutters on the door, he closed the shutters on the window, he grabbed him, he gave him a big abrazzo, took him home, introduced him to his family, and then introduced him to quite a number of people who were now presently active in the underground opposition that exists in Spain against the present government.

It's only one, these are only one or two of many stories that can be told.

SN: May I add one more point. I imagine you're going to run out of time soon.

One of the things that I think your audience would want to know, and that is, what's the situation now? And while I don't want to discuss what the situation is in Spain from what I heard, and I was recently in Paris, and I met Spaniards who are working in the underground, who are coming back and forth, and who told me what was going on, spoke very enthusiastically about a popular united movement that's developing on a broad basis against Franco. But they say, "But you, the United States, is going to be on our back if we have any trouble. You've got your bases there, and if these bases are attacked or some trouble begins over there, it's going to be your troops that are going to join along with Franco against us just as you're doing in Vietnam today."

So we of the Lincoln Brigade and our friends are very anxious to support a move in the United States Senate, you know, to have a hearing on the Military Aid pact. And we hope the day is coming when the United States' government is going to stop supporting Franco to the tune of over two billion dollars in the last decade. It started off with Eisenhower, it's going on to this day. And we hope that message reaches your audience and that when the campaign starts, they'll help us in this campaign to end this pact with Franco.

SG: In this connection, in the last couple of years it was reported in the press, in *The [New York] Times* and the rest of the press, that the United States' forces in Spain had joint maneuvers with the Franco army.

SN: Right, right.

SG: Now, obviously, from present-day conditions, Spain is not threatened from the outside . . .

SN: No, by nobody.

SG: . . . and it's quite obvious that the only kind of threat would come from the people themselves. And I question, I question the reasons that the government of the United States could give for such participation.

SN: I'm going to tell you something. As long as you have Nixon in power, he's going to find the formula. We had to attack to protect our boys who were being threatened. And that's going to be his statement, just as he says it in Cambodia and in North Vietnam and in other places. That's going to be his statement, so that's not going to be a guarantee for us unless we make sure that that pact is broken.

SG: We may be getting close to . . . . Well, we don't have too much time, but I want to say this. I've often thought, you know, 35 years is a long time. It's a short time when you look back at it, but it's quite a long time.

And I've often said, you know, put the question to myself: would I, if I had to live my life over again, go to Spain, because the pressures of life and the different type of life that we have now could change a person's outlook on things. But I think that the vast majority of the Spanish Vets would answer that they would do it all over again. It was worth it, and we're proud of it.

And of course there are people in this country who are still giving false impressions of what we really stood for. In fact, we're on the attorney general's list as being un-American for fighting for a democratic way of life against fascism. Now what could be more illuminating than this? At 35 years after the struggle in Spain, reactionaries in this country are making it their business to keep us on the un-American activities lists. And it's a tragedy for this country that the people who went to Spain, who fought in Spain for democracy, are not given the proper recognition that they should get.

LC: It's interesting in that connection, Sam, that during World War II, after some initial hesitations on the part of certain reactionary officials, American military figures had no hesitation in accepting our talents, our energies, and our lives in the cause for which this country was fighting.

For example, I myself enlisted as a private, came out of World

War II as a captain. I participated in all of the major fighting in Europe and in the European Theater of Operations, from the assault landing on D-Day to the meeting with the Russians. I had no difficulties in the American Army, and nobody discriminated against me, although there were men in the American Army that had fought in Spain that for some peculiar reason were discriminated against.

Yet, out of the rather small number of vets compared to the total number (there were 13 to 14 million in the American Army), sixty of us—sixty of us—became commissioned officers, many of us on a battlefield basis. Many of us were decorated, with the Distinguished Service Cross, the Silver Star, the Bronze Star, what have you. And many many more became non-commissioned officers in the American Army during World War II.

Nevertheless, what Sam says is still true. And it is really a very very sad observation on the realities that exist in our country.

SG: I had a little different experience than you in the Army. I was in the Army Air Corps for close to four years, and I was a staff sergeant. And I was called into G-2, which was on the intelligence at . . . that time. I think it's still G-2.

LC: Yes, it is.

SG: And I was questioned for about an hour on why I went to Spain. Of course there was a young lieutenant who did the questioning, and he wasn't aware of what the political situation in Spain was at the time, and he was looking at me in amazement when I explained to him the reasons for going and what was actually going on there.

And I was told by someone in my unit on one of the airfields here in the States—it was Lachman [?] Air Base . . . outside of Converse, Ohio—that there was someone all the time at my outfit keeping an eye on me. This was pretty reliable. So they still, even though you were in the Army, they were still. . . . And they knew that . . . your philosophy, your political philosophy, coincided with the principles of the struggle against fascism, there were still reactionaries who were pointing the finger and saying there's something wrong with this guy.

SN: Yeah, we never did live down the stigma of being "premature anti-fascists" to this day.

TE: I was going to say that. It's always that you're still that today.

SN: Right. We're on the Attorney General's list to this day.

TE: I guess that's it. Thank you

SN: Thank you, Tony.

LC: Thank you very much.

SG: Thank you. [inaudible]

FOR FURTHER READING

The literature on the Spanish Civil War is voluminous. The starting point for researchers is Hugh Thomas, *The Spanish Civil War* (New York: Harper and Row, Publishers, 1977). Five important works on the American experience are Vincent Brome, *The International Brigades, Spain, 1936–1939* (New York: Morrow, 1966); Peter N. Carroll, *The Odyssey of the Abraham Lincoln Brigade: Americans in the Spanish Civil War* (Stanford: Stanford University Press, 1994); Cary Nelson and Jefferson Hendricks, eds., *Madrid 1937: Letters of the Abraham Lincoln Brigade from the Spanish Civil War* (London: Routledge, 1996); Arthur H. Landis, *The Abraham Lincoln Brigade* (New York: The Citadel Press, 1967); and Robert A. Rosenstone, *Crusade of the Left: The Lincoln Battalion in the Spanish Civil War* (Lanham, Md.: University Press of America, 1980). For specific information on the Mac-Paps, see Victor Howard and Mac Reynolds, *The Mackenzie-Papineau Battalion: The Canadian Contingent in the Spanish Civil War* (Ottawa: Carleton University Press, 1986) and William C. Beeching, *Canadian Volunteers: Spain, 1936–1939* (Saskatchewan: Canadian Plains Research Centre, University of Regina, 1989). Carl Geiser's memoir, *Prisoners of the Good Fight: The Spanish Civil War, 1936–1939* (Westport, Conn.: L. Hill, 1986) includes an account of how Lawrence Cane saved his life when he was captured. The web site of the Abraham Lincoln Brigade Archives, located at http://www.alba-valb.org/, provides a wealth of information about Americans who fought in Spain, including an on-line version of the veterans of the Abraham Lincoln Brigade periodical, *The Volunteer.* A novel, set in Buffalo, New York, which captures life within the Communist Party from 1939 until the 1960s is Harvey Swados, *Standing Fast* (New York: Doubleday, 1970).

Of the many works published on World War II, those that speak most directly to the experience of Lawrence Cane include Stephen E. Ambrose, *Citizen Soldiers* (New York: Simon &

Schuster, 1997); Stephen E. Ambrose, *D-Day, June 6, 1944: The Climactic Battle of World War II* (New York: Simon & Schuster, 1994); Mark Bando, *Breakout at Normandy: The 2nd Armored Division in the Land of the Dead* (Osceola, Wisc.: MBI Publishing Co., 1999); Martin Blumensen, *Breakout and Pursuit* (Washington, D.C.: Government Printing Office, 1961); Hugh M. Cole, *The Ardennes: Battle of the Bulge* (Washington, D.C.: Government Printing Office, 1965); Trevor N. Dupuy, David L. Bongard, and Richard C. Anderson Jr., *Hitler's Last Gamble: The Battle of the Bulge, December 1944–January 1945* (New York: HarperCollins, 1994); Gordon A. Harrison, *Cross-Channel Attack* (Washington, D.C.: Government Printing Office, 1951); Max Hastings, *Overlord: D-Day and the Battle for Normandy, 1944* (London: Cape, 1982); Judy Barrett Litoff, David C. Smith, Barbara Wooddall Taylor, and Charles E. Taylor, *Miss You: The World War II Letters of Barbara Wooddall Taylor and Charles E. Taylor* (Athens: University of Georgia Press, 1990); Charles B. MacDonald, *Company Commander* (New York: Ballantine Books, 1947); Charles B. MacDonald, *The Seigfried Line* (Washington, D.C.: Government Printing Office, 1963), John Man, *The D-Day Atlas: The Definitive Account of the Allied Invasion of Normandy* (New York: Facts on File, 1994), and William L. O'Neill, *A Democracy at War: America's Fight at Home and Abroad in World War II* (New York: Free Press, 1993).

INDEX

INDEX